Wayfarer Denman's

Crawley Revisited

1835 - 1945

ISBN 0 9521300 0 9

First published by Nâdine Hygate, 1993
216 Ifield Road, West Green, Crawley, West Sussex, RH11 7HY

British Library Cataloguing-in-Publication Data
A catalogue record for this book is available from the British Library.

Produced and typeset by Performance Publications, Billingshurst.

Printed in Great Britain by East Sussex Press, Crowborough.

Contents

For those who remember.

Acknowledgements

East Sussex Records Office - Lewes

Sussex Archaeological Collection

Sussex and Surrey Courier

Corporation of London, Greater London Records Office and Library

West Sussex County Records Office - Chichester

For their encouragement and help: Brenda Young and Charles Kay

Sayed M. Rafiq Zahedi Shah

Unless individually acknowledged, all illustrations are the property of the family.

Preface

As it is almost 50 years since the death of Mr. Denman, this book has been compiled in two sections.

The first section is biographical and has been taken in the main from his own writings and his family's recollections. During his lifetime Crawley developed rapidly, and he records many events in the prosperous community, from village to town.

In the second section his writings have specifically been recorded ad verbatim, about "Historical Crawley". As Mr. Denman interviewed people over a period of sixty years, and many were aged at the time, we have a verbal recollection from villagers as to Crawley's life and times. Illustrations have also been selected mainly from his own collection to reflect this. At the time of his writing, many of the statements could not be substantiated by documentation records, as records were not so readily accessible to the public as they are today. Therefore, excerpts written in italics are from research in Public Records to verify or clarify Mr. Denman's statements.

The events which are given in this book are but a glimpse of the vast amount which flowed from Mr. Denman's pen.

N.D.H. 1993

Introduction

Poo Bah

> A remarkable man retired today from Crawley postal service - he was not only head postman here until this afternoon, but he is the Poo Bah of Crawley being:
>
> County Councillor
>
> Rural District Councillor
>
> Parish Councillor
>
> Justice of the Peace and Officer of nearly 30 other institutions.
>
> He is the town's busiest man.
>
> "This evening," he told me, consulting his diary, "I attend a school managers' meeting at 6.30, and the Co-operative Society Committee at seven, and go on from there first to the British Legion Committee and then to take the chair at the Cricket Club committee."
>
> This is quite a usual evening for Mr. Denman.
>
> Evening Standard Friday 31st December 1937

Who is this man? Why was he considered remarkable?

To understand his achievements we need to look at this description in the context of his time. A time when in society everyone knew their place and position in the hierarchy. A village had its gentry and its villagers, then the strangers. One did not mix one with the other.

When history is recorded the names which come to mind are those of the gentry, intellectuals, great craftsmen or artists, but the ordinary people, faceless figures in a crowd, only hover in the shadows and their contributions to life and their achievements go mainly unnoticed. From these shadows came such a man, his way of life no different from the majority of people who lived at the same period of time.

Why should he be remembered?

From birth, he began a love affair, a love affair with Crawley which remained with him until the day he died. The strength of purpose which moulded him is deep-rooted in his heritage. His family history is not just his history but a reflection of Crawley and the ordinary man of that time.

When first I began assembling together material for Mr. Denman's biography, as a supplement to his writings and collection of articles relating to Crawley, it was to be just that - his biography. But the more I delved into the past, the more fascinated I became. This led my research back further than intended. However, while a family-tree has been included, I have concentrated on one hundred years of the family, from 1843 to 1945.

(Any reader who can prove their family connection I shall be happy to hear from.)

Cameos of uncles, aunts, brothers and sisters, father and mother, give glimpses of Crawley and the surrounding area, in the Victorian era, leading through the 1914-1918 war, culminating at the end of the second world war. These serve as a background to the central figure of my study, but each made their own contribution to the life of the area.

The name Denman is frequently found or heard in Sussex, particularly near to the Sussex/Surrey border. From the name's origins, it is not surprising to see why.

It comes down to us through the mists of time, from when the great forests of Andriaswold covered the area. During that era herds of pigs, or swine as they were known, were kept in small clearings in the forest, each herd being looked after by a man and his family. In Anglo-Saxon times these clearings were known as "Dennes", hence the pigs' owners were known as Denne men, a job description used as a means of identifying individuals. So, as the years passed by, and surnames came into being, "John" the Denne Man became John Denman.

Families tended to stay generation upon generation in one area. In early times people named their children after kings and queens or names heard from the Bible. Thence, after their parents, brothers and sisters. So the result is many people with identical names, but totally unrelated one to another, except perhaps by several generations distance. Such a common name as Denman has proved to be a hazard in trying to link people together, and in the very early years something of a conjecture. From the point at which my Denman biography begins, however, it is fact and not fiction and can be authenticated.

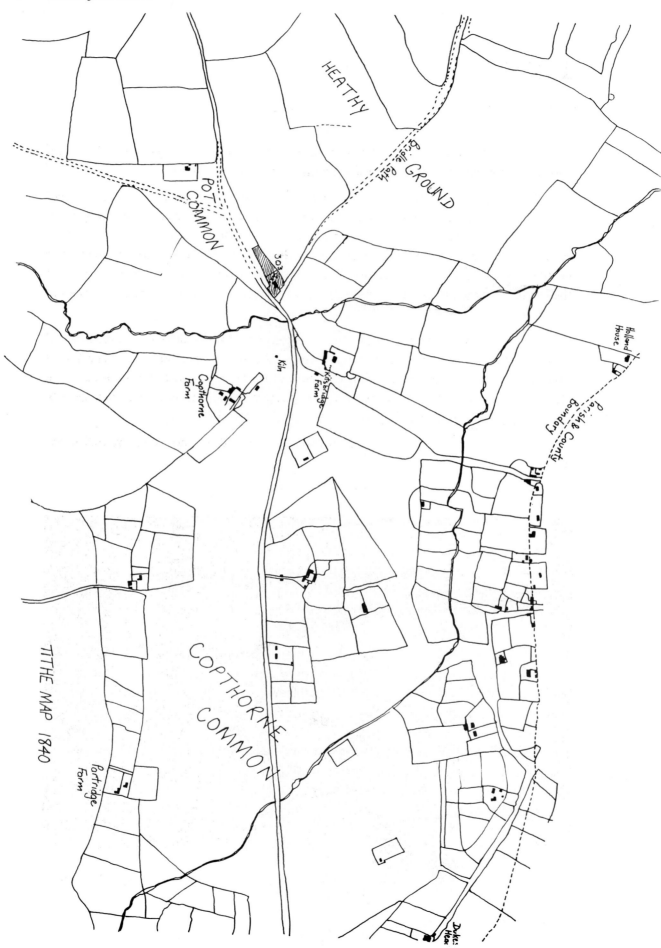

HEATHY

Bridle Path

GROUND

POT COMMON

303

Kiln

Copthorne Farm

Kitsbridge Farm

Holland House

County Parish Boundary

TITHE MAP 1840

COPTHORNE COMMON

Partridge Farm

Dukes House

Links

Early in the eighteen hundreds there lived in a large clearing on Pot Common (303) Copthorne, Thomas and Eliza Denman with their children.

At this time Copthorne consisted of several isolated farms and many small scattered cottages on the large areas of common land which were surrounded by thick forests. There were a huddle of little cottages near to what was to become the village green, the school not being built until 1842. Several ale-houses nearby, perhaps, the best known being the Abergavenny Arms which came into prominence at the turn of the century when cockfighting and bare fisted boxing took place on the field opposite to it.

The Denman home was a thatched cottage surrounded by a vegetable garden and orchard. There were chickens and a pig. Internally, the ground floor rooms had hard earth floors and low-beamed ceilings. There was a large fireplace with hooks in the chimney for hanging the cooking pots, or smoking and roasting meat, wood being easily come by from the surrounding forests and nearby sawmill.

Water was obtained from a well, and an "earth closet" was housed a small distance away.

courtesy of Peter Brunt

courtesy of Peter Brunt

James Denman's cottage is on the right - 1915

At this time the cottage was their own, though when the thatch fell into disrepair, they could not afford to replace it. So the Blunt family of Crabbet Park repaired it in exchange for the land which was in extent 2 rods and 22 perches. Thomas continued to live in the cottage for a rent of 2/8 per annum payable to the Rector of Worth.

(In later years, (1870) Kitsbridge Cottages were built on the site and the old cottage became derelict. One feature of the family home, however, remains to this day, a giant yew tree. Thomas' son James, with his family lived at Kitsbridge Cottage until his death in 1919.)

Thomas was born in Worth in 1798, and possibly in this cottage, though his wife was formerly Eliza Wood of Charlwood. Thomas worked for the Blunts at Crabbet Park as a roadman. It is here that he may have met Eliza working as a servant in the house.

Thomas and Eliza had eleven known children, though the large gaps between the ages of some of them suggest there may have been others, but the beginning of their family was in the days before registration was law.

The eldest was Martha born 1831, but dying at 6 months old, Peter born 1833, followed by William, Eliza, Thomas, Mary, John in 1843, James, Jane, Elizabeth and Sarah in 1853. Unfortunately, the girls were not registered and only traceable when a marriage took place or from the census of the period.

Early in Thomas and Eliza's married life Queen Victoria ascended to the throne. When she made her visit to Sussex on 5th. October 1837 stopping at "The George" en route, all the country folk from the surrounding area came to Crawley to try to catch a glimpse of the new Queen. Surely, Thomas and Eliza would have been amongst them, their home being less than four miles away? A good description of the event is given by Henry Burstow of Horsham who was but a boy at the time.

> "Accordingly about seven o' clock in the morning Bill in nothing but his rags, and I, with nothing more than the clothes I stood up in, started off, trusting to luck to lead us the right way and fill our little bellies. We trudged on alone, through Roffey, hoping for a friendly waggoner to give us a lift, but none came along. At length we got to Pease Pottage, where we saw a large archway made of evergreens, with "Victoria Regina" worked on it in various coloured Dahlias. We were mightily impressed and felt we must now tread the ground very lightly. Here we waited until Horsham 'Rookery' boys came up, when, hearing that the Queen's chaise would change horses in Crawley, and thinking we should get a straighter and longer stare at her there, we decided to go. We found Crawley very gaily decorated and crowded with people. All the school children were penned in like sheep, awaiting the Royal arrival, and under orders to sing when called upon. We, the Horsham contingent, now getting very hungry, crowded ourselves together in a bunch close to the "George Hotel", carefully hiding in our midst our ragged and tattered little companion, lest the Queen when she came might see him and perhaps, we thought, order his head off. Presently the Queen and her mother, in a post chaise, with postboys and outriders, and escorted by a large number of yeomen from the neighbourhood, each carrying a white staff, drove up to the Hotel, close to us boys. The Crawley folk cheered tremendously, but the sight of these two very ordinary-looking women by no means satisfied our

youthful but elevated ideas of Royalty; worse! It did not appease our hunger, now thoroughly aggravated by the information that the Crawley youths were to have a big feed as soon as the Queen was gone. "Which is the Queen then, Harry?" asked Tom Vinall of me. "Why, the young'un, I suppose" I answered crossly. I felt disappointed and hungry enough almost to be uncivil, and as the crowd sang "God save the Queen" etc. I could not help thinking He would be attending to a more necessitous case, if instead of sending her victorious He sent us Horsham boys something solid to eat, together with a new suit of clothes and a pair of boots for Bill Etheridge. With the Queen gone, the Crawley people dispersing, and without a farthing between us Horsham boys, we now had to face the seven miles walk home..."

For the most part, in common with their neighbours, life was very hard for the Denmans. They were desperately poor by today's standards, or were they? There was food aplenty in the countryside, with rabbits and birdcatching and fish for a supplement to their own livestock and home grown vegetables. Fruits in summer and autumn giving a balanced diet. Sugar and tea would be a rarity and luxury for them, tea being 6 s. and 8 s. and 10 s. per lb and moist sugar 6d and 8d a lb. For sweetening of food honey was normally used.

One very filling dessert was known as "Hasty Pudding" perhaps even used as a substitute for porridge.

A kettle of water/milk mixture was boiled over the fire, and flour was gradually added whilst continually stirring the mixture until it thickened into a porridge-like consistency without being lumpy. Then it was removed from heat and honey was added until of sufficient sweetness.

Nothing was discarded which could be of use. So when chickens became too old for egg producing, the flesh was stewed. Meantime the chicken feathers were used for fillings of coarse covered pillows and cushions.

Pigs lard was usually the only source of oil available to the family. One use was to manufacture crude light wicks. A dish of liquid fat with cotton threads floating in it could be lit to give small illuminating flame, or common rushes taken from a pond, dried, then coated in fat were held in a pair of pincers mounted on a wooden block. To prepare the rushes for use as lights, you first cut each end of the rush leaving a piece about 18 inches in length. Remove most of the outer green skin exposing the white pithy interior. Using a gresset, which is a shallow iron dish set on three legs and with a long handle, stand it in the fires embers so that the fat it contains melts. Lay the prepared rushes in the gresset until they are sufficiently coated with grease. Allow them to dry thoroughly. When a rush is placed in the pincer holder, only a small section protrudes for lighting. As the rush burns away, it is gradually eased manually through the holder. (Candles of tallow were a luxury they could not afford.)

In winter the children had their chests smeared with lard, then wrapped around with strips of cloth, before adding layers of clothing, in order to try to prevent them from catching colds.

With such a large family one wonders how they were all accommodated in such a small cottage. However, many children started full time employment at the age of 10 to 12 years, and often lived at the place of their work, so seldom were they all at home together. This simplified the sleeping arrangements, boys being in the loft and girls downstairs. It has been known that six children occupied one double bed, three at the top and three at the bottom end!

Thomas was keen to improve his children's lot in life, for all of them received some schooling, although he, and his wife were illiterate. The eldest two children probably went to a dames school for a limited period, whilst the other children were educated at Copthorne Village School. The school which was built on land given by the Blunts opened in 1842. Being a rural school, attendance fluctuated depending on the seasons, as many were required to work on the farms. From an old school log book kept by the Head teacher, one gets an insight into some of the difficulties encountered when trying to instil the 3 R's into the pupils, as their attendance was not that consistent. Though the log is dated 1879, little would have changed in the intervening years and it reflects a typical school year.

Log 1879

April 30th. A great many children away getting flowers for their Maypoles.

May 1st. Half the school absent - carrying said Maypoles around the village.

June 4th. Several of the children not at school this week - gone to Bark scraping.

(Bark scraping - The curing of leather requires tannin, and this can be found in high quality in oak bark, and to a lesser degree in alder, beech and willow, the tannin being in the inner layers of the bark. The best time for removing the bark is May/June. It could be done before the tree was cut down or after felling. Sometimes, particularly on oak, a small section was taken every eight years so that the tree remained growing. The cut bark was stacked on racks or poles and allowed to dry thoroughly for several weeks. The cut and dried bark was then steeped in pits of water. The leather skins were soaked in this liquid for 4 to 12 months.)

June 11th. School very low this week owing to it being Whitsun week and two club feasts on close here.

June 28th. School very low, weather fine so a great number busy getting the hay in.

July 26th. Harvesting commenced in some places - makes it low.

Aug 2nd. School very low. Closed for Harvest holiday until Sept 2nd.

Sept 2nd. Commenced school this morning - a great many families gone to hop picking.

Sept 27th. School still low - a great many families back from the hopping. Am expecting a larger school next week.

Oct 4th. A greater number at school this week - the children which are back from the field work are seemingly very dull and giving a great deal of trouble to break them in again.

Oct 18th. Weather very fine, school not as large as I expected - a great many picking Acorns.

Nov 18th. Average for the week ended 73. Several on Monday not at school gone to get work tickets for their parents and some of the elder boys gone to beating.

Nov 21 and 22nd. Boys gone beating.

Dec 20th. Several boys again off beating - some of the children during the week gave deal of trouble by going some distance from the school sliding, caned three and kept the rest in after school.

A mention is made in the School Log of the children going hop picking. The Denman children accompanied by their mother went hop picking each year in Kent. They travelled by wagon or cart along with other families from Copthorne. Picking of hops was a form of earning pin-money by the wives. The older children would help with the hop picking or by looking after the young ones, but in general it was a holiday for them. For the most part the men stayed at home continuing with their usual occupations. The pin-money would be extremely useful in purchasing new winter clothing.

Having briefly shown something of Thomas and Eliza's daily life the scene is set.

Abergavenny Arms 1880s

Dukes Head

Village Glimpses —1840 - 1870

What of Crawley at this time? Was it really the sleepy non-descript village that travellers would have us believe, not worth a mention in Sussex history? Crawley was a rural community, much dedicated to farming and during the day few people would be about in the village as all would be engaged about their daily business in the countryside, and at night early sleepers due to early rising.

In the previous century where now is the High Street was common land which extended to beyond "The Sun" where people kept ducks, geese and chickens, and cows

MASTER CHARLES.   W.H. IN A FIX.

or goats grazed. With the development of the turnpike road, the bridle track gradually widened to form a roadway and the greens contracted in size to make room for pathways and cottages. The great forests of Worth and of Tilgate extended from the south, skirting the Church and extending almost to Ifield Lane corner.

Over the years "Crawleyites" had been used to seeing foreigners as they passed through on their way to the great port of Shoreham or to the iron forges. But the coming of the stage coach for mass travel, as well as the private chaises opened up new horizons and brought new commercial business.

For the visitor as well as the inhabitants what was Crawley like?

The memorable 'Drive to Crawley'

by courtesy of P. Allen

Upon entering the village proper from the north one would be faced with a very unpleasant sight and smell! Just before the bend on the London Road near the junction with Black Dog Lane (Woodborough Road) was Clappers.

At one time Clappers was just a pond fed by streams which due to the slope of the terrain flowed from Goffs Hill, Springfield and Broadfield. During the winter/spring months this pond overflowed right across the highway to the other side. To enable people to traverse the morass of mud and water a Sussex Clapper bridge was built. This consists of loose wooden planks raised on logs or stones and purely for pedestrian use. Sometimes there was a handrail. Hence this part of the village became known as the Clappers. However, with the expansion of building, this pond became a cesspool. An open ditch commencing to the rear of the George Inn, and following behind the cottages below, towards The Sun, took the sewage from that side of the street to Clappers. Later, with the lands south of the church being developed the problem became worse. There was an open drain into the fields near the church and running for some distance beside the Three Bridges Road. Another went behind the church and parallel to the street, passing in a conduit near the Rectory, but becoming an open sewer near to the building itself. This ditch fed into several small ponds where cattle drank, and was supplemented by two streams which carried human and farm effluence, the whole network again converging at Clappers.

The problems of Crawley drainage were not resolved for another forty years, as agreements could not be reached by the appropriate authorities and landowners. One of the major difficulties being that Crawley lies within three parishes: Worth, Ifield and Crawley, each with its own governing body, and Worth's higher authority being the East Grinstead Union, while Crawley and Ifield lie within that of the Horsham Union.

So Clappers was not a place where one would wish to linger, neither was it a favourable introduction to the village.

Progressing around the corner there was an unhindered vista of greens, trees, quaint cottages with their pretty gardens, and with a sprinkling of larger, more ancient plaster houses. Looming above all, the lofty branches of the renowned elm tree. To the left just before passing through the North Tollgate were situated "The Magazines." This was a group of some fifteen hovels each with its pocket-handkerchief sized plot of garden, so named as the site had originally been an army ammunitions depot. Gunpowder and shot were stored to supply the armies as the soldiers marched south towards Shoreham for embarkation, some of the last ones being those going to fight in the Napoleonic wars. Some soldiers were billeted at The Magazines with their followers-on, and at other cottages around the village. Passing through the tollgate, a few yards to the right hand side of the street opposite Furnace Cottage (Boscabel) was the entrance to the Smalls Lane, the roadway which led towards Horsham, and by track to Ifield, though a more usual route to Ifield was via Hutt's Lane or Langley Lane, Smalls Lane being the only westerly roadway until Pease Pottage was reached.

On the left past the Elm and Dr. Smith's home The Tree, with its wisteria covered walls, stood an old Tudor cottage with its Horsham slab roof. Adjacent to this, the fields of the only working farm on the High Street, thence a motley of cottages on either side, some of clapperboard, some of brick, until we reach The George Inn with its unusual gallows sign straddling the road, and linking it to the Annexe.

Beyond this junction there were but few houses, some in the upper square and near to the church itself. By this time Three Bridges had a railway station, but the branch line through to Crawley was not completed until 1848. To bring the rail line through to Crawley necessitated in the cutting down of many hundreds of trees, and a sawmill was set up near to what was to become Station Road corner. It was at this period of time that this end of the village began to expand.

Three Bridges Road did not exist during the 1840's but was a very narrow track wending its way between farm buildings round to the rear of the Church and White Harte Farm, and continuing toward Three Bridges to meet the lane to Malthouse Farm and was known as Worth Lane.

We also have Ifield Lane, another track which gave access to the blacksmiths at the rear of Millers' shop. Also, Ockenden's builders yard and two or three cottages. The way through to meet the Horsham Road was barred by a large pond which covered the now Victoria Park spreading to almost meet Smalls Lane.

The National School was opened on land in this vicinity in 1831, paid for by monies raised by the Robinson family, a prominent Quaker family of the area. The school was non-denominational. This increased the traffic along Ifield Lane, and in the '50's when Jenner opened his broom makers business on land which is now Victoria Road and leading to Spencers Road, part of the pond began to be filled in, so a connection was made with the Horsham Road. Where now is "The Swan" was a beer shop with a smithy behind, later becoming known as The Westgreen Arms, while The Crown was a cottage selling beer. The lane did not become a more permanent thoroughfare until the beginning of the 1880's, when Major Manton Pipon, the then Lord of the Manor of Ifield had the rest of the pond filled in, and the road given a better surface. At this point in time Smalls Lane started to become obsolete.

Returning to the centre of the village we find it a very thriving area. In 1845 there were 19 shops, including a hairdresser, Mrs. Louisa Russell whose business occupied a room at the White Harte Farm, and 12 service establishments plus the Post Office, and an Insurance Agent. Also a licenced carrier of goods to London departing Mondays and Thursdays, returning on Wednesdays and Fridays. By 1855 the number of shops had increased to 20, and Mrs. Louisa Snelling and William Tully had opened shops in West Green. Crawley had also acquired a veterinary surgeon, named Hampton Raywood.

In a cottage to the south of Ifield Lane, on The Street was a business run by James Pickett. (This site in later years became the drapery department of Crawley Co-op.) Mr. Pickett had a small workshop attached to his cottage where he made pattens and clogs. Mention has already been made of the state of the road ways at certain times of the year. There were no footpaths, and with the constant churning up of the mud by carriage and animals, it was difficult to walk. To assist people to traverse the highway

Crawley Rectory: Rev Charles Augustus Fowler 13 June 1849

Mortgage securing £200 with interest.

'The within named John Fisher Hodgson being nominated by the ordinary Patron and Incumbent of the Rectory of Crawley etc to receive and apply the money authorised to be borrowed by mortgage of the Glebe tithes and rents and other profits and emoluments of the said rectory for the purpose of building a parsonage house and offices belonging to such a living.

Courtesy of Mrs R. Odey

women in particular wore pattens or clogs. Pattens were shaped like the sole of a boot, but made of wood and had a leather toe piece and a heel, and raised two inches to three inches from the ground by means of irons from toe to heel, like the blade of a skate, and worn over the shoe. Clogs were made the same as pattens, but minus the iron work. That pattens and clogs were necessary in The High Street even to the end of the 1880's is shown by a comment in "Simmins Advertiser" (the local newspaper): "From Dr. Martins (Northgate) down to Gas-house cottages the footpath is impassable in wet weather being flooded, and after the water has gone, the mud is so deep that females cannot use it unless they wear pattens."

With the great influx of visitors and the increase in trade it seemed that new buildings sprang up almost overnight, and permanent residents to the village required more amenities. So began the development of the area now known as Robinson Road. Firstly, it was called Church Road, then New Road, and Post Office Road, guidance being from the properties developed there.

Off Worth Lane in 1845 was built the Monastery for the Fransican Friars, built by the Crawley firm of Messrs Ockenden. There was a little brick-built school on the right side of the carriageway, and here many well-known Crawley people had their early education. The school mistresses were the Misses Booker who lived in Robinson Road.

About this time the National School came more and more under the influence of the Church until they took over completely. So the Robinson family decided once again to build another non-denominational school, paid for by public subscription, and land was duly purchased in the new development of Church Road. By 1854 the school was opened, and described thus in February 1855: "A commodious school room with masters dwelling house attached has been erected and used for the purpose of the schools a considerable time; and such has been the success with respect to the building fund that in addition to £310.15.0 subscribed up to January 1854, £159.12.4 more has been raised amounting altogether to £470.7.4. The Committee have expended in purchasing land, building etc. the sum of £478.0.1 which is £7.12.9 in excess of the fund. This included everything done up to the present month, some fencing and the building of a small woodshed, which together we estimate to cost about £30 remain to be done, both of which it is hoped will be accomplished before the end of 1855. Thus when the whole has been completed, about £510 will have been spent."

About this time religious fervour began to manifest itself in Crawley, and non-conformist movements began. Prior to this the only non-conformist church in the area was at Ifield, The Friends Meeting House which had come into being in 1676, but at this time it was for strict Quakers only. The nearest chapel was The Independent Chapel at Staplefield. For several years Charles and Lucy Court and three friends walked to Staplefield every Sunday carrying their lunches. After some time they decided to hold such gatherings in Crawley. Strange though it may seem in these days, they were not permitted to hold a meeting of any kind without the permission of the Bishop of Chichester, so a licence had to be obtained, and strangely enough, the licence had to be read on licensed premises. (Was there ever a partnership between Church

Vine Cottage is on the left

Mark Lemon

courtesy of H. Frost

and beer?) Six people assembled in an upstairs room in The Star and Garter (later Mr. Yetman's shop) often known as The Drum and Monkey, a house of not very good repute, and the licence was duly read out and the meeting held.

The movement spread and ultimately it was decided to build a Congregational Church in Crawley. Land was purchased in 1858 and the Church was completed in 1859, in New Road on the opposite side of the road to The British Schools, and slightly to the west.

A Bethel Chapel was opened at the far end of New Road, on the same side as the School in 1858 for strict Baptists. The Temperance movement began to escalate, and infiltrate people's leisure time, though it would be another twenty-five years before a Baptist Church was built.

During the 1850s and 60s the business and industries which continued to thrive in the village centre were still much related to farming activities and coaching. A corn and cattle market were held on alternate Wednesdays in a field at the rear of the White Hart Inn. Smithies and wheelwrights were kept very busy. All must have been chaos on these particular days, with cattle returning to their homes for milking, chaises and carts, and no one way system for the traffic.

Another type of traffic arrived. With the advent of the railway, Crawley had its first commuters on a regular basis. Gentry from several miles around would travel to London, leaving their horses or carriages at the Railway Inn, which at that time was a pretty little cottage with a front garden, and stables to the rear. Perhaps, the best remembered commuter was Mark Lemon, who became the first editor of the magazine "Punch". He came to Crawley in 1857 to live in a cottage which was on the west side of The Street approximately half way between Robinson Road and the railway line, known as Vine Cottage. (In later years Wilson's shop was built over the front garden. This became Forest Stores, and is now an estate agents.) Part of his garden still exists, though somewhat derelict. He became well integrated into the local society as did his many literary artist friends, the best known being Charles Dickens and John Leach, the artist.

Mark Lemon describes Crawley in one of his books under the name of "Snugton".

> "At the southernmost end of the little village of Snugton stands a small cottage, remarkable for nothing but its somewhat picturesque gable end and pretty conservatory. It is a neighbourly sort of cottage, attaching itself to a row of smaller houses, and scarcely shutting itself away, by low wooden railings, from its opposite neighbour, a most industrious wheelwrights shop (later Tizards Shop) where saw and adze or hammer are going from morning till night making pleasant sounds of labour, and keeping the south end of the village wide awake. Not that Snugton is a drowsy village. Oh no! There is the blacksmith's lower down, that tells you when it is daybreak by the hard breathing of its bellows, and the clink, clink of its anvil; and, when its meal times, by the silence of its iron tongue. And then midway there is the once famous posting-house that could not contain itself in the days of glory, but stepped out on the village green, and built a sort of house of ease to the mother hotel, to which it is conected by

a long beam supporting the sign of St George and the Dragon, which hangs lazily in summer and swings and screeches on winter nights. True, 'First pair out!' is now rarely heard, but there are thirsty souls enough in Snugton to keep the centre of the village from stagnating. There are shops, too, on the other side of the way, where men and maids can deck themselves out in all kinds of rustic finery.

Then there is the barber - or, as he delighteth to style himself, hairdresser - whose bow-windowed shop (part of an old inn that afforded good entertainment to man and horse in the days of Queen Bess) is full of lures for fish, stuffed birds, and toys for children, plainly indicating that the barber has more sympathy with the sports and pastimes of his neighbour than cutting, and curling, and shaving for a penny. There are always gossips to be found at his threshold. Over the way at the corner of a by-road is a perfect pantechnicon: tea, sugar, ten penny nails, candles, bacon, crockery, bread, ironware, butter, gunpowder, mops, Epsom Salts - in short, everything that is required by a civilised Englishman in a small way. Ask for the sweet meats made up on the premises, mind you they defy competition.

If you walk on, you will see there is a dear old English village green, with three venerable geese, and at the proper season a hopeful family of goslings, eating their commons. Those geese I believe, are (like Guildhall pigeons) the property of themselves, and live in the old hollow elm at the north end of the green. That old tree was once a great headed giant, and stood boldly alone in the centre of the green, but time and the winds have robbed it of its branches, and what remains of it has been preserved by the piety of the good doctor of the village, who has fenced it around with turf, marigolds stocks, and sunflowers, which even the three geese respect and spare.

We have passed the Post Office. I question if St Martin's-le-Grand can hold its head higher in a proper way, or show more business and bustle. Having said a word to our excellent friend the shoemaker, whose lapstone 'makes music all day long,' we have taken a peep at the rectory, lying back snug among its plashed hedges and trellised walks, and now stand at the doctor's wicket. You need not do so if you are sick, weary, or sad; the door is always open for such to enter, and find relief, solace and those bright, sweet young faces clustered at the window are lighted up by hearts both warm and good. God bless bright faces!

You can't be dull at the north end of the village, for the kennel of the P- hounds is here, and

'Dido and Bendigo, Merry Lass and Towler'

keep up an almost continual chorus from their tuneful throats, occasionally varied by the rating of Mr Bowker the huntsman. A few steps further and we come to the barbican (or turnpike-gate) and its faithful guardians, the gate-keeper and his missus; and, having bid them 'God-den,' let us return to the cottage at the south end.

It has as you may see, a hedge-row of roses running along the side, with a background of yew, thick and tall enough to have a bower cut in it. Here is another hedge of honeysuckle and roses mingled together with a dwarf jessamine tree, almost as white as the twelthcake with blossoms."

At this time The Vestry Committee (forerunner of The Parish Council) decided to try to improve some of the local amenities. The first public clock was erected in 1855 over the cottage/shop adjacent to Mr. Charles Messer's cottage. This shop later became

Lillywhites the tailor. Gas was brought to the area in 1858, a "gas house" having been built to the north of Blackdog Lane. Debates were held regarding lighting The Street. After due consideration it was decided to erect five lights, though a month later two extra were added. Each light cost £2.12.6, and they were placed by the Railway Station, near to the Church Road on The Street, Church Walk entrance, The Tree, and at the end of the cottages on the west side of The Street. The two additional ones were: one at the N.E. corner of The George Hotel and one adjacent to The White Hart Inn and John Wrights. As well as improving the main thoroughfare by lighting, a footpath was laid in 1859. Made of stone slabs, it extended from Worth Lane to The Rising Sun Inn and was 4 ft wide.

From old diaries, we learn that by the 1860's Crawley had had a resident doctor for more than one hundred years. The Dungate family were a family of doctors, the father John practising in London, with some patients in the county of Sussex. Whether he himself practised in Crawley is not clear, but the diaries are in three different handwritings with dates of entry, but in some cases several years lapsing between entries.

Charles Dungate's writing ends in 1751, and the diaries recommence in 1784 written by John Dungate Junior who at that time was 49 years old and had already been working for several years in Crawley. So, perhaps, he took to keeping the diary on the death of his relative.

The practice of John Dungate was vast. Amongst his memoranda is a list of patients, their places of abode and the amount due from them, which will give some idea of the extent and arduous nature of his practice. For patients not only resided in Crawley and Ifield parishes, but also in Slaugham, Cuckfield, Ardingly, Balcombe, Charlewood, Horley, Hoathly, Copthorne and even Croydon and "Rygate". When one considers the state of Sussex roads at the time, and having to do all the rounds on horseback, it was no easy task.

At the time of his death in 1798, John Dungate lived at Elm Tree Cottage. John Dungate had a young assistant, one Robert Smith, whose age would have been about 24 years. "His salary was £20 per year, out of which he paid his own washing."

In 1798 Robert Smith married and moved to "The Tree", setting up his practice and no doubt inheriting many patients connected with his predecessor. So began the long association of the Smith family with Crawley. This Robert Smith died in 1828 and the practice was continued by his son Thomas (Robert, the eldest, practising in London) who had as his assistant, one Dr. Timothy Martin from Wales, and one apprentice, John Leech, "who was much given to drawing on his bedroom walls!" Dr. Timothy Martin married a daughter of Mark Lemon, and one of their daughters married Dr. Sidney Matthews.

The welfare of the Crawley inhabitants, not just their physical well being, began developing. Two very important safety measures were introduced. The first was the formation of a Prosecuting Society. Instigated by the Vestry Committee, it consisted of a group of respected gentlemen who were to apprehend any wrongdoers, this being in the days before an established police force. Anyone caught committing a misdemeanour would be brought before the appropriate Manor Court for judgement, or in serious cases such as murder, to either Lewes or Horsham gaol and the assize court. When policemen were in fact introduced, Crawley had two men, one for either side of The Street, and when on duty neither must transgress to the other one's territory. This strange state of affairs was brought about due to the fact that one side was Worth Parish under the jurisdiction of East Grinstead and the opposite side of The Street being Ifield, answerable to Horsham and West Sussex.

It was decided to form a Fire brigade, there having been many serious farm fires, of barns and stacks in recent years, as well as loss of animals and houses. This was a purely voluntary body of men, and was to remain so until well into the 1920's. The brigade was inaugurated on 10th. August 1866.

During the 1860s coaching travel began to wane as a means of transport through to Brighton. So much so that The Rising Sun Inn near to the North Tollgate was no longer a staging post for horses. The commodious stables were taken over by Mr. Lee Steere, then followed by Charles Bethune as the headquarters of Crawley Foxhounds. Mr. Bethune engaged the famous Jack Press as his huntsman. Jack Press' daughter married Mr. Edward Dean who kept a dairy and grocers shop. Mr. Dean secured the licence of The Rising Sun Inn, and established the present Sun Inn on the opposite side of the roadway some 250 yards to the north in 1864. The old Sun gradually ceased to operate as an inn.

With reference to Foxhounds, the question of Crawley Sporting activities for the period is introduced, and mainly they reflect the country pursuits of this time. As well as foxhounds, a pack of beagles were kennelled at the Holmsbush and Buchan Hill Estates. Harehounds, too, hunted Crawley district, but these came from Paddockhurst.

Cricket was played on The Street greens. Crawley, being such a small parish, could scarcely raise its own cricket team, and the persons most proficient in the sport lived mainly in the Ifield parish. Ifield Cricket Club was founded in 1804 and their home matches were played upon the village green. At frequent intervals a team known as Crawley and Ifield played matches, so a combined effort on these occasions occurred.

The year 1866 seems to be an auspicious year in the social activities of the community when we have the introduction of the "Crawley Athletic Sports." This comprised both walking and running races which took place on The Street, followed by horse and pony racing. So there was racing both for the local inhabitants and nearby gentry. In fact people came from all over the county even from as far as London to participate or enjoy the sights. Indeed, an enjoyable day out for all concerned.

During this same year was organised at the George Hotel "The Great Exhibition". Special trains and fares were advertised from Victoria to Crawley, to enable people to venture from the capital to see this wondrous sight. The exhibits were a motley of

The site of The Sun Hotel, showing the grocer's shop of Edward Dean
which originally was there in 1864.

1876: The Railway Inn when still a pretty cottage. To the left, the gateway entrance
to the stables built by Simmins.

F. RUSSELL,

PRESERVER OF SPECIMENS IN NATURAL HISTORY,

Stationer, Bookbinder, Bookseller,

TOBACCONIST, VENDOR OF STAMPS,

AND

HAIRCUTTER,

NEWS, ADVERTISING, & PRINTING AGENT,

DEALER IN CUTLERY,

PICTURE FRAMES, AND PRINTS,

AT THE

GENERAL FANCY EMPORIUM,

CRAWLEY, SUSSEX.

AGENT TO THE BRITON LIFE ALLIANCE FIRE

AND

ACCIDENTAL DEATH ASSURANCE OFFICES.

AGENT TO G. F. SALTER & Co., DYERS, PLUMASSIERS, &c.

O yes! O yes! I'm not the town crier, but I wish to make a noise in the world, like some of my betters,

And as I can't be a Member of Parliament, nor an Archbishop, Lord Chancellor, barber surgeon to the Queen, nor a distinguished man of letters,

I have opened an Omnium Gatherum at Crawley, in the County of Sussex, right in the centre of the village,

Where I'll sell you all I profess to have on the spot, or by procuration, at a very small profit, and without any pillage.

Vases and workboxes, wax fruits and wax flowers, so natural they cheat the roving bees, whether common or humble;

Glass shades, bread, fruit, and cheese mats, fishing tackle, clocks, watches, and Albert guards to save your tickers a tumble.

First-rate engravings, picture frames, looking glasses, concertinas, spectacles, preserved specimens of birds, beasts, and fishes as old as the creation.

Lustres, China ornaments, vestas, fancy reticules, ornamental cut paper, portemonnaies, enough to hold the wealth of the nation.

Albums, pipes, one shilling clocks—yes, only a shilling!—wool mats, writing desks, combs, brushes, and razors that would cut your poorest relation.

Crotchet hooks, walking sticks, fancy baskets, musical instruments, cabinet ware, finger rings in gold or silver, for civil service or use matrimonial!

Electro-plated spoons and forks, brooches, cosmetiques, bird cages, tooth brushes, jewellery, perfumery, home made, foreign and colonial.

Tunbridge ware, fancy stationery, worked slippers, clothes brushes, oil paintings, photographs of the living celebrities, and several of the great departed;

Figures in *terra cotta*, Parian, Alabaster, barometers, thermometers, stereoscopes, microscopes, and telescopes, that can shew you when the Great Eastern has really started.

Backgammon, chess, and bagatelle boards, cigar cases, newspapers, cutlery, japanned papier maché goods, pocket knives with handles of horn, or

Ivory, cigars, tobacco pipe cleaners, pouches, match boxes, scissors, lucifer matches, pistols and guns that will shoot straight or round a corner.

Elastic bands, trinket holders, whatnots, hand mirrors, leather bags, quills, pen holders, and steel pens that spell and write grammar like Lindley Murray.

Crotchet mats made to order, feather dusters, razor strops, watch stands, Vesuvians (safety ones), that won't go off in a hurry.

Ladies' companions (very chaste), egg boilers, account books, key rings, Zealand twine, ink, luggage labels, hedge-hog caps—such traps for garotters;

Tea caddys, blank cards, pins, hair wash, pomade, pencils, sealing wax, Leach's Alabastrine for mending broken China, Russian waterproofing to keep dry your trotters.

The mechanical autoperipatetikos, the magic apokathartikon, so mysterious I cannot here explain,

Bill files, cricket bats (such willow, bound to make a *Grace*-ful score), pocket books, and puzzles that give good training for the brain.

Berlin wool, complexion powder, dessert papers, letter weighers elementary musical works, in German, French, and our dear native tongue,

From the works of Great Handel, to the slap-bang penny song book to suit all tastes and lung.

Memorandum books, tooth picks, monograms, tracing paper, Pharoah's serpents, magic photographs, and other clever mysteries;

Camels' hair, pencils paint boxes, clips, gum bottles, Roulette boards, books of fiction and different kinds of histories.

Young artiste's drawing books, steel knitting pins, tatting needles—all needles except the needle gun.

Ledgers, cash books, double and single entry, poetry of the most serious nature and verses full of fun.

Marking ink, envelopes – official sizes, adhesive and stamped, with plain or gorgeous crest.

Despatch bags, toilet trays, almanacks, photo frames to hang up the image of those we love the best.

Dram bottles, ivory tablets, comic cubes, bread and butter plates in wood, satchels, Mavors' spelling books, and comic *cartes*,

Church services and hymn books, Christmas and New Year cards, scented sachets, valentines and Cupid's missiles, warranted to smart all hearts

Playing cards, India-rubber pipe cases, conjuring tricks, walnut desks, Tivoli boards, tourists' cases, perfumed soaps, pink, mauve, green, and almost every shade.

I receive contributions for that most useful and well disciplined body of men – the Crawley and Ifield Fire Brigade.

The above are a few of the numerous and extending variety of articles which may be had or procured as aforesaid at my Omnium Gatherum.

And I assure lives in the Briton, Medical, and General Life Office and insure against loss by fire in the Alliance. I also shave men (not the ladies) and lather um

With the sweetest of soaps, use the softest of brushes. I cut the hair of ladies and gentlemen, little boys and girls, schools and families of more than twenty by contract, and not by the new fangled machinery.

I insert advertisements, print circulars, bill heads, hand bills on the shortest notice, and supply periodicals at home and by post; I am agent for G. F. Salter and Co., who dye silks, satins, feathers, and repair crinolinery.

Make up ladies' own hair, titivate gentlemen's wigs, like my great prototype FIGARO, the original *largo al factotum!*

So now, gentles, you know what I can do and what I can sell, and if you see anything here that you want, be kind enough to note 'em!

artifacts loaned by the local gentry and their friends and included paintings, china and stuffed animals. A description of the event was written by Harry Lemon, son of Mark Lemon.

Penny readings of these tales were read to the public at the National Schools for evening entertainment. Some have been collected together in book form under the title "Tales of Serena Woritts" and were published by Frederick Russell.

Mr. Frederick Russell became a well-known character in the village of Crawley and the surrounding area. He first established himself as a barber, setting up in the room above his mother's shop in the Old Whyte Harte. By the mid 1860s, he had extended his accomplishments to embrace taxidermy and antiquities, and opening the first "multi-store." This was opened in the cottage facing the upper square and went under the grand title of "Russells Emporium", its contents being numerous and diverse. Each small room must have been an alladin's cave of treasures, as shown by the advertisement on the opposite page.

During this period of time, "The Street" became a thriving business area which needed supporting industrial development. While a few builders, tinmen and painters had premises in this vicinity, the most suitable expansion area was to the west of The Street in the triangular area encompassed by Smalls Lane and the West Green. Here several industries were developed.

Behind the George Inn, bounded by Ifield Lane and Smalls Lane, the Ockenden family established their builder's business in 1824 and later their funeral establishment. Their home "The Croft" and builders premises still remain today, though somewhat altered. When the pond in the area was drained and filled in on their land, they built the shops known as "The Market Place" in Ifield Road and the houses in St. John's Road along the boundaries of their property. Also, building the first fire engine house, and storing and maintaining the engine, the family having a long association with the Fire Brigade.

Another industry in the area with which another branch of the Ockenden family was associated was brewing. There were four breweries in Crawley at this time, the largest being that owned by the Ockendens, though not established by them. They owned two sites, one in West Street, where now extends Gadstones workshops and parking facilities and Ball's Off-licence. The other on the corner site of Robinson Road and The High street, part of the land being taken from the School's playground. These premises had long and spacious cellars and vaults, and did a big trade extending miles around Crawley. For many years the Ockendens, the Mitchells and the Gates families (all inter-married) were owners of nearly all the licensed premises in the High Street and also the breweries. (Those who like a glass of beer, will never know what real beer tastes like. In those days, a pint of beer cost 1½d (½p) and there were few houses in Crawley that did not have a 4½ gallon cask - 3s.9d (18p) brought in, tapped ready for use.)

1875

Top: The Street facing North

Below: The Street facing South

from old faded photographs

The other two breweries were sited, one in The High Street owned by Chantlers, and later developed into The Brewery Shades, and the fourth on the corner of West Street and Oak Road owned by Holders. Holders just died out. Mitchells took over The Brewery Shades, and the Southdown Brewery acquired Ockendens in later years.

Along the Ifield Road opposite to the West Green was a pair of small cottages, one with a lean-to extension. This was the house of Mr. Budgen and his wife. Here he carried on the business of cooperage, baths, wash-tubs and beer casks predominating. This business gradually died with the advent of metal washing vessels.

Crawley and Three Bridges was at one time a centre of the broom making trade, and during the year, thousands, possibly hundreds of thousands of brooms, both birch and heath, were sent to various markets. All materials came from our woods and forests, not a single outside material was needed. Crawley had two large broomyards with their stacks of birch and heath, rods and sticks. One was at the corner of West Street and Springfield Road owned by a man named Biggs, the other, by far the largest, was where Victoria Road stands leading through into the meadow where now is Spencers Road. To reach the broomyard, a cinder track led between the School and pond in Ifield Lane (now Victoria Park) and the owner Jesse Jenner lived in the cottage now known as 1, Victoria Road.

On the left hand side of the track were large stacks of birch, heath and faggots, large sticks from which the bands to bind the brooms were split, osiers (willows) etc. Near to Jenner's house commenced the wooden workshops. The first was a making shop; the second the handle shaving shed. Then came a much larger making shed with a long shed at right angles, the centre being used as a store shed. The end buildings were additional making shops. Facing the first run of shops was a similar lot except that one had an open front and was used for the truck on which the brooms were conveyed to the railway station. The whole formed a kind of quandrangle and at the rear were the cattle pens, a pleasure farm and a slaughter house used by Mr. Spencer Smith.

At the old forge in North Road, Nat Goring (blacksmith) used to fashion the knives and hooks used by the broom makers. In the spring, the broom makers visited the forests and trimmed the birch from the trees which had been felled. These were tied in neat bundles or faggots and carted to the broomyard. The same happened to the heather after it had flowered. The large sticks were cut in the woodlands and also carted to the broomyard. These sticks had to be thoroughly soaked before they could be stripped for bands for the brooms. Osiers were gathered to finish off heath brooms and broom heads.

To secure the heath (heather) and the birch for making brooms was no light task. The men used to go to Shelley Plain, Grouse Road and Grouse Farm, and parts of Buchan Hill for the heath, and Tilgate and Buchan Hill for the birch. If possible, the largest bundles were carted to Crawley. There the birch for broom making was trimmed from the bough, the remainder being made into faggots, or if straight enough, into beansticks. Large faggots (for fire) could be purchased at 3d (1p) each or £1 per

CRAWLEY

*1875 Ifield Lane. The gate and field beyond is the site of Spensers Road.
The cottage is 10, Ifield Road.*

hundred, and beansticks (really straight good sticks) at 6d (2½p) per 50 sticks. Other by-products were "the headings" - the birch headings - which were chopped before the sticks (handles) were inserted. These made excellent kindling wood, and if a very strong fire has to be maintained, heath seeds can be strongly recommended. The choppings from the broomsticks were also much sought after.

To make a broom, whether of birch or heather, a quantity of the material was selected and rolled out evenly in the lap, by hand. Some of the thinner birch was doubled up to make the body and then was tightly buckled round, and the whole rolled with the feet until it became the desired size and shape. Then came the banding. The bands had to be prepared overnight and it required strength and skill to secure these bands. Imagine a stout stick or pole some 1½ - 2 inches in diameter and 5 - 6 feet long. A neat nick was made and then strips were peeled off and the end was shaved to an incredible thinness and pliability. Two of these strips went round the broomhead, which had its thick end evenly chopped, a handle inserted and then a wooden peg driven through the handle. A neatly executed piece of work! Broomheads were used among merchandise when being shipped. They made excellent "buffers" and when the ship arrived at its destination, the broomheads were sold and the handles attached.

Broom making was not only a long and hard job, but it was very poorly paid. To make anything like 25s to 30s a week (£1.25 - 1.50p) the workers would have to sit up till 10 o'clock at night drawing the bands and cutting the pegs. Soon after 6 a.m., they were there (they were on piece-work) and had to continue until late, and then after a break for tea, go on for hours drawing the bands. The principal makers at this place were Jenners, Sippets, Izards, Sherlocks and the Stanfords (William Stanford set up his own business in North Road after Jenners closed) also Denman. To this broomyard came one - John Denman, walking daily from his home at Copthorne.

P.A.

Horley to Balcombe Road 1903 near to Pound Hill crossing with Worth Lane.
Showing Peter's Lime Avenue.

P.A.

Three eldest sons of Maria & William 1888

Cameo

The Siblings

Here it is appropriate to return to the Denman children introduced earlier. Through pictures and brief descriptions of their adult life, the reader will have a flavour of the working class society and a glimpse of the fashions and environment of that era.

Living on part of the Crabbet estate, all the boys found employment there except for John. Peter, the eldest, worked as a labourer at Kitsbridge Farm when he first started work. Later, he worked maintaining the forests surrounding Crabbet Park. As a young man he planted the avenue of lime saplings which extended along the Horley-Balcombe Road for some 2 miles. Some of these trees remain today. When first married he lived in a cottage at Wakehams Green (now the site of the garden centre) later moving to one of the cottages on Church Lane, Worth, where he remained until his death in 1913 aged 80.

Thomas finished school at the age of ten, working as a carter boy at Toveys Farm. Later, he worked on Crabbet estate as a gamekeeper. Unfortunately Thomas was killed while at work in a machinery accident at the age of 36 years, leaving a young widow, formerly Jane Vigar and two small children, Annie and John Arthur. Widow Denman later married Alfred Wilding.

The home of Peter Denman and his family, in Worth Lane. This group of three cottages was adjacent to Worth School near to the old Workhouses. The picture shows Esther and Minnie with their mother. Esther became Mrs Peter Dench and Minnie, Mrs Maurice Langridge.

William worked as a servant at Worth Park for the Montefiores, though upon marriage he moved to a small thatched cottage along London Road at County Oak near to Jordans Farm. John, as previously mentioned became a broom maker. Also in his youth John became a local champion bare-fisted boxer, fighting on the field opposite to the Abergavenny Arms. William and John had a double-wedding at Worth Church on Christmas Day 1863, William marrying Mary Pollard and John marrying Ann Langridge. It was not unusual for the servant classes to marry on Christmas Day as this was often the only free day which they had during the year. John with his wife lived in a small cottage in Coomber Wood until just after his father's death in 1874, then he moved his family to Crawley.

James, the youngest son and last to marry, was a game-keeper for Crabbet. When Kitsbridge Cottages were built on the land containing their family home, Thomas and Eliza moved to the new premises with their son James and youngest daughter Sarah. Upon James' marriage in 1873, the parents went to live with John. James and his family remained at Kitsbridge and James continued to work as a gamekeeper until his death in 1919.

The girls appeared a little more adventurous, as mostly their marriages took them away from the area, and they became absorbed within their husband family.

Mrs Montifores School, Worth

Class of 1878 - Minnie Denman front row first on the right,
who later married Maurice Langridge.

P.A.

Peter Denman 1833 - 1913

PETER DENMAN m Mary Buckland
1857

Mary Ann	William Stemp
William	Maria Watson
Annie	Charles Twinn
Jane	unmarried
Peter	Emily Sargent
Ellen	George Perkins
Hester	Peter Dench
Kate	died 7 hours old
Minnie	Maurice Langridge

THOMAS DENMAN   m Jane Vigar
(1839 - 75)

1862   m   Alfred Wilding

Annie	Arthur Trigg
Thomas Edward	died aged 10 months
John Arthur	Ellen Billson

JAMES DENMAN   m Jane Reeves
1873

George	Minnie Potter
William	Isabella Buckland
Jane	Fredrick Clements
Elizabeth	unmarried
James	Elsie Barnett
Alice	Thomas Deighton
Ellen Annie	Thomas Maynard
Mabel Florence	died aged 4 years
Edith May	married late in life

James Denman 1845 - 1919

WILLIAM DENMAN m Mary Pollard d. 1878
1863 m Rebecca
Bredan
(widow)

Emily Jane	—	Thomas Denman
William Henry	—	died 4 days old
Mary Ann	—	Thomas Gorringe
Son	—	died 20 hours old
Peter Bredan	—	Stepson

William Denman 1835-1903

Eliza, the eldest daughter, married Thomas Jenner, a son of broomdasher Jenner. Thomas did not follow his father's trade, but was a butcher. In fact, a mobile butcher, as he visited farms and private homes slaughtering pigs for their owners consumption. Upon marriage in 1860 to Eliza he set up a pork butchers shop in The Street, Crawley, where he sold pork pies, brawns and sausages as well as having a slaughter house to the rear. Late in 1868 he sold the business to Mr. Yetman and moved to Vauxhall Bridge in London opening another shop, where he became very prosperous.

Mary did not rove far from home marrying Edward Vigar of Copthorne. He lived at 'The Prince Albert', his father being the landlord and builder of this establishment. Edward Vigar followed the building trade and built up a very thriving business in the village and many of the houses remaining in the older part of the village are testimony to his skill.

Jane and Elizabeth went into service, Jane as a housekeeper to an elderly couple at Three Bridges, where she remained for several years. Elizabeth gave birth to an illegitimate daughter, Olive, in 1871. When Elizabeth married Alfred Parmenter, a

Mary Vigar 1841-1914

railway engineer, in 1874, her daughter moved with her. Finally the Parmenter family moved to Lewes where in retirement they had a Fish and Chip shop until the end of the first world war. Their declining years were spent at Rodmell, where Olive, who did not marry, looked after them. At present, no further information can be found regarding Jane and Sarah.

Eliza Jenner & family   Elizabeth & Alf Parmenter

Family Cottage - Copthorne

William James Denman
(standing)
and brother Jack (1891)

W.J. Denman

Childhood and Youth

William James Denman was the third, and youngest son of John and Ann Denman. He first saw light of day on 20th December 1877 in the upstairs room above the barbers shop of old Mrs. Russell in the Ancient Priors, then known as The White Harte Farm. Why he was born at this house is unclear, unless old Mrs. Russell also acted as a midwife, for the Denman family lived at Tichborne Cottages, Ifield Road, opposite to the west green. This pair of cottages were minute, each with one small living room, a scullery and two tiny bedrooms. The cottage which the family occupied was the end one nearest to Ifield Lodge, their small garden plot having the river as its boundary. This river flowed from the top of Goffs Hill, supplemented by several springs, passing under the railway line near to the crossing gates, down Prospect Place, under Turners Farm House and crossing Ifield Road whence it sped merrily on its way towards Clappers. (These two cottages were demolished by the new town commission in 1959/60.) There were but few cottages in the area at the time. Just a group of eight Tichborne Cottages on one side of the green, Turners Farm and six more cottages on the other side of the green. While on the curve of Horsham Road were one or two pairs of isolated cottages. Shop extensions on the front of the first pair of cottages were occupied by "Major" Moore who sold fish. "Fine haddocks, fine kippers and new bloaters" sounded throughout the town practically every day. The next door was the bakery and sweet shop of Mr. and Mrs. J. Till. The West Green Arms, and the cottage known as The Crown Beerhouse. The west green, being common land was used for grazing of goats, chickens and ducks. Also there was some of the area used as allotments. Here John Denman had a large, vegetable plot. William was christened at St. Margaret's Church, Ifield on 3rd. February 1878, one of his sponsors being James Waghorn (for whom he was named) an elderly shoemaker, who was the last tenant of the North Gate Toll cottage.

A tiny, wiry, little boy with a mass of thick black hair, Willy tagged along with his brother Jack (John) who was some two years older than himself, and his friends, being led into all kinds of mischief. One incident he most vividly recalls relates to the time when the development of Horsham Road was having the new areas of Alpha Road, or Paradise Alley as it was known, constructed. At the spot where the houses of Sunny side were to be built, remained the roots and stump of a very large oak tree. The intrepid explorers decided to blow it up. From old Benny's (William Bengo Benny) general store which was on the bend of the road opposite the west green, and a veritable cave of goodies to delight any small boy's heart, was purchased a quantity of gunpowder. The gunpowder was packed around the roots, the fuse set and lit. The little gang retired

99 High Street - the first cottage on the left

The house next door. In the doorway Mrs John Court, George Court,
Joe Court, Dean's bakers boy, ?, C. Messer, H. Briggs, ?,
Joe Heathfield W.J.D. Clarence Parsons

to take shelter at a safe distance to watch the results. They waited, and waited but nothing happened. Finally, the youngest, almost four, Willy was elected to go to investigate. As he approached the tree root and bended down, the gunpowder exploded, taking with it all Willy's hair, eyebrows and eyelashes and leaving him distinctly black! One can imagine his mother's reaction and the consequences to brother Jack upon their return home. Needless to say, Willy only recalls not requiring a haircut for many months. "I well remember going when I was a youngster to the back steps of 75, High Street, where Mr. Jimmy Denman (no immediate relation) used to cut hair at 1d for children and 2d for adults. At the rear of the premises there is a sort of well at the back door and smaller boys had to stand on the top step and the bigger boys on the second. At that time there was only one professional barber, Fred Russell. One remembers the "barber of the steps" did not politely ask - a little to the right or left please, but a quick twist of the hand sent the head into the required position."

At the age of five young Will was enrolled as a pupil at west Crawley National School. To attend this school payment of half a penny a week was made, while the British School in New Road charged one penny per week. (There is no equivalent amount in today's monetary system, as it is less than 1p. Sufficient it is to say as a comparison that the same amount purchased two bars of chocolate in those days.) The curriculum consisted of the three "R's", some history and geography, and, of course, Religious instruction. As to Willy's performance as a pupil, we can only surmise, as there are no family records. Judging by his performance in later life with his pen, command of English language, and descriptive talent, he was a very apt pupil. Schooling must have been a revelation and joy to his enquiring mind, an instrument by which he could further his knowledge through books and writing. He learned where he could, and now he held the key to recording many things stored in his memory. (Willy's near neighbour Mr. Harry Holder, a roadman well over 80 years of age at the time, regaled young Willy with many stories of his youth when he was a postboy riding the coach horses.) Even at an early age, Willy appears to have had an insatiable appetite for knowledge, particularly with regards to the history of the area. From his work in later life we know that he was very sensitive, taking great pleasure in observing things of nature and beauty and possessing of a photographic memory. Little could he have dreamed, as he worked away in the classroom, that one day he would return there as a School Governor, for that position was reserved for the local gentry and wealthy tradesmen, and his family did not fall within either of these categories.

As previously mentioned, Willy was a mischievous little boy, though the pranks were usually harmless, and as he became older, he was usually the ringleader of the group. Care and planning were required for these escapades, as punishment and ire of his father were somewhat swift if caught and rather painful. Despite his small size he was also a very good athlete.

In 1881 the family moved from Tichborne Cottages to The Street. The house was a timber framed building circa 1441, which had been divided into three small cottages during the early 18th. century. Their cottage was later numbered 99, though for the

*John and Ann Denman with some of their children in 1897.
Standing: Vashti, Jack, Thomas, Will, Kate. Seated: Olive and Nell*

next fifty years, it was referred to as "Denmans." Situated next to "The Mychelles Farm" with the garden orchard with its well, between them, and the Long Green stretching way in front of the row of cottages, which at this time was bereft of trees, but the centre of many village activities. Here village cricket was played on a Saturday and on summer evenings, and other entertainments took place. So most of his childhood recollections take place in the vicinity of The Street, though he reminisces about roaming the surrounding woods and fields, skating on Bewbush ponds and fishing at Ifield millpond. His descriptions of the activities pursued by the boys give an insight into the pastimes of the young in this era. Favourite games of the period would appear very unexciting to today's youth.

Some games were seasonal as Hoops, tops, marbles and hopscotch. Many involved much running and shouting, like Hide and Seek, Paperchasing, Chivvy, Chibby I and My knocker your knocker, the last being played across the lower Square and Greens. A piece of string was tied to a knocker on one side of the street and carried across to the knocker of the house opposite. When the knots were tied, a sharp knock was given on one knocker and when the door was opened, it raised the knocker on the other side of the street, the shutting of the first door banging the knocker on the second. Annoying perhaps but simply mischief.

Jump, Tiddy Wagtail involved using a piece of wood, a stone and a stick. The piece of wood was laid on the ground with a stone on one end of the wood. Using the stick, the player hit the wood at the opposite end to that of the stone, the object being to see who could catapult the farthest. Elastic shooters (catapults) were common then and an owner of one would imagine himself "a tough guy", though the shooters were mainly used to see who could shoot the furthest and be most accurate at a target.

Willy recalls a time when about thirty boys were lying in the mangers of the coaching house at the White Hart playing "I spy". "We had wetted our faces and rubbed brimstone matches over our faces and hands, and when 'man out' as we thought threw open the door, we all jumped up and yelled. It was P.C. Gower! He yelled out too. We must have looked weird with all the phosphorous running up and down our hands and faces. Before he could do anything, we were gone."

Two games, or rather sports we would call them, have not been mentioned, cricket and football. Crawley had its own cricket team, and while the boys coached by the rector still played on the long green, 'The Club' played on a field at the rear of The White Hart. Many of the large estates surrounding Crawley, such as Worth Park, Crabbet and Paddockhurst had their own teams, providing local "derbies". School teams were also encouraged.

Football was introduced to the area by The Reverend Barrett-Lennard. He taught the Sunday School boys and choir boys the rudimentary skills of the game. Brother John was one of this group, and as usual Willy was 'tagging along', and stood watching the boys' antics. Suddenly, a voice boomed: "Willy, why are you not playing?" "Please, Sir, I don't know how," said the small boy. I have never seen a football before. The

Reverend gentleman fetched the ball and placed it about six yards from me and said, 'Now, run and kick hard.' I did so, and oh my relief, when I found that my foot was still attached to my leg!" So commenced his second great passion in life. For, when Crawley football club was formed, Willy became a player member at the age of twelve in 1890, an association which was to last for the rest of his life.

In common with all the other children, William attended Sunday School and Church twice on a Sunday as a member of the choir. In fact, the National School provided all the members of the choir, and continued to do so until the 1940's. It is presumed that William did not attend Sunday School at St Mary Magdalene's, West Crawley, but at St John's, for he had as his teachers the Misses Smiths. He speaks of west green Sunday School, but may mean pupils who attended the National School building. The highlight of the year was the Sunday School treat. Willy won his first penknife for good attendance, along with the Lord's Prayer printed on a large card, all in fancy colours. It was presented on the last occasion that the treat was held at the Old Rectory, Ifield. The children had been taken by wagons to the old house, and tea was served from long tables upon the lawn, while beneath some of the trees were large brown pans full of lemonade for the thirsty children.

In future years, the Sunday School treat was held at Crawley Rectory. The eldest group of children were also invited to partake of tea with the Misses Smiths, inside of the room in Crawley Elm Tree. (The Congregational School held treats in Gravely's fields - now Goffs Park Road/Horsham Road corner, while the Baptist children used Crosskeys meadow - The Broadway/Queens Square area.)

It appears that the boys were not content to belong to one church, because several also belonged to the Baptist Church in order to join their drum and fife band. This band was formed under the direction of a Mr. Coombes, who was employed at Mr. Spencer Smith's. The band went further afield for its treat - Eastbourne. Well, the great day arrived, but first there had to be a parade, headed by the band. With green baize bags slung each side, the little group marched down Station Road, up Three Bridges Road and High Street, to the Railway Station with all the excursionists walking two by two. The band were only "safe" (said Mr. Coombes) with two tunes - "What a friend we have in Jesus" and "Onward Christian Soldiers", and these were played both at Eastbourne on the way to The Wish Tower and Crawley on the return.

"The fife and drum did not last long. We got tired of attending every little function and with only being allowed to play the same two hymns. Unofficially, some of us tried other tunes in the coachhouse of the White Hart yard and it was agreed to break out a bit. It was customary for Mr. Coombes to state: "You will commence with" (he would mention which of the two hymns) and at the conclusion he would hold up his baton for six paces and on the seventh we had to follow the second hymn. Judge his surprise and anger when 'British Grenadiers' sounded. I was adjudged the ringleader (rightly too) and told my services were not wanted and as the others upheld me, that finished the Baptist school fife and drum band."

John Denman continued the tradition of his childhood by taking his own family hop picking each summer in Kent. So, William had a holiday each year. Probably, he also earned pin-money when older by delivering milk or working in the barns of the farm which adjoined the family plot of land, run by Mr. Tyler.

When William completed his formal education at the age of twelve and a half years, he went to work for Mr. Tyler full-time. He drove a pony and cart collecting and delivering milk as far as Hutt Farm and surrounding houses. At this time his friends called him "Fatty", but in the way of small boys, this name denotes he was the very opposite. Then, on 5th. November 1894, Willaim embarked on his future full-time employment. At the age of sixteen, he was accepted by Mr. C. Mitchell as an employee of Crawley postal services. He must have worked exceedingly long hours, as amongst his tasks was to meet the night mail coaches. This was both for the collecting and dispatching of mail. The horse drawn coaches continued until 1st. June 1905. The horses were changed at The Black Swan, Peas Pottage, and then Chequers at Horley. The guards went right through, but the drivers returned to Brighton. The guards were armed with a blunderbuss, bayonet, a truncheon, a pair of handcuffs and a whistle. The motor coach era started on 2nd. June 1905 and was a very tame affair by comparison to the horsed coaches. At that time no fewer than 112 horsed vehicles were conveying mails at night time.

Will's job was to oversee the loading of the mails for East Grinstead, and the van which took mail to places on the Surrey and Kent border. At this time William, occasionally joined by brother Jack, was the eldest child living at home, with four younger sisters. This generation of Denman children enjoyed on the whole more diverse occupations to that of the previous generation, at least the boys did, and travelled further afield in the process.

Thomas the eldest (named for his grandfather) joined the Royal Marines on H.M.S. Colossus serving in Hong Kong and fighting in China in The Boxer Rebellion, among other postings. Like his father, he was also a very good boxer. In 1894 he married his cousin Emily Jane, at St John's Church. At this time he was based at Portsmouth. William could scarcely have known this elder brother as he was 12 years older to him.

John (Jack) was apprenticed to a saddlemaker, and later worked for Mr. Miller's Saddlers business on The Street. When of an age, he became a regular soldier joining the 12th. Lancers, a cavalry regiment. His first experience of battle was in The Boer War in South Africa.

The two eldest daughters, Annie Jane and Elsie, worked for the Montifores at Worth Park as housemaids. Annie married John Johnson on Christmas Day 1886, a cowman on the estate, and Elsie married Albert Mitchell, a carpenter of Crawley and an ardent campanologist. This wedding also took place on a Christmas Day, 1892. After marriage, Elsie and Albert's first home was in Princess Road, where they stayed for the next twelve years, before moving to an apartment in The Ancient Priors in 1904.

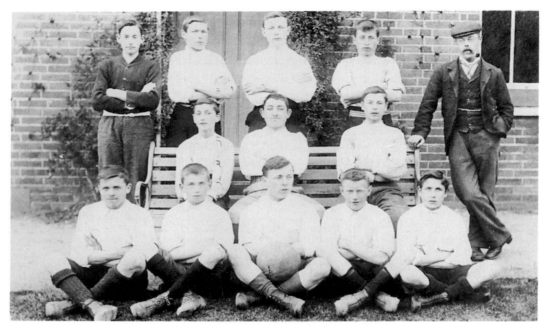

P.A.

Crawley Football Club 1890. Bill Denman first left middle row.

Crawley Cricket Club 1892. Bill, front row, right.

Both pictures taken beside The Sun Hotel.

Whilst William, now called Bill, worked very hard, he also played very hard. As previously mentioned, he joined Crawley Football Club in 1890, and the Cricket Club in '92. By the time he was 14 years old, he was assistant Honorary Secretary of the Football Club, and by 16 years of age he was Honorary Secretary of both clubs, as well as a team player. A good athlete, he joined Crawley Harriers Athletic Club, and Crawley Cycling Club.

When not working at the Post Office or partaking of sporting activities, Bill was busy collecting items of local knowledge by talking to all elderly inhabitants and making notes of their information. From the age of 17, he began writing articles for publication in press and magazines.

During the first 25 years of Bill's life, Crawley experienced rapid changes of development from a relatively small village to that of a thriving small town. Many incidents of national interest occurred also at this time. These happenings were recorded by him, and if he was too young at the time of the event, he sought out informants in later years. So we are able to visualise the community in which Bill lived and worked, before the turn of the century.

Elsie Denman married Albert Mitchell 25 December 1892.
Elsie was the third child of John and Ann Denman.

All the Inhabitants of Crawley and Ifield, 1881

Crawley Parish

No. of Assessment.	Name of Occupier.	Name of Owner.	Description of Property.	Name or situation of Property.
1	Bowers, Stephen	Johnson, Mrs.	House, shop, and garden.	Crawley Town.
2	Burgess, S. C.	Himself.	,, ,,	,,
3	Caffyn, C.	Himself.	,, ,,	
4	Crawley Gas Company	Themselves.	Mains and works.	Clappers.
5	Chantler, George	Himself.	House, shop, and garden.	Crawley Town.
6	Gates, Robert, Executors of	Montefiore, J. M., Esq., Executors	Land.	,,
7	,, ,,	,, ,, ,,		,,
8	,, ,,	,, ,, ,,	Hotel.	,,
9	Ellis, George	,, ,, ,,		,,
10	Gravely, T. and Son	Gravely, Thomas	House, shop, and garden.	,,
11	Gravely, Thomas	Himself.	House and garden.	,,
12	Kelsey, H. A.	,,	House, shop, and garden.	,,
13	Knight, Ephraim	Blunt, W. F. Esq.	Land.	Tushmore.
14	Little, Charles	Russell, Frederick	House, shop, and garden.	Crawley Town.
15	Lennard, Rev. J. B.	Himself.	House and garden.	Rectory.
16	,, ,, ,,	,,	Tithes.	,,
17	,, ,, ,,	,,	Land.	Crawley Town.
18	,, ,, ,,	,,	,,	Back of Town.
19	,, ,, ,,	Smith, T., Esq.	,,	,,
20	Muggridge, John	Tusler, James, Executors of	House, shop, and garden.	Crawley Town.
21	,, ,,	,,	Land.	,,
22	Miller, Milton	Johnson, Mrs. A.	,,	,,
23	Mitchell, William	Himself.	Post Office.	,,
24	,, ,,	,,	Land.	,,
25	Martin, T. H.	Montefiore, J. M., Esq., Executors of	House and garden.	Crawley Town.
26	Nightingale, William	Caffin, Mrs.	Land.	Black Dog.
27	Nelson, Miss	Saillard, P., Esq.	House.	Buchan Hill.
28	Penfold, John	Himself.	House, shop, and garden	Crawley Town.
29	Pronger, James	Saillard, P., Esq.	House and land.	Shelley Farm.
30	Bedford, John	Buckle, Rev.	Land.	Part of Jordans.
31	Robinson, Jos. and H.	Montefiore, J. M., Esq., Executors of	House and land.	Manor Farm.
32	Russell, Frederick	Himself.	House and shop.	Crawley Town.
33	Rowse, James	Leach, J.	House and garden.	,,
34	Randall, Stephen	Chantler, George	Beer house.	,,
35	Saillard, P.	Himself.	Forest land.	Forest.
36	Saillard, P.	,,	,,	Whines of Shelley.
37	Steele, Mrs	Sandeman, Mrs.	,,	Bucks Coppice.
38	Seamer, Isaac	Smith, Mr.	House.	White Hart Inn.
39	Smith, Misses	Montefiore, J. M., Esq., Executors of	House and garden.	Crawley Town.
40	Smith, T. H.	Smith, Misses	,,	,,
41	Smith, Spencer	Himself.	Warehouse.	,,
42	Tyler, Stephen	Churchwardens of Worth.	Land.	Clappers.
43	Wright, John	Caffin, W., Executors of	House land and barn.	Crawley Town.
44	,, ,,	Blunt, W. T., Esq.	House and garden.	,,
45	Wilkins, John	Himself.	House and shop.	,,
46	Weedon, Joseph	Stacey, John	Land.	Worth Lane.
47	Cooper, Thos.	Dean, Mrs.	House and garden.	Clappers.
48	Cheale, Mrs	,,	,,	,,
49	Davis, John	,,		,,
50	Easton, Job	,,		,,
51	Green, E.	,,		,,
52	Harrington, James	,,		,,
53	Homewood, Luke	,,	,,	,,
54	Jenner, Chas.	,,		,,
55	Parsons, Miss	,,		,,
56	Potter, Wm., Jun.	,,	,,	,,
57	,,	,,	,,	,,
58	Semple, Dr.	,,	,,	,,
59	Thompsett, Thos.	,,	,,	,,
60	Botting, Benjamin	Mitchell, William	,,	,,
61	Broom, Henry	,,	,,	,,
62	Briggs, G.	,,	,,	,,
63	Cheal, George	,,	,,	,,
64	Court, William	,,	,,	,,
65	Holmwood, J.	,,	,,	,,
66	Soper, James	,,	,,	,,
67	Burgess, S. C.	Russell, Frederick	House.	Crawley Town.
68	Dench, William	,,	House and garden.	,,
69	Denman, William	,,	House.	,,
70	Snelling, John	,,	House and garden.	,,
71	Skinner and Court	,,	House.	,,
72	Denman, James	Johnson, Miss A.	House and garden.	,,
73	Holder, Henry	,,	,,	,,
74	Jones, Thomas	,,	,,	,,
75	Pollard, Peter	,,	,,	,,
76	Pollard, Peter	,,	Workshop.	,,
77	Humphrey, William	,,	Workshops.	Crawley Town.
78	Gravely, Thomas	Himself.	House and garden.	,,
79	Parker, Sydney	Gravely, Thomas	,,	,,
80	Barnes, —	Gravely, Henry	,,	,,
81	Dewdney, William	,,	,,	,,
82	Botting, John	,,	,,	,,
83	Messer, Stephen	Chantler, George	,,	,,
84	Chantler, George	Himself.	Warehouse.	,,
85	Tingley, James, jun.	Biggs, Thomas	House and garden.	,,
86	Tingley, James, sen.	,,	,,	,,
87	Hall, Mrs.	,,	,,	,,
88	Ede, Mrs.	Dalton, Miss A.	,,	County Oak.
89	Ellis, —	,,	,,	,,
90	Killick, Frank	,,	,,	,,
91	Soan, William	,,	,,	,,
92	Bridger, Mrs.	Tusler, James, Executors of	,,	Cross Keys.
93	Fuller, George	,,	,,	,,
94	Bridger, Richard	Webley, Ambrose	,,	Worth Lane.
95	Brench, Richard	Montefiore, J. M., Esq., Executors of	,,	Manor Farm.
96	Reen, Philip	,, ,,	,,	,,
97	Nightingale, William	Smith, Mr.	,,	Crawley Town.
98	Pronger, James	Saillard, P., Esq.	Cottage.	Shelley Farm.
99	Denman, William	Caffyn, Brothers	House.	Crawley Town.
100	Hall, A.	Lennard, Rev. J. B.	Lodge.	,,
101	Bark, Samuel	The Gas Company.	Cottage and garden.	Clappers.
102	Botting, John	Montefiore, J. M., Esq., Executors of	House and garden.	,,
103	Biphiek, Mrs.	,, ,, ,,	,,	Old Workhouse.
104	Godsmark, Richard	,, ,, ,,	,,	,,
105	Johnson, Mrs.	,, ,, ,,	,,	,,
106	Johnson, Thomas	,, ,, ,,	,,	,,
107	Lidbetter, James	,, ,, ,,	,,	,,
108	Messer, Mrs.	,, ,, ,,	,,	,,
109	Fuller, Mrs.	Wilkins, John	,,	Crawley Town.
110	Denman, John	,,	,,	,,
111	Knight, Ephraim	,,	,,	,,
112	Knight, Ephraim	,,	,,	,,

All the Inhabitants of Crawley and Ifield, 1881

Crawley Parish

No. of Assessment.	Name of Occupier.	Name of Owner.	Description of Property.	Name or situation of Property.
116a	Martin, David	Rendle, William	House and garden	Crawley Street
117	Murphy, —	Cutler, Miss	„	West Green
118	Miles, Henry	Jacques, Thomas	„	Ifield Road
119	Nightingale, William	Pipon, Major, Executors of	Land and brickfield	Gossip's Green
120	Ockenden, George	Himself	House and shop	Crawley Street
121	„	„	Brew-house and premises	New Road Brewery
122	„	Staveley, Pepper George	Land and buildings	Gossip's Green
123	Ockenden, John	Himself	House and garden	West Green
124	„	Biggs, William	Land	Part of Burstow Mead
125	Ockenden, Charles	Himself	House and garden	Laurels
126	„	„	Brew-house	Station Brewery
127	Osbourn, Henry	Osbourn, Henry	House and shop	West Green
128	„	Staveley, Pepper George	Land	Part of Goff's Hill Farm
129	Ockenden, Henry	Stacey, John	House, shop, and garden	Crawley Street
130	Parsons, George	Heath, Mary	House	Amberly Farm
131	„	„	Land and buildings	„
132	Penfold, John	Society of Friends	House and premises	Meeting House
133	Penfold, Frank	Trist, George	House	Collins's Farm
134	„	„	Land	„
135	Pipon, Manaton, Executors of	Pipon, Manaton, Executors of	Land, buildings, & shooting	Duxter's Farm
136	„	„	House	„
137	„	„	Land, buildings, &c.	Park and other land
138	„	„	Land and shooting	Part of Ginham Farm
139	„	„	„	Part of Ewhurst Place
140	„	„	Rough Land	Hyde Hill
141	„	„	House and garden	The Cottage
142	„	„	„	White House
143	„	„	Plantation	Stafford
144	Phillips, Thomas	Mitchell, John	House and garden	Fern Cottage
145	Pook, Mrs.	Simmins, William	„	London House
146	Pace, Henry	Russell, Frederick	House and shop	The Terrace
147	Pronger, Richard	Blunt, Wilfred	Land	Hogg's Hill
148	Pronger, James	Himself	„	Part of Whitehall Farm
149	Pimm, Mary	Farmer, James	House and garden	Rusper Lane
150	Pickett, Caleb	Jacques, Thomas	„	Crawley Street
151	Paine, William	„	„	Ifield Road
152	Penfold, Widow	Scott, Mrs.	„	Ifield Churchyard
153	Penfold, George	Weeks, Henry	„	New Town
154	Reeves, Mary	Ockenden, John	„	Church Road
155	Robinson, Joseph	Sumner, William	„	Lowfield Heath
156	Redford, John	Buckle, Matthew Hughes	„	Jordan's Farm
157	„	„	Land and buildings	„
158	„	Little, Mrs.	House and garden	Rose Cottage
159	Razzall, William	Lewin, Mary Emily	House	Ifield Green
160	„	„	Land	„
161	Robinson, Joseph	Robinson, Joseph	„	Church Road
162	Rawson, Helen	Montgomery, Hon. F.	House and premises	Ifield Lodge
163	Rich, Henry	Warren, Stephen	House and garden	Royal Oak
164	Sayers, Thomas	Cook, Richard	„	New Town
165	Smith, Spencer	Steadman, Miss	House	Little Buckswood
166	„	„	Land and buildings	„
167	„	Mrs. Montefiore	Land	Sun Meadows
168	„	Smith, Spencer	House, shop, and garden	West Sussex House
169	„	„	House and shop	Crawley Street
170	Soule, Henry May	Soule, Henry May	House	Whitehall
171	„	„	Land, buildings, & shooting	„
172	„	„	Laundry	„
173	Sanders, William	Pipon, Manaton, Executors of	House	Langley Farm
174	„	„	Land and buildings	„
175	„	„	Shooting	„
176	Simmins, William	Himself	House and garden	Crawley Villa
177	„	„	Coal shed, yard,& steam mill	Near Station
178	Simmins, Stephen	Simmins, William	House and shop	Bank Buildings
179	Simmins, George	Himself	Land	Part of Collins's Farm
180	„	„	House and garden	Bank Buildings
181	„	„	Printing office	„
182	Stavely, Pepper, Gen. Augustus	„	House, garden, and premises	Woldhurst Lea
183	„	„	Land and shooting	Gossip's Green
184	„	„	House	Lodge Woldhurst Lea
185	„	„	Land	Part of Goff's Hill Farm
186	„	„	„	New Town
187	Smith, Thomas	Blunt, Wilfrid	„	Old Workhouse
188	Smith, Caleb	Smith, Amelia, Executors of	House and meadow	West Green
189	Smith, Spencer	Smith, Spencer	Land	„
190	Steadman, Thomas	Mitchell, Henry	House and premises	The Swan
191	Soan, George	Montefiore, Mrs.	House, shop, and garden	Crawley Town
192	Smith, Mary	„	Land	Brickwall Field
193	Sayers, John	Himself	House, shop, and premises	Hope House
194	Pipon, Manaton, Executors of	Pipon, Manaton, Executors of	House	Stumbleholme Farm
195	„	„	Land and buildings	„
196	„	„	Shooting	„
197	Short, William	Himself	House	Little Park Farm
198	„	„	Land and buildings	„
199	Smith, Albert	Smith, Spencer	House and garden	Jessamine Cottage
200	Sherlock, George	Smith, Albert	„	West Green
201	Sayers, Amos	Biggs, William	„	Crawley Street
201a	Sprake, Charles	Himself	„	Richmond Villa
202	Smith, Spencer	Cutler, Miss	Land	Part of Turner's Farm
203	Sumner, William	Sumner, William	Land, brickfield, & buildings	West Green
204	„	„	„	Part of Goff's Hill Farm
205	„	Simmins, William	House and garden	Near Station
206	Shepherd, —	Sumner, William	„	Lowfield Heath
207	Strudwick, James	Cutler, Miss	„	West Green
207a	Stone, George	Blunt, Wilfrid	Land	Part of Malthouse Farm
208	Soan, Mary	Weeks, Henry	House and garden	New Town
209	Tizard, George	Simmins, William	House, shop, and garden	Bank Buildings
210	Taylor, Edwin	Hughes, Mary	House and shop	The Terrace
211	Tusler, Helen	Tusler, James, Executors of	House and garden	Perryfield House
212	Turner, William	Russell, Frederick	House and stables	New Town
213	Tyler, Stephen	Tyler, William	Land	Lowfield Heath
214	„	Blunt, Wilfrid	Land and buildings	Popes
215	Trist, George	Himself	Land, buildings, & shooting	Prestwood
216	„	„	House and garden	Prestwood Cottage
217	„	„	Land and buildings	Upper Prestwood
218	Thornton, Amos	Caffin, Peter	House and garden	Church Road
220	Verrall, Jane	Scott, Mrs.	„	Ifield Churchyard
221	Wylam, Edward	Himself	Land	The Elms
222	„	„	House and garden	„
223	„	„	Land	Part of Goff's Hill Farm
224	Wheeler, Mary	Simmins, William	House and garden	Westfield House
225	Wales, Ephraim	Tusler, James, Executors of	„	The Crown
226	Wright, John	Blunt, Wilfrid	Land and shooting	Part of Collins's Farm
227	Warren, Walter	Pipon, Manaton, Executors of	Land and house	Ifield Wood
228	Weedon, Joseph	Tyler, William	House and shop	The Terrace
229	„	Mitchell, John	„	„
230	Wood, William	Pipon, Manaton, Executors of	House	Ifield Court Farm

To be continued next week.

All the Inhabitants of Crawley and Ifield, 1881

Crawley Parish

No. of Assessment.	Name of Occupier.	Name of Owner.	Description of Property.	Name or situation of Property.
231	Wood, William	Pipon, Manaton, Executors of	Land and buildings	Ifield Court Farm
232	"	" "	Shooting	
233	"	" "	Land and buildings	Part of Ginham Farm
234	"	" "	Shooting	
235	"	Wood, William	Wind and steam mill	Ifield Green
236	"	Pipon, Manaton, Executors of	Recreation ground	Ifield Common
237	"	Wood, William	Enclosed land	Ifield Green
238	Webley, Ambrose	Blunt, Wilfrid S.	Timber yard	Near Crawley Station
239	"	Simmins, William	House and garden	Walnut Cottage
240	Webley, Frederick	"	"	Bank Buildings
241		"	"	
242	Walder, Foster	Ockenden, John	"	West Green
243	Watherston, Helen	Watherston, Helen	"	Crawley Cottage
244	"	"	Land	
245	White, —	Maclean, Charles	House and garden	New Town
246	Wilson, William Thorburn	Farmer, James	"	Bowman's Lodge
247	Watts, —	Stacey, John	"	Church Road
248	Wright, —	Staveley, Pepper. Geo. Augustus	House	Lyons Farm
249	"	"	Land and buildings	"
250	Warner, John Thomas	Little, Mrs.	House and garden	Perryfield
251	Wright, Mary	Smith, John	House and shop	Ifield Street
252	Wales, Daniel	Bisshopp, Robert	"	New Town
253	Webley, Ambrose	Pipon, Manaton, Executors of	Land	West Green
254	late Armstrong	Staveley, Pepper George	House and garden	Summer Lodge
255	Empty	Hardwick, E. H.	"	The Hollies
256	late Amsden	Little, Mrs.	"	Holly Lodge
257	late Parsons	Himself	Wheelwright's shop	Ifield Street
258a	Empty	Sumner, William	House and garden	West Green
258	Eli Yetman	Jacques, Thomas	"	Crawley Street
259	late Farncombe	Mitchell, Thomas	"	Poplar Villa
259a	late Aaron	Farmer, James	"	Ifield Wood
260	late Pointer	Cook, Richard	House and shop	New Town
261	Yetman, Eli	Jacques, Thomas	House, shop, and garden	Crawley Street
262		Stacey, John	Orchard	Smalls Lane
263	Booker, —	Parsons, Mary	House and garden	Lowfield Heath
264		Mockford, George	"	New Town
265			"	"
266	Blunt, Wilfrid	Blunt, Wilfrid	Tithe rent charge	
267	Birch, Mary, Executors of	Birch, Mary, Executors of	"	
268	Blaker, Rev. R. N.	Blaker, Rev. R. N.	"	
269	Hutchison, Timothy	Hutchison, Timothy	"	
270	Hurlock, Mrs., Executors of late	Hurlock, William, Executors of	"	
271	Lewin, Mary Emily	Lewin, Mary Emily	"	
272	Budgen, John	Budgen, John	"	
273	Tusler, James, Executors of late	Tusler, James, Executors of	"	
274	Wilson, Charles	Wilson, Charles	"	
275	Wells, Jane	Wells, Jane	"	
	COTTAGES AT 15 PER CENT.			
276	Bristow, James	Biggs, William	House and garden	Crawley Street
277	Elsey, Phillip	Brown, Thomas	"	Ifield Street
278	Langley, —	Beard, George	"	Buckswood
279	Tusler, —	Ault, Mrs.	"	West Green
280	Thornton, Henry	"	"	"
281	Still, —	"	"	"
282		"	"	
283	King, Mark	Christie, Capt., Executors of	"	The Mount
284	Razzell, Frank	Clarke, John Farrand	"	Ifield Park
285	Charman, Edward	Charman, Edward	"	Tushmoor Cottage
286	Rapley, Frank	"	"	
287	Smith, —	Chester, Thomas William	"	Ifield Park Lodge
288	Holmwood, James	Gatti, Carlo, Executors of	"	Lowfield Heath
289	Court, Henry	Gates, Mrs.	"	Church Road
290	Hole, Henry	Hole, Henry	"	New Town
291	Hooker, Robert	Hooker, Robert	"	"
292		Longden, Charles Scudamore	"	Oakwood Lodge
293	Lindfield, James	Lindfield, James	"	Westfield
294	"	"	"	
295	Waghorn, James	Redford, John	"	Crawley Gate
296	Simmons, —	Pipon, Manaton, Executors of	"	Langley Lane
297	Elsey, —	" "	"	Finches Lane
298	Rapley, James	" "	"	Bonnett's Lane
299	Knight, James	" "	"	
300	Burtenshaw, —	Staveley, Pepper George	"	Gossip's Green
301	Wales, John	Smith, Albert	"	West Green
302	Wallace, Mrs.	Smith, Spencer	"	Ifield Road
303	Tullett, Edward	Tullett, Edward	"	Small's Lane
304	Wilkins, Stephen	Wilkins, Stephen	"	Lowfield Heath
305	"	"	"	"
306	"	"	"	Ifield Green
307	Wilkins, Miss	"	"	Providence Cottage
	COTTAGES AT 25 PER CENT,			
308	Heathfield, Henry	Bisshopp, Lucy	"	Crawley Street
309	"	"	"	"
310	Gardner, William	"	"	"
311	Plume, Frederick	Biggs, William	"	"
312	Hooker, Robert	"	"	"
313	Holder, Charles	"	"	"
314	Sayers, Richard	"	"	"
315	Holder, John	"	"	"
316	Leach, William	"	"	"
317	Cawley, Widow	Bates, James	"	Worth Road
318	Morley, Joseph	"	"	"
319	Patching, John	Buckle, Matthew Hughes	"	The Hut
320	Budgen, John	Budgen, John	"	New Town
321	Netley, Henry	"	"	"
322	Mitchell, Eli	"	"	"
323	Hilliar, Alfred	"	"	"
324	Upton, James	"	"	"
325	Godsmark, George	"	"	"
326	Lillott, Henry	Brown, Thomas	"	Gossip's Green
327		Pipon, Manaton, Executors of	"	Rusper Lane
328		" "	"	
329	Penfold, Thomas	Cook, Richard	"	New Town
330	Briggs, —	"	"	"
331		"	"	"
332		"	"	"
333		"	"	"
334	Snelling, Oliver	"	"	"
335	Thornton, Edward	"	"	"
336	Sayers, James	"	"	"
337	Chester, Thomas	Chester, Thomas William	"	Park House
338	"	"	"	Ifield Wood
339	"	"	"	"
340	Heathfield, Henry	Charlwood, Frank, Executors of	"	Crawley Street
341	Morley, Julius	" "	"	"
342	Little, Mrs.	" "	"	"

To be continued next week.

All the Inhabitants of Crawley and Ifield, 1881

Crawley Parish

No. of Assessment.	Name of Occupier.	Name of Owner.	Description of Property.	Name or situation of Property.
843	Easton, Frank	Charlwood, Frank, Executors of	House and garden	Crawley Street
844	Geal, James	Chantler, George	,,	Tushmoor Cottages
845	Sumner, Isaac	,,	,,	,,
846	Harding, Harry	,,	,,	,,
847	Deadman, Jane	Deadman, Jane	,,	,,
848	Godsmark, Richard	,,	,,	,,
849	Constable, John	,,	,,	,,
850	Cannon, Jesse	,,	,,	,,
851		,,	,,	,,
852	Thompsett, Thomas	,,	,,	,,
853	Cannon, Jesse	Deadman, Henry	,,	,,
854	Parsons, Robert	,,	,,	,,
855	Chipperfield, James	,,	,,	,,
856	Ware, Thomas	Dalton, Miss	,,	County Oak
857	Booker, William	,,	,,	,,
858	Denman, William	,,	,,	,,
859	Lucas, Widow	,,	,,	,,
860	Tyler, Thomas	Farmer, James	,,	Ifield Wood
861	Wales, Thomas	,,	,,	,,
862		,,	,,	,,
863	Gribble, Sarah	,,	,,	,,
864	Budgen, Mary	Freeman, Sarah	,,	West Green
865	Biggs, Widow	,,	,,	,,
866	Denman, Widow	,,	,,	,,
867	Flint, Henry	Trist, George	,,	Hilly Barn
868	Funnell, John	,,	,,	Lower Barn
869	Gadd, Edward	,,	,,	,,
870	Hill, James	,,	,,	Bonwicks Cottages
871	Booker, Edward	,,	,,	,,
872	Denman, John	Garner, —	,,	Tichborne Cottages
873	Cooper, Albert	,,	,,	,,
874	Nicholson, Jesse	,,	,,	,,
875	Doyle, Michael	,,	,,	,,
876	Knight, John	,,	,,	,,
877	Holder, Thomas	,,	,,	,,
878	Penfold, Thomas	,,	,,	,,
879	Charman, James	,,	,,	,,
880	Holden, Caleb	Pipon, Manaton, Executors of	,,	Gossip's Green
881	Sharman, Walter	,,	,,	Ginhams
882	Hollman, John	Hollman, John	,,	Church Road
883	Hilder, Charles	,,	,,	,,
884	Hole, Mary	Johnson, Mrs.	,,	Crawley Town
885	Wales, Frederick	,,	,,	,,
886	Gadd, Edward	Mitchell, Henry	,,	Rusper Lane
887	Charman, Henry	Homewood, Edmund	,,	,,
888	Botting, Thomas	,,	,,	,,
889	Merritt, James	,,	,,	,,
890	Lidbetter, William	Lidbetter, William	,,	West Green
891	Stoner, Stephen	,,	,,	,,
892	Holder, Peter	,,	,,	,,
893	Knight, William	,,	,,	,,
894	Jupp, James	,,	,,	,,
895	Holder, John	,,	,,	,,
896	King, Alfred	,,	,,	,,
897	Pierce, John	,,	,,	,,
898	Elsey, Thomas	Lewin, Mary Emily	,,	Workhouse Cottages
899	Knight, James	,,	,,	,,
400	Lesgatt, William	,,	,,	Ifield Street
401	Monk, Henry	,,	,,	,,
402	King, Michael	,,	,,	,,
403	Whiting, William	,,	,,	Tweed Cottages
404	Rapley, Widow	,,	,,	,,
405	Rapley, Richard	,,	,,	,,
406	Brown, Thomas	,,	,,	Danns
407	Watson, Thomas	,,	,,	,,
408	Ford, Benjamin	L. B. & S. C. R.	,,	West Green
409	Ongley, Alfred	,,	,,	Snell Hatch
410	Ploughman, Thomas	,,	,,	Gossip's Green
411	Foster, Joseph	Mrs. Montefiore	,,	Crawley Town
412	Hollman, James	,,	,,	,,
413	Dobell, —	Maclean, Charles	,,	New Town
414	Kennaway, William	,,	,,	,,
415	Lee, Maurice	Osbourn, Henry	,,	West Green
416	Sippett, —	,,	,,	,,
417	Morgan, —	,,	,,	,,
418	Pellem, Jam.	Ockenden, Charles	,,	Crawley Town
419	Thornton, Widow	,,	,,	,,
420	Hole, James	,,	,,	New Town
421	Edwards, William	Ockenden, George	,,	West Green
422	Leney, James	,,	,,	,,
423	Pickard, Peter	,,	,,	,,
424	Cannon, Jesse	,,	,,	,,
425	Snelling, Louis	,,	,,	,,
426	Leney, Thomas	,,	,,	,,
427	Wales, James	,,	,,	,,
428	Mitchell, James	,,	,,	Crawley Street
429	Brasier, James	Potter, John	,,	New Town
430	Denman, George	,,	,,	,,
431	Denman Michael	,,	,,	,,
432	Pullen, Maurice	,,	,,	,,
433	Collison, Widow	,,	,,	,,
434	Nightingale, William	,,	,,	,,
435	Potter, Joseph	,,	,,	,,
436	Lidbetter, Peter	Pipon, Manaton, Executors of	,,	Hyde Cottages
437	Shaw, Ambrose	,, ,,	,,	Ifield Green
438	Stone, Jesse	,, ,,	,,	Rusper Lane
439	Whiting, Thomas	,, ,,	,,	Ivy Cottage
440	Penfold, John	,, ,,	,,	Finches Lane
441	Moon, William	,, ,,	,,	,,
442	Charlwood, William	,, ,,	,,	Rusper Lane
443			,,	,,
444	Penfold, Phillip	Penfold, John	,,	Gossip's Green
445	Gander, William	,,	,,	,,
446	Pierce, Widow	Pearless	,,	Crawley Street
447	Soper, Henry	,,	,,	,,
448	Thornton, Henry	Penfold, John	,,	Clappers
449	Court, Widow	,,	,,	,,
450	Leney, James	Mitchell, Charles	,,	West Green
451	Lovett, Joseph	,,	,,	,,
452	Bellchamber, Charles	,,	,,	,,
453	Thornton, E.	Mills, Henry	,,	New Town
454	Tullett, Edward	Russell, Frederick	,,	,,
455	Jeffery, John	,,	,,	,,
456	Chantler, Thomas	Soule, Henry May	,,	Rusper Lane
457	Saddington, —	,,	,,	,,
458	Cooper, William	,,	,,	Whitehall
459	Sumner, —	,,	,,	,,

All the Inhabitants of Crawley and Ifield, 1881

Crawley Parish

No. of Assessment.	Name of Occupier	Name of Owner.	Description of Property.	Name or situation of Property.
460	Shaw, James	Shaw, James	House and garden	Lowfield Heath
461	"	"	"	"
462	Thornton, Jonas	Sumner, William	"	West Field
463	Rofe, John	"	"	"
464	Elliott, Isaac	"	"	"
465	Brewer, George	"	"	"
466	Hayler, William	"	"	"
467	Sayers, —	"	"	"
468	Simmonds, Michael	"	"	"
469	Barnes, Edward	"	"	"
470	Stone, Harry	Pipon, Manaton, Executors of	"	Stumbleholme
471	Ridley, Edward	Stacey, John	"	Small's Lane
472	Tidy, Stephen	"	"	"
473	Sargent, —	"	"	Lowfield Heath
474	Reem, Isaac	"	"	"
475	Martin, Thomas	"	"	West Green
476	Snelling, William	"	"	"
477	Gawman, Peter	"	"	"
478	Adamson, William	"	"	"
479		Staveley, Geo. Augustus Pepper	"	Gossip's Green
480		" " "	"	"
481	Verger, William	Simmins, William	"	Station Yard
482	Knight, Richard	"	"	"
483	Cannon, Jesse	Sayers, Edward	"	West Green
484	Roser, Widow	"	"	"
485	Botting, Widow	"	"	"
486	Sumner, Edward	Killick, Silas	"	Bogle Row
487	King, James	"	"	"
488	Rice, Amos	"	"	"
489	Penfold, Widow	Smith, Amelia, Executors of	"	West Green
490	Lovett, Widow	"	"	"
491	Shaddock, James	"	"	"
492	Francis, Joseph	"	"	"
493	Lindfield, James	"	"	"
494		"	"	"
495	Sayers, John	"	"	"
496	Moore, Thomas	"	"	"
497	Till, William	"	"	"
498	Adamson, Henry	"	"	"
499		"	"	"
500		"	"	"
501	Thornton, —	"	"	"
502	Jenner, Thomas	"	"	"
503	Dale, George	"	"	"
504		"	"	"
505	Coates, William	"	"	"
506	Jenner, Jesse	"	"	"
507	Ongley, Alfred	"	"	"
508		"	"	"
509	Wales, Allen	"	"	"
510	Funnell, Sarah	"	"	"
511	Short, Frederick	"	"	"
512	Penfold, —	"	"	"
513		Tusler, James, Executors of	"	New Town
514		"	"	"
515	Holloway, William	Trist, George	"	Prestwood
516	Penfold, Thomas	"	"	"
517	Chart, Edward	Wright, John	"	Worth Road
518	Terry, Thomas	"	"	"
519	Warren, Stephen	Warren, Stephen	"	Ifield Green
520	Brooker, Arthur	"	"	"
521	Lovegrove, —	"	"	"
522	Brown, William	"	"	"
523	Batchelor, —	"	"	"
524		"	"	West Field
525	Taylor, —	Wilkinson, William	"	"
526		"	"	"
527		"	"	"
528	Tullett, George	"	"	"
529	Hitchman, Thomas	"	"	"
530	Johnson, —	"	"	"
531	Parsons, —	"	"	"
532	Doyle, —	"	"	"
533	Ellis, Widow	Pipon, Manaton, Executors of	"	Rusper Lane
534	Holcomb, —	" "	"	Ifield Wood
535	Sayers, Henry	" "	"	"
536	Baker, Stephen	" "	"	Gossip's Green
537	Thornton, William	" "	"	Ifield Court
538	Lambert, W.	" "	"	Ginhams
539	Strudwick, Peter	" "	"	Ifield Green
540	Nichols, Walter	" "	"	Ifield Mill Cottage
541	Wood, Thomas	Wood, William	"	Ifield Green
542	Fuller, Stephen	"	"	New Town
543	Denman, Daniel, jun.	Wilkinson, William	"	"
544	"	"	"	"
545	Cook, Edward	"	"	"
546	Yetman, Mary	Yetman, Syrus	"	"
547	Weller, Henry	"	"	"
548	Bellamy, —	"	"	"
				Grand Total

Supplementary Ifield Parish

No. of Assessment.	Name of Occupier.	Name of Owner.	Description of Property.	Situation of Property.
	Dean, Edward ..	Buckle, Matthew Hughes George ..	Land..	Clappers .. ..
68	A Greenfield, Wm...	Trist, George	Land and buildings ..	Bonwick's Place .. ..
A	" ..	"	Shooting	" .. ..
A	" ..	Executors of late Captain Christie	Land..	Part of Bonwick's Place Farm .. ..
A	" ..	" James "	Shooting	" .. ..
59	B Gardner, Humph..	Harley, Robert	Land.. " ..	Part of Ewhurst Place ..
182	B " ..	"	Land and buildings ..	Duckster's Farm ..
	B Harley, Robert ..	"	Woodland	Part of Ifield Court ..
	C Longley, James ..	Longley, James ..	Steam mills and buildings	Part of Collins's Farm ..
	Martin, T. H. ..	Martin, T. H. ..	Land..	Crawley Town ..
144	D Pronger, Jas. ..	Pronger, James	"	Part of Whitehall..
129	E Penfold, Frank ..	Trist, George	House	Ifield Wood.. ..
	F Trist, George ..	"	Land..	Part of Bonwick's Place Farm
214	Wood, William ..	Harley, Robert	Land and buildings ..	Ifield Court.. ..
	G Winfred, — ..	Winfred, —	House	New Town .. ..
	G Winfred, E. ..	Cook. Richard.. ..	"	" .. ..
	G	"	"	" .. ..
	G	"	"	" .. ..
	G	"	"	" .. ..
	G	"	"	" .. ..
400	H Knight, John ..	Garner, William ..	"	West Green.. ..
	I Humphrey, William..	"	West Park Cottages
	I	"	"	" .. ..
	I	"	"	" .. ..
	J Hole, Henry ..	"	New Town .. ..
	J	"	"	" .. ..
521	K Coates, Mary ..	Powell, Thomas ..	"	West Green.. ..
	L Lee, Maurice ..	Executors of Major Pipon ..	"	Ginhams Cottage ..
	L	" "	"	" .. ..
	M Soan, James ..	Soan, George	"	Lowfield Heath ..
	M	"	"	" .. ..
	M	Simmins, William ..	"	Near Railway Station ..
	M	"	"	" .. ..
	M	"	"	" .. ..
	N Wilkins, Stephen	Wilkins, Stephen ..	"	West Park ..
	N	Wales, Daniel	"	" .. ..
	N	"	"	" .. ..
247	Blunt, Wilfred ..	Self	Tithe rent charge	
248	Trist, George ..	"	"	
249	Blaker, Rev. Rchd. Nathaniel	"	"	
250	Hutchinson, Tim. ..	"	"	
251	Hurlock, Mrs., Executors of ..	"	"	
252	Lewin, Mary Emy.	"	"	
253	Budgen, John ..	"	"	
254	Tusler, James, Executors of ..	"	"	
255	Wilson, Charles ..	"	"	
256	Wells, Jane ..	"	"	

These lists were compiled for the new rating valuation for the area.

Crawley's Awakening

The dawn of the 1880s heralded a new era in the development of Crawley. Since the coming of the railway, and the gradual decline in coach travel to Brighton, Crawley life had become more tranquil. Many wealthy business men from the city had acquired and built up, country estates in the surrounding areas. Now, commenced their slow demise, in the interests of "villadom", and the land to the south, and south west of the railway line was built upon.

The Magazine hovels were at last declared unfit for human habitation, and in any case the soldiers were long since gone. So began the building of "Newtown". This was the area encompassing West Street, Denne Road and Oak Road, the whole area once known as the Springfield, and including what is now known as Goffs Park. An apt name due to the many underground streams which emerged in varying places, to the surface. Despite modern drainage there are still some of these streams remaining. It led credence to there being a vast supply of underground water at Goff's Hill, and hence to Charles Longley, boring for water, and building the waterworks at the top of the hill, when mains water was installed in the town.

Springfield Road development was of several imposing villas while the cottages were in the streets to the rear. Richard Cook had purchased most of the land in this region of the village with the exception of Goffs Park and he was responsible for building the houses in "Newtown". Richard Cook's own home and offices were at the junction of West Street and Springfield Road, and his works in later years off Newlands Road.

On the opposite side of the Turnpike Road, between the railway line and Malthouse Lane was the brickworks of Sumners at East Park. Mr. W. Sumner had opened a brick yard in the Gossips Lane area where the bricks were made by hand. Bricks being in great demand, he invested in steam machinery capable of turning out 14,000 to 20,000 bricks daily. The whole of the steam plant was transferred to a site near the railway station, where he secured land highly suitable to his purpose. Sumners had a mortgage with James Longley. of Turners Hill, and when Sumners were in financial difficulties in 1881, James Longley foreclosed and took over the site. It was ideal for James Longley's thriving business expansion, being situated so close to the railway, and he had his own little siding direct to the works. The family lost no time in establishing their new workshops. The first steam-powered joinery to be set-up in Sussex was installed, and its engine remained in good working order until the joinery works were gutted by fire in 1924. The chimney only remained, and today serves a modern boiler, a reminder to the past.

James Longley's company built all the houses in East Park east of the junction with Malthouse Road and some of the individual villas of Goffs Park Road.

Many city gentlemen wanted country retreats, or weekend residents and the surrounding area of Crawley seemed ideal to them, being easily accessible by train. Cycling became all the rage and Crawley was not so far from town for a day's outing.

So, after a few leisurely years, Crawley Street once again became a busy thoroughfare. Many of the village cottages were adapted to accommodate the increase in trade. Pretty cottage gardens gave way to shop-window fronts. Parlours became tearooms or coffee houses, catering for the "day trippers". Perhaps the best known of these establishments was "The Bay Tree" Coffee House. This was established in the home of Mr. Charles Messer, Senior, in 1878 shortly after his marriage to Mary, a domestic, who worked at The Tree house for Dr. Smith. It proved a very successful venture as the era of cycling was in the air. At first one saw the old velocipede, then the boneshaker, quickly followed by the penny farthing bicycle and then the safety. Mr. and Mrs. Messer were the first to cater for the new trade. They sold their business to Mr. and Mrs. Shaw who soon tired of the catering trade and took up the machine side.

Mr. Shaw, Senior, had worked for the Premier Cycle Co. It was at the Bay Tree works that the first motor cycle was built - the engine being built onto the back stays and forks. When this machine was first tried out, Crawley High Street was crowded. The motor cycle was ridden to the Chequers at Horley and back, in what seemed an incredibly short time.

On the opposite side of the road, just below Mr. Gasson's shop, was another cyclist company, that of Messrs Hooker and Sons, and here was made the Crawley cycle,

The Bay Tree Coffee House - note the Horsham Slab roof.

Crawley Bicycle Club.

Runs—Season, 1882.

June 21.—East Grinstead, Railway Hotel.
  „   28.—Horsham, *via* Pease Pottage, Black-Horse Hotel.
July 5.—Box Hill, *via* Norwood Hill, "Beehive."
  „   12.—Cuckfield.
  „   19.—Club Races, Crawley.
  „   26.—Dorking.
Aug. 2.—Cowfold, "Red Lion."
  „   9.—Billingshurst.
  „   16.—Merstham, *via* Redhill.
  „   23.—Bolney.
  „   30.—Caterham.
Sept. 6 —Ashington.
  „   13.—Newdigate, *via* Rusper.
  „   20.—Box Hill, *via* Norwood Hill.
  „   30.—Brighton.

Bicycling

A large number of the bicyclists resident in the town and neighbourhood met at the Railway Hotel on Wednesday last, when it was decided to form a club to be known as the Crawley Bicycling Club. The uniform agreed upon was dark grey tweed braid tunic, breeches, black stockings, and huntsman's cap. Badge to be white shield with light blue lettering. The first run is appointed for Wednesday next, the start to be made from headquarters, the Railway Hotel at 6.30pm.

Simmins Weekly News May 1882

PROPOSED BICYCLE CLUB.—Under the presidency of Mr. F. A. Webley a meeting was held at the Railway Hotel on Wednesday evening to consider the advisability of forming a bicycle club for Crawley and district. After some discussion the meeting was further adjourned till Wednesday next, when all those who take an interest in the bicycle world are invited.

BICYCLE RACE.—On Tuesday evening a bicycle match took place between Peter Tullett, Arthur Thornton, and Charles Sayers. Tullett started at scratch, Thornton had 100 yards start, and Sayers one minute. Thornton met with an accident opposite Albert Cottages, thus leaving the race to Tullett and Sayers. The course was from the White Hart Hotel to the Lion at Lowfield Heath and back. The time for each being—Tullett, 19min. 27secs.; Sayers, 20min. 50secs.

Jack Hooker - Sussex Champion   *Courtesy of R. Carmen*

(previously the business had been owned by Kenning and Holder) and this in turn had a good market. Frank Kenning and Fred Holder were noted pace-makers with their tandem, and they were used to help the London to Brighton and back record breakers. Jack Hooker became a Sussex champion. It is from this works that toe-clips were first introduced.

Crawley Cycling Club, founded in 1882, had its headquarters at the Railway Inn.

Let us return briefly to Mr. Messer as he was a great character in the village. Born in Crawley in 1848, and dying 10th. November 1915, he had spent the whole of his life in Crawley. Like the majority of boys of those days, he had very little schooling, as a matter of fact he could not read and hardly write, yet he was able to hold his own in conversation and he had a happy knack of seeing the humorous side of life and could keep a company well amused by his jokes and quips.

At a very early age he commenced work, and gradually worked his way up to the position of estate bricklayer at Tilgate and he was well known as a very able and efficient workman.

It is, however, with his public life that we are concerned. At the age of nine years he became a choirboy at Crawley Church, but he proved such a mischievous boy that he was a considerable source of anxiety to the choir master (Mr. J. Sayers). The Rector of the Parish was the Rev. Soper and he recognised that Charlie was not a bad boy, but just an imp of mischief. He conferred with the verger, Mr. Stephen Bowers, who advised giving the lad some office, some responsibility so to speak, believing that would sober him. So we find him appointed assistant verger, his duties being to help with the seating, to see books were in order, to place fresh water in the vestry, and in the tower. This did not lessen the spirit of fun, but only so far as the church was concerned. It was the time he sprinkled snuff and pepper in the gallery and caused much sneezing thereby. One occasion when in a hurry he actually dropped from the gallery onto the floor of the chancel! He succeeded to the office of verger at the retirement of Mr. Bowers, and for over fifty years he carried out the onerous duties, never missing a practice night (then twice a week), never once missing a single service, except when illness laid him aside. The church was his all and what is more, he began to look upon it as "all his" for all with whom he came into contact, it was 'my' church.

From early days Mr. Messer was fond of singing and jokes. He formed what was for many years a most successful Band of Minstrels - The Gohawk Minstrels, some 18 in all, Mr. Messer being the Chief. At the funeral of Mr. Messer was a wreath with the inscription "In loving memory of a Sunday School Scholar" - Misses Smith. In Misses Smith's eyes their pupils never grew up!

Adjacent to The Bay Tree were the cottages of the Heathfields, the spot at one time "The Place" to all Crawley children, for it was here that Miss Heathfield had her sweet shop, and from the back at night emerged Mr. Heathfield with his hot sausage rolls. It was here, too, that one saw scores of pots of auriculas, as Mr. Heathfield made a hobby of these flowers and when in bloom they made a glorious sight.

In 1903, these cottages were amalgamated with The George Inn with a "gate-room" bridging the gap between them. This then became known as The George Shades. The Heathfield family moved to two cottages on the opposite side of the Street. Mr. Shaw remained, and expanded his business to incorporate motor accessories.

In other areas of the Street old cottages were removed and new buildings erected. Extensions to sides and rear of cottages became evident. At last the problem of Crawley drainage and sewage had to be resolved, due to the growth in population.

The Simmins family had much to do with improvements in the commerce of the community, being, amongst other things, auctioneers and owning stables at the rear of the Railway Inn. In March 1881, Mr. Simmins launched the first Crawley Newspaper, or rather news sheet, being only one page, costing half a penny. Known as Simmins Weekly Advertiser, it was the forerunner of what became The Sussex and Surrey Courier. Printed in the house next to The White Hart Inn, in what was the first Post Office, it was an instant success and doubled in size. After two years, the printing works moved nearer to the railway, to the building which in later years became Willets Shop.

The gas works were added to, and a new gasometer erected in order to meet the demands of an increasing consumption.

Another business venture which was to have a profound effect upon the way of life in Crawley for many years was the formation of the Crawley Co-operative Society. First registered on 2nd. November 1888, the Society was formally inaugurated and commenced trading on December 10th. 1888. "Actually there had been a co-operative store in Crawley for several years before the Crawley Society was founded. It was a branch store of the Horsham Society, and had been opened in April 1882. From some cause or another, the Horsham Society did not flourish, and in Crawley there seems to have been a feeling that the service given was not satisfactory.

By the latter half of 1888 the Horsham Society was clearly on its last legs. The Brighton Society had, at that time, actually acquired a building-site in Horsham with a view to opening branch premises. The Crawley Stalwarts were evidently dissatisfied with either alternative. Hence they set up a provisional committee and proceeded to take the steps necessary to establish a Crawley Society of their own.

Basically, its membership from the start was drawn from the ranks of the railway workers. But with them, and giving the Society its initial impetus, was a sturdy company of workers in the local building industry. Workers in the local nursery (Cheals) and on the then flourishing farms in the area added their quota likewise. Only very exceptionally has anybody been active in the Crawley Society who was not a plain wage-worker.

At the time of its registration, the membership of the Society totalled 20, of whom the majority were building trade workers. Both the first President and first Secretary were builders; of the Committee, seven were builders and two railwaymen. After 16 weeks of trading, its membership had risen to 82. By the end of the year, it had reached 103. The second hundred was reached after nine years' trading.

The first new departure of the Society was the setting up of a Bakery early in 1891. The site, however, at the extreme end of the Westfield Road, was ill-chosen for a counter trade, while the Society was not yet big enough to undertake house-to-house deliveries. In the end, the Bakery was abandoned in the third quarter of 1892." - From *Fifty Years, compiled by W.J. Denman and T.A. Jackson - issued in celebration of its Jubilee by The Crawley and Ifield Co-operative Society Ltd.*

With the trading area expanding to the railway line and beyond, we find a busy shopping venue developing in the upper Street. Mark Lemon's cottage was extended at the front to give us Wilkins Grocery Store while, at the other end of the terrace of four cottages, Mr. Albert Smith sold his home on the corner of New Road, to Mr. Charles Mitchell, to house the Post Office, as the building next to the White Hart had become too small for their needs. (Mr. Albert Smith was something of a traveller, for he spent 6 months in New Zealand during 1881/82, and upon his return published an account of his travels. Also, he gave illustrated talks, using the 'magic' lantern in the National School for the local inhabitants.)

Ockendens brewery flourished on the corner opposite to the post office. Adjacent to John Penfold's shop, an old tenement was pulled down and replaced by Spencer Smith's splendid 'modern' warehouse with its deep cellars. This building was used as a model by Mr. Warren in the 1890s when he established his shop and home on the opposite side of the highway. With ever more people moving into the West Green area, and it being in the Parish of Ifield, it was considered appropriate to have a small chapel built in the area, it being a considerable distance to St. Margarets, Ifield. So, monies and donations were collected, and in 1881, St. Mary Magdalene's Church was built on the corner of Prospect Place and Alpha Road. This had an harmonium, usually played by Grace Martin (Dr. T. Martin's daughter) and its own choir, and Sunday School.

1884. John Penfold's shop. On the right is the entrance to Worth Lane.
To the left is Spenser Smith's new warehouse, being used as a furniture store.

Parsonage House was built facing the church for the young curate-in-charge. Here, the first public lending library was installed by the Rev. Aubrey Blaker.

The school in West Green also required enlarging to accommodate the extra pupils. There was a Teachers House between the Infants and mixed school (at this time it was one oblong room sub-divided by partitions.) This the Rev. Barrett-Lennard had pulled down in 1879 and by using the space thus available both schools were enlarged, and a new teachers House built on a plot of land adjacent to the school facing the Ifield Road. In November 1882, an extra classroom was built at the rear of the school for the use of the Infants. A separate building for Infants was not established until well after the turn of the century. The pond on the opposite side of the track to the school was properly filled in and grassed over. It was bought by Mr. Goddard, and presented to the school for use as a playground.

Meanwhile, the Temperance Movement gained apace in the area. We have a Reading Room set up by Sarah Robinson by "The Sun" public house! It was there they taught married women to read and write at afternoon lessons.

Also, it was like a workingman's Club during the evenings, as well as giving Religious Instruction. A West Crawley Temperance Band was formed. (In later years, this became the West Crawley Silver Band.) The Old White Hart Farmhouse, which

The cottage on the right is the Old Parsonage house demolished in 1879.
The double gates are the entrance to the Rectory.
When a new Lodge was built the driveway was diverted to the right of the Lodge.

courtesy of Rev. M. Goode

Ecclesiastical Dilapidations Act, 1871.
Diocese of Chichester.

23, Bedford Row, w.c London,
9th November 1877

My dear Sir

Crawley Rectory

I have no hesitation in advising you that your proposition to erect one good cottage in the place of the existing building at the Rectory Gate would be advantageous to the benefice. Possibly some of the roof timbers might be reusable.

Believe me Yours very truly
Lacy W Ridge

Rev. J. B. Lennard.

Bishop's Registry,
Chichester.
5th January 1878

Dear Sir

I write to inform you that I have received a letter from Col. Clitherow in which he consents to your pulling down the Old Buildings at the Rectory Gate and the same has been duly filed in this Registry

I remain Dear Sir
Yours truly
R. G. Raper

Secretary to the Lord Bishop

Revd J B Lennard

had in recent years been sub-divided and occupied as two shops with living accommodation, was refurbished and opened as The Old Whyte Hart Temperance Hotel (now known as The Ancient Priors.) We also have Terry's Albany Temperance Hotel being built, where now is The Embassy Cinema.

The Baptist Church was finally built in 1883 along the Station Road, after several mishaps. At the opposite end of the Station Road, a Police Station was opened in 1884.

The 1890s saw more rapid progress in the village's development. After several years of complaint as to the hazards encountered when crossing the railway track in the vicinity of the Station, Richard Cook and Sons built the railway subway, and to stop the residents of the East Park area crossing the tracks haphazardly, also built what became known as The Monastery Bridge.

At this time also, Cook's started to build St. Barnabas Church on the West Green Common, completing the structure in May 1893. However, upon its inauguration, it was decided to dedicate the church to St. Peter.

At this time Crawley homes were serviced by a garden well for drinking water, tapping into the limitless supply of underground springs. But it was decided to drill for

The Handcross Bus 1880s, owned and driven by Mr Will Ledbetter.
Departures and return were twice daily.

water in order to set up a network of piped water to homes, earth closets, still being all the vogue, and cesspools often being sited near to wells, giving health problems. Charles and James Longley, with others, formed a syndicate, and decided in 1898 to bore for water. A test bore hole was sunk at the top of Goffs Hill, just off the Goffs Park Road, and water was finally struck at a depth of 950 feet.

Prior to this in 1895, a Cottage Hospital was opened in New Road, in what was previously the Servants Home next to the School. So, the health of the community became more adequately catered for.

While all the building and new commerce was being developed, the social amenities and leisure pursuits had not been forgotten. Different societies and clubs abounded, catering for all tastes. Not only were brass bands formed, but the Hazeldene Orchestra, under the auspices of Mr. Moses Nightingale, The Crawley Harmonic Society, The Crawley Blackbirds and The Gohawk Minstrels, all giving regular performances at The George Assembly Rooms. Indeed, the Assembly Rooms became a 'mecca' for all such types of entertainment for the gentry and traders. We find announced in Simmins Weekly Advertiser of November 11th. 1882: "We have pleasure in announcing that on 25th. and 29th. December, theatrical performances will be given at The George Assembly Rooms under the auspices of Mr. Charles Dickens and Dr. Martin. The pieces selected being "The Sheep in Wolf's Clothing" by Tom Taylor, and "No Song, No Supper", an operetta by Storace. The proceeds after defraying necessary expenses will be given to local charities." Charles Dickens actually took part in this play, as well as did members of the Martin and Romer families.

The Assembly Rooms also saw the gaiety of Hunt Balls, and Quadrille classes, as well as many varied and numerous dinners being hosted at The George Inn dining rooms. The working class entertainments were mostly held at the schools, and at the end of the century, St. Mary Magdalene Church, became the Parish Room and the centre of social adventures as an alternative venue.

Outdoor pursuits continued in abundance, not only with the formation of the Bicycle Club, but we see the first Crawley Cricket Club in 1881. Also Ifield Club, and Crawley and Ifield Club! Several clubs for shooting activities and Rifle Club. It was not until 1890 that the first football club was formed.

So, the once small village community began to flourish and expand. Perhaps the largest single impact influence on the continued expansion of Crawley's prosperity was the "coming" of the "Motor Car." In the previous century, it had been the coaching era, next the railway, and, lately, bicycles; now came the combustion engine. It became "the thing" to have day trips to Brighton. Once again the London-Brighton Road began to hum with activity bringing business of a different kind. Crawley needed to adapt to this new phenomenon which brought not only cars but charabancs of day trippers and even the first mechanical buses to their midst.

In 1900 Mr. C. Gadson was a frequent traveller along the London-Brighton Road with his charabanc, and often on his travels, he came upon the familiar scene of a broken

The Brewery, late 1880s. This is a 15th century timber-framed house. The right hand-wing is the original brewery, known as such since the mid 1600s. The central area is of a later period making a narrow tunnel-like entrance leading to the cellars and making an extension to the left-wing which is the shop and home of Mr. E. Chantler. Note the Horsham slab-roof on the original building. The gateway entrance leads to a monumental mason's yard, and following the pathway further brings us to the laundry run by Miss Sarah Hygate and her mother.

Above can be seen Mr Chantler with his delivery cart.

down motor car defying every effort of its owner to restart it. He was one of the first of those few men who recognised in the newly-invented motor a potential source of income for anyone conversant with the technical details of their working. He decided to put his knowledge of motor engineering into practice, and in 1902 bought a partnership in Bannister's which was next door to Nightingale's shop in the Brighton Road, and there began to cater for the ever increasing number of motorists who chugged toward Brighton in their uncertain vehicles. Finally Mr. Gadsdon bought out Bannisters and a year later he started a garage of his own on the opposite side of the road. There he enjoyed an exclusiveness that is almost unbelievable today. For many miles up and down the road Mr. Gadson was the only one to whom the distressed motorist could turn for assistance, for he was the only one who could and would give it. Appeals to bonafide blacksmiths and horse drivers was of no avail: they would look with disgust upon the stranded vehicle and pass by on the other side.

Mr. Gadson says that in those days one had to be an engineer, a blacksmith, a solderer and a magician rolled into one to render effective aid in case of a breakdown. One was never quite sure whether the car in which one was hurrying to a break down would not itself come to grief. The steep hill at Hogs Hill was the site of many such

Two views of the west side of The Street.
Above: looking north, and below towards the South.

courtesy West Sussex Library

1893. West-side of The Street between the railway-crossing and Robinson Road. The trees are in the garden of Vine Cottage. Next to the trees on the left almost hidden from view except for the pointed roof is the home of Miss Chitty which became the Westminster Bank.

calamities. While a team of horses could draw a coach up the steep incline, it proved to be a disaster to the combustion engine. So a cutting was made through the hill, and the roadway diverted, to accommodate these new-fangled machines - a route which is still in use today. Times have changed: flint surface has given way to macadam; where there was one car, there are now thousands and Mr. Gadson no longer sells petrol at 4s. 6d a gallon.

1902. Bannisters Shop

The Diamond Jubilee 1897

Dancers: Violet Hibbs, Louie Pavey, May Kilner, Mildred Hearsey, Louie Carthew, Gertie Lee, Beatrice Carthew, Priscilla Godsmark, Minnie Miller, Laura Rocer, Nellie Bartley, Beatrice Parsons, Nellie Hewett, Lily Short, Daisy Morley and Kate Holmwood

Crawley Jubilees

1887—1897

Sir: The great Jubilee Carnival which was Crawley's contribution to the national festivities will recall to we older folk who have seen three Jubilees and two Coronations the festivities in Crawley at previous Jubilees. Though taking a schoolboy part in the 1887 Jubilee and the possessor of a good memory, I would like to recount a few memories of that day of celebration and facts given to me by the late Mr. Moses Nightingale.

The 22nd June, 1887, was a wonderful day, the weather being perfect, everybody happy and the town gaily decorated. The Jubilee day opened with a peal on the bells of Crawley Church, followed by services of thanksgiving in all the churches. At one o'clock the children from all the schools marched to the Square, where a procession was formed, headed by the Crawley Town Band, then the children (683 of them), with the Crawley Temperance Fife and Drum Band bringing up the rear. On arrival at the cricket ground the National Anthem was sung. During the afternoon games, sports, &c., were indulged in. Tea was partaken of in companies of about 200, including all visitors, who were waited on by various ladies of the town and teachers of the various schools. The tea tables were handsomely decorated with flowers given by Messrs. J. Cheal & Sons. At 8 p.m. the children were again called together and, preceded by the Band, marched to the Upper Green to witness the planting of the Jubilee oak. Lord de Blaquiere (who then lived at "Springfield," Mrs. Parbury's residence), dressed in the Court dress of a naval officer, did the planting. The tree was presented by Messrs. J. Cheal & Son; the silver spade with which the planting was done is still with Messrs. Cheal (1933). The singing of the National Anthem closed a glorious day.

To commemorate the event small medals with the impression of the Queen's head a 1 the words, "Victoria, Queen, born May 4th, 19," were presented to the smaller children, and a larger medal to the elder children with the inscription : "To commemorate the Jubilee of the reign of Queen Victoria, 1887."

The Diamond Jubilee of Queen Victoria was celebrated on 20th June, 1897. This was a general holiday in the town and the largest fête it has been my privilege to witness here. The various committees were at work for months. The proceedings began at 12 mid-day and did not finish until 10 p.m. All Schools, Fire Brigade, Bands, Cricket, Football and Cycling Clubs took part in the procession (dressed in appropria costumes), the day's proceedings, which included a procession of children dressed in costumes to represent all the Royal Family, including Queen Victoria as she was in 1837 in addition to 18. , with their maids of honour. The Queens of England, Mary, Elizabeth and Ann, with their ma is of honour. All our Colonies were represented and various countries ; all sports of the reign, inventions, manufactures, advertisements, and a company of soldiers and sailors. The afternoon's festivities included Maypole and Swedish dances, and concerts by the school children, ventriloquial entertainments, washing and hat trimming competitions for men, nail driving and cokernut shies for women. Concerts by the Harmonic Society and Band and a huge dance on the cricket ground finished this memorable day.

I have a photograph of this event, which I will be pleased to show.

These facts given to me by such an authority should prove of great interest to those who took part or saw last week's celebrations. Thanking you in anticipation,

Yours faithfully,

W. J. DENMAN.

19, Station Road, Crawley.

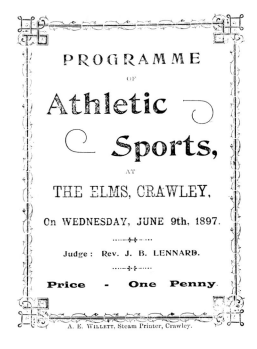

PROGRAMME

OF

Athletic Sports,

AT

THE ELMS, CRAWLEY,

On WEDNESDAY, JUNE 9th, 1897.

Judge : Rev. J. B. LENNARD.

Price   -   One Penny.

A. E. Willett, Steam Printer, Crawley.

W.J. Denman   *2nd 440 yards Handicap*
1st 100 yards
2nd 440 yards Obstacle Race

1886. Looking North towards the railway crossing.

1900. The bank now replaces Nightingales.

courtesy of L. Collins

1908

1915

P.A.

Black Dog Lane c. 1903

Looking north along the Brighton Road, viewed from Hogshill.

Sports of the '80's

Crawley Recollections.

Crawley has always had a name for sport, particularly before football became so popular and other sports have taken a back seat. Public tastes have changed and many of the annual events have fallen into oblivion. Cricket always appealed to the public, and in 1881 we had Ifield Cricket Club, Crawley Cricket Club and also the Ifield and Crawley Club. The Three Bridges Central Railway Cricket Club was formed in that year and there was yet another club of which little was ever known—Poundhill Cricket Club, which apparently had matches with Lowfield Heath but, as far as I can ascertain, only with that club.

For instance, we find that on September 6th, 1881, under the heading of Lowfield Heath: A cricket match was played here between Lowfield Heath and Poundhill Clubs, terminating in favour of the home team. Wickets were pitched at 11, and long before the game was played out it was seen that the Lowfield Heath party had the best of it. E. Gasson was captain of the home team, and William Dench of the Poundhill Club. These clubs play annually for a new ball. A capital luncheon was provided at the White Lion. The chair was occupied by Mr. E. Gasson, and the vice-chair by Mr. John Wilkins. About 30 partook of the repast. I have pointed out in previous articles that every possible occasion was seized on to have a dinner or luncheon.

On Good Friday, 1881, the first cricket match of the season was played in a field in the rear of the White Hart Hotel. W. Hayler and Thomas Denman were chosen captains. It was a rather remarkable circumstance that the captain of one team should get the highest score of the day (48) and the other captain had nought to his credit. Hayler's team in their first innings scored 77, and in the second innings 42. Denman's team in the first innings made 36, and in the second innings 89. Hayler's team thus won by four runs.

In the same year out and home games were played between teams raised by Mr. Latham, of Ifield Rectory, and Mr. J. Bucknell, of Worth Hall, and, of course, dinners followed. It was in the return game at Worth Hall that I find recorded for the first time the name of G. F. H. Banks, who opened the innings with E. Bucknell for Worth Hall. Ifield Rectory made 37 and 38; and Worth Hall 41 and 28. Thus Ifield Rectory won by six runs. At Ifield previously the Hall won by 71 to 52.

On Thursday, September 21st, 1881, there was a game of exceptional interest. Worth Park v. Crabbet Park. The latitude then allowed by editors to their correspondents can best be illustrated by the following reproduction of a report of the proceedings: This match, probably the last of the season, was played at Worth Park on Thursday when some very interesting play was shown on both sides. Crabbet Park won the toss and went in first. They kept pegging away till at the end of the innings the useful total of 76 had been piled up, the principal contributors being J. Weller (18) and J. Dunnett (12). It may therefore be said J. "done it" well and J. "weller." No less than five wickets fell before the clever bowling of W. Dench, who also nipped Kenning's aspirations in the bud by catching him when only one removed from the much dreat duck's egg. J. Frost (rather early in the year, by the bye, for this gentleman to be at work) must be held responsible for extinguishing the hopes of three of the Worth Parkites. In the first innings of Crabbet Park a total of 60 runs was put together before the last man, Francis, was left not out. This innings—chiefly remarkable for H. Budgen's score of 29, including two 3's and seven 2's—was also notable for G. Gates's neatly made 14, which included four 2's.

It will be seen that at this stage of the game, each team having played one innings, the totals were: Worth Park, 76; Crabbet Park, 60. Crabbet Park followed on for a second innings and had nine of their men dismissed for 32 runs (a rather low average) when darkness set in and stumps were reluctantly drawn, the result of the match being, without doubt, considerably in favour of Worth Park.

On December 26th, 1881, there was great excitement in the town as J. Hawkins had backed himself for £5 to run 10 miles within one hour, the start to be from the Sun Inn and the course to be one straight in London Road and turn about each mile. The roads were in anything but proper trim for the occasion, a drizzling rain having made them very wet and muddy. There was a crowd of quite 700 to witness the event. Mr. John Ockenden was the starter and at 31 seconds past 2 Hawkins commenced his task. Mr. Edward Dean saw fair at one end of the course and Mr. George Dean the other. The first two miles were accomplished in 11 mins. 35 secs.; the next two in 23 mins. 35 secs.; and the fifth mile was done in 29 mins. 30 secs. Here the race came to an end, Hawkins complaining of a pain in his side. Had the road been in the same state as on Christmas Day it is not unreasonable to suppose that the 10 miles would have been covered in the time agreed on.

A walking race followed, the contestants being Newton Parsons and Frederick Heathfield—two miles in 17 minutes—Heathfield allowed 30 secs. start. Both were in excellent form for walking, but through the bad state of the roads Parsons, though beating Heathfield, was one minute over the prescribed time.

At this time shooting was very popular, there being a pigeon shooting club and a sparrow shooting club. On New Year's Day of 1882 there was a match at Black Dog Farm, lent by Mr. W. Nightingale. The conditions were eight birds apiece to be shot in sides of eight, the first four of each team having an extra bird to make up for an absent member. There were two traps, H. and T., 21 yards rise, with the use of two barrels. Only one on either side succeeded in scoring 8—J. Smythe (whose side proved winners by 41-39) and H. Brown.

Sparrow shooting matches were also in great favour. A well-known Lowfield Heath sportsman (name not given) backed himself to kill 30 out of 50 sparrows rising from five traps. This took place in a meadow at the rear of the Plough Inn, Three Bridges. The bet was won, whereupon a well-known Crawley shooter bet a level sovereign that he could shoot 40 out of 50, and this he did.

The annual shoot of the Crawley Sparrow Club marked the big day of the year. In the rear of the White Hart was (and is) a large, airy room which had very small meshed netting in place of windows, and here sparrows were collected and fed awaiting the shoot. For some weeks before this event men went round after dark with very long nets with which the ivy on buildings were covered and then poles were rattled in the ivy which drove the frightened birds into the nets. Stackyards were hunted in the same way. Whether one agreed with sparrow shooting on these lines or not, there could be no question that sparrows were not such a nuisance to the farmer as they are in these days.

One sport which caused a great to-do was coursing. The Crawley and Horsham Fox Terrier Club held annual meetings in a meadow at the Sun Hotel when silver cups, silver collars and cash prizes were competed for. The Rev. John Barrett Lennard (Rector of Crawley) made devastating attacks on the "ruffians who were responsible for this cruel and wicked sport." Letters in the columns of this paper "for" and "against" went on for a long time, and eventually coursing stopped. There was an annual hare hunt—usually at Ewhurst. It was in 1882 that the Crawley Bicycle Club was formed.

— — — WAYFARER.

W.J. Denman

The Adult Years

Bill Denman continued to work hard and play hard. In fact, when not at his postal duties all his spare time appears to have been devoted to sport. In summer, cricket and running, and in winter football, his great sporting passion. When Bill decided that he should settle down and marry, this event, or date, had to be accommodated around the sporting calendar! The year 1903 became a momentous year not only for Crawley Football Club, but also for him, the year of his marriage. Married on 15th. April 1903, to Helen Fielder of West Street, the ceremony took place on a Wednesday, due to the fact that all Saturday afternoons were occupied with football! Three days later it was the final of the Mid-Sussex Football League Challenge Shield, which the Crawley team won for the first time in their history. The headquarters of The Crawley Football Club was the Railway Inn, and their field was at Malthouse. (In those days Crawley Football Club Supporters wore red geraniums in their buttonholes to show which team they supported.) Bill's normal playing position was left-wing.

Upon marriage, Bill and his wife first lived at Ticehurst, 10, Station Road. Here their three eldest children were born. Life moved on at a leisurely pace, the young family struggling for survival in common with all their neighbours. Wages of a postman being very low, Bill started to supplement his income by selling his writings about Crawley to newspapers and magazines.

The first upheaval in their lives came towards the end of 1906. Bill's eldest brother Thomas' wife died in childbirth, shortly followed by Tom who was heart-broken by his wife's death. This left three orphan children. Mabel 11 years old, was adopted by Bill, and the two youngest were taken by Elsie Mitchell. So the children were able still to see each other every day.

With a growing family to feed, Bill acquired a large plot of land off the Three Bridges Road as an allotment. In actual fact, it was an orchard and garden. Over the years it acquired some forty apple, pear and plum trees, as well as other fruit and a vegetable plot. There were also several chickens, for eggs and meat. He also bred rabbits for food.

In later years, this land was sold to Sussex Electricity Supply Co. who in turn sold it for building to Mr. Avery in 1930. (Crawley first experienced Electricity in August 1908. After a week of testing the generator, electricity was switched on in the town, on Saturday and Sunday free of charge.) On the occasion of Bill's Silver Wedding, he planted a Sussex Forge Apple Tree, which survived in Mr. Avery's garden. Each year

WEDDING OF MR. W. J. DENMAN. — Crawley Parish Church was crowded on Wednesday afternoon on the occasion of the marriage of Mr. W. J. Denman, third son of Mr. John Denman, to Miss Fielder, fifth daughter of Mrs. and the late Mr. Geo. Fielder, of Springfield-road, Crawley. The families of both bride and bridegroom have been resident in the town for many years, and the bridegroom particularly has made himself exceedingly popular by his great interest in and work rendered on behalf of local sport. Mr. Denman is the secretary of the Crawley Football and Cricket Clubs, and there is probably not another person in the town who has worked so hard in this direction than he. His abilities on the field—no matter whether cricket or football—have gained for him a good deal of popularity, which has been increased by his ably discharged secretarial duties. The congregation at the church included many local devotees of sport, and many were the good wishes expressed for the future welfare and happiness of both bride and bridegroom. The church looked exceedingly pretty, the Easter decorations still remaining, and the interesting ceremony, conducted by the Rector (the Rev. H. B. Lennard), was witnessed by the large audience with much pleasure. The bride looked very charming in a costume of grey material trimmed with white, and wearing a white picture hat to match, and she was attended by her sister (Miss Gertrude Fielder) and Miss Vashti Denman (sister of the groom) as bridesmaids, these being very prettily attired in brown dresses trimmed with blue silk. Miss Fielder was given away by her brother (Mr. Geo. Fielder), and Mr. Wm. Wells, of Worthing, accompanied the groom as best man. The happy couple received a large number of very useful presents and the hearty congratulations of all who know them.

Football, 1903

until Bill's death, Mr. Avery supplied Bill with a basket of apples from this tree. (This is approximately the site of Mothercare in Haslett Avenue.) Bill showed the same enthusiasm for gardening as he did in other activities undertaken, and over the years became the holder of three Royal Horticultural Society Banksian Medals, in addition to many other gardening trophies.

In 1909, the Denman family moved to the opposite side of the Station Road, to number 19, adjacent to Mr. Cox's the wheelwright. Mr., Cox, Senior, had four houses built, which eventually became the property of his children. Number 19 was owned by Kate Cox, and Tom Cox continued his father's business at number 17 until his death when the property was purchased by Harrison's the builders.

When the family first lived at number 19, there were no mod-cons. Oil lamps were used for lighting, and cooking was done on the kitchen range.

Winifred, the eldest daughter, recalls one tea time, the oil lamp which hung above the dining-room table fell, and set the tablecloth alight. After this, her father insisted on gas being connected to the house.

Number 19 was served by a well shared with 17 and worked by a hand pump. Tap water was not connected to the house until several years later, after the children caught fever, thought to be caused by contaminated water. To heat water for washing or bathing, there was a large brick copper, with a chimney in the corner of the scullery, and baths were taken in an enamel tub, and later a zinc tub.

The three eldest of Mr. Denman's children, Winifred, William (George) and Gladys attended the National School at West Green. Meanwhile, Mabel, who wished to become a nurse, had gone to train at Shoreham Hospital. In common with all their friends, the children had, in many ways, a carefree, though in some respects a somewhat regimented, existence. Toys were few, and the children were inventive of their own amusement. Mr. Yetman provided pigs' bladders, which were blown up and used as footballs by the boys, while girls had whipping toys and hoops. The children could roam through fields and woods for miles around without coming to any harm.

Every Sunday, the family attended church twice, morning and evening service. Then, in the afternoon, there was Sunday School for the children. During the summer evenings, there was the "promenade" in the High Street. Earlier, there would be a walk, in your "Sunday best". Usually, the Denmans would follow the same route going to Three Bridges along the roadway, round the Hazelwick Mill, back via Blackdog Lane and up the High Street to the Lower Square. The children were required to walk sedately in front of their parents. While the parents stood by the rails in front of the White Hart, the children sat on the wall around the George Hotel Annexe with their friends, listening to the band play. As a treat, they had a small bag of sweets from Miss Heathfields and a comic each. Each child chose a different comic so that they then could share and have three to read: "Chips", "Comic-cuts" and "Tiger". On Sunday mornings during winter months, the muffinman, who came from Horsham, walked

The family 1907: Mabel (standing)
George, Winifred, Gladys

Baby Winnie

The three eldest children with baby Thomas

24 September 1906 - Bill on right with bat.

A NOVEL CRICKET MATCH was played on the Crawley ground on Wednesday, the rules which obtained a hundred years ago being observed, while all the players wore high hats and other garments in conformity with the fashion that prevailed a century since. And very odd indeed they looked in tall "toppers," cravats, braces and side whiskers, many being perfect *fac-similes* of old time cricketers, as seen in the various old prints now in existence. Some of the hats were exceedingly ancient, the one worn by Mr. Bartley being over 150 years old, whilst Messrs. Green, H. Harms and Oliver had secured very high hats, which were absolutely identical with those in vogue in 1800. Not a few of the players defied their true identification, and Mr. Melling, especially, looked the centenarian he represented. Underhand bowling was, of course, the order of the day, and any batsman fortunate enough to compile twenty notches had to retire. The respective elevens were chosen and captained by Mr. Green and Mr. Melling and the game was a most interesting one, Mr. Green's side eventually winning very comfortably. A fair number of spectators were present, though not nearly as many as would have congregated on a warm July afternoon, but those who did take the trouble to attend were repaid by the amusement the game afforded. The antics of some of the players caused a good deal of laughter. To run after a ball and to keep one's hat on was no easy task, and the effort to do both frequently ended in disaster. After the match the teams, together with a few friends, sat down to dinner at the Railway Hotel, Mr. Melling serving a capital meal. This was followed by a smoking concert, during which various toasts were honoured. The score of the match is appended:

MR. GREEN'S XI.

W. J. Denman, retired	20—not out	17
W. Wilkins, c and b Taylor	19—b Neal	0
T. Bartley, b Taylor	0—c Melling, b Taylor	1
A. T. Harms, retired	20—b Taylor	0
H. Stocken, retired	20—b Taylor	10
E. Nightingale, b Beer	2—c Beer, b Neal	3
E. South, lbw, b Oliver	1—b Neal	12
J. Wilkins, c and b Oliver	4—b Neal	0
J. Morley, not out	4—b Neal	0
C. Purle, st Beer, b Oliver	1—b Taylor	0
C. E. Green, b Taylor	0—b Neal	0
Extras	2 Extras	2
Total	**93 Total**	**45**

MR. MELLING'S XI.

A. E. Taylor, b South	17	H. Melling, not out	1
H. Beer, c Green, b Stocken	4	O. Cove, b Wilkins	2
S. Bridger, c Bartley, b Stocken	0	C. Traynor, b South	1
S. Hawtrey, b South	3	D. Spittles, st South, b Wilkins	0
H. T. Oliver, lbw, b South	7	Extras	4
E. S. Neal, c Stocken, b South	14		
F. Rich, c and b Wilkins	6	**Total**	**59**

Umpires; Messrs. J. G. Sims and J. Wells.

1909
Trial trips for coaches between Brighton and Crawley were started in May, to last for a period of 3 months. The coaches were 'The Viking' and 'The Venture'.

H.M.S. Delta

through the streets carrying his tray of muffins upon his head and ringing his handbell to let the people know of his coming. A real treat for afternoon tea on winter days.

Perhaps the most exciting times for the children of Crawley to look forward to were Fair Days, and Winifred, George and Gladys were no exception. They also had the advantage of their grandparents' house being alongside the greens where all the amusements were set up, the swing-boats being right outside of their front door. Around 6.30 p.m. the night before Fair Day, the gypsies in their horse-drawn vans started to converge upon the village centre, coming from all directions: Woolborough, Black Dog and Worth Lanes, from Lowfield Heath and Ifield. By morning the greens were transformed into a veritable children's wonderland. Each year saw the same families on their regular pitch. Outside of The George Hotel stood an old lady with her toy and sweets stall - humbugs, brandy snaps, toffee apples, etc. There were the Boxing Booth, Fire-eaters, a circus of performing fleas, and a tent where you could be tattooed, and many others. The entertainments did not commence until evening after the business of the cattle fair had been completed. By the morning of the following day, all had disappeared, that is until the next time.

At the end of 1912, 29th. December, Bill's father, Broomdasher Denman died after a long illness. Prior to this, the two youngest of Bill's sisters married: Olive to Alfred Hygate of 97 The Street, and they left Crawley for London as Fred was employed by Napiers, the aeroplane firm as an engineer. Nell (Ellen) the youngest of the family emigrated to Canada just before her father's death, where she married Harry Wiles. The other two girls married in Crawley: Kate to Harold Hearsey and Vashti to Charles Payne, while brother Jack married Harold's sister, Mildred, at The Crawley Baptist Church.

Tragedy struck the small family, when Bill and Helen's second son, Thomas John, who was four years old, died in 1913 of pneumonia. This may have been a complication of the fever which all the children had, and led to the mains water being connected to the house.

Around this period, Crawley Post Office used the railway for sending mail in bulk, though, sometimes, a van would be used across country to outlying areas away from this facility. Within the village area, there were three deliveries of mail per day. Bill did not learn to drive, so, whereas he previously fetched or delivered mail from the coaches, he transferred to carrying out the same procedure to and from Crawley Station, as well as sorting and delivering locally. The heavy wooden trucks with their metal wheels pulled by a wooden handle were little different from those seen today. They made a terrible noise when being trundled along the street. One winter of severe snow over the Downs caused problems with the postal distribution. On arrival at Crawley Station, early one morning, Bill and his mate were told that the track between Three Bridges and Lewes was closed due to heavy snow. So without consulting the Postmaster, the two set off for Brighton pulling the loaded truck, instilled in their mind that the post always gets through regardless! It was well after dark when the pair returned to base. Not content with delivering the mail to Brighton, from whence it could reach Lewes depot, they also returned with the mail for Crawley!

The outbreak of the First World War in 1914 sees Bill joining the 1st Essex Regiment when it came his turn for call-up. He was nearly forty years old; by 1916 he had achieved the rank of corporal. After some preliminary training at Great Yarmouth, he went to France. He worked in the cookhouse section, and while there met up with his two nephews, just a few years younger to himself, the sons of his eldest sister Annie: James and William Johnson. They were regular soldiers and had marched into the camp on their way to the front. Knowing this was their uncle's regiment, they sought him out, and all three had "a night on the town." Bill was the last member of the family to see them alive. James was killed in 1915 and William at the Battle of the Somme.

Throughout the time he was away from home, he wrote to his family every single day, usually a postcard, but sometimes letters, not only to his wife but his children also and vice-versa.

At this time, there was a large tented army camp at Pease Pottage, many of whom were Canadian soldiers. So Crawley High Street continued to hum with activity. The George Hotel offered not only beer but extra food. The Denman women, Elsie, Kate and Vashti, were with others employed in providing this sustenance. Bill's wife, although initially engaged in this activity, was forbidden to continue. She had enough to do, with looking after her family and helping the children to maintain the large allotment and orchard and animals.

In a fervour of patriotism, Crawley's superb Athletics track and cricket field to the north of the village was ploughed and planted with corn, never to return to its former glory.

Along with many hundreds of other soldiers, Bill was a victim of gas. This caused severe breathing difficulties, and probably was the initial cause of his relatively early death. It also made all his teeth rot and they were extracted by the army surgeon with a pair of pliers and without anaesthetic as the lesser of two evils. After convalescence, Bill returned to his unit until demobilisation, whence he returned to his family and postal duties; also, to his beloved football and cricket, although he could not play so frequently, being replaced by a younger generation, but continued as secretary. He finally "hung-up" his boots after 38 years with the Club, but continued with his cricket for a further two years. His writing continued apace, and he was the reporter for sports around the Crawley area for the local newspapers, writing under the title of "Onlooker."

In May 1920 Bill's youngest son, James Fielder, was born. He was educated at The Council School in Robinson Road.

The return to peace brought many changes to the villagers' way of life, not least to Bill's. He decided to enter Public Service. The local governing bodies, the Parish Councils, adhered strictly to the boundaries of the parishes. Hence, we find Bill standing as a candidate for Ifield Parish although his home was barely 100 yards from St. John's Church. He was elected to the Council in April 1922, and in the autumn of

The War Years

I sit in the deepening twilight
My toughts dear heart of thee
In our cosy nest, a lover's nest
Which awaits me beyond the Seas
What though the time goes slowly
And my heart is weary - I ween
Yet I know there will be love and Sunshine
When I come to thee my Queen.   21/7/17
No Crown is won by waiting
A battle must be fought
But the victory won is worth the Strife
If love is the laurel sought
For love will conquer all
For ever and for aye
Honours may perish and pass away
But love endures for aye.   12/8/17
Though Seas may roll between us
And years may pass away
Yet neither pace or time can dim
The love that endures for aye.
My love is not like the red, red rose
Of which the poets sing
For the rose it blooms then blows away
A useless shattered thing
My love can never shattered be
Or like rose petals blow away
For it is fed by thoughts of thee

Who gives me love for love alway.   26/8/17
God sends his glorious sunshine
To warm dear Mother Earth
.To gladden hearts and lovers
Who prove their souls worth
For love is like the sunshine
So pure and bright and free
And I thank God our Father
For giving thee to me.   7/7/18
No flower so sweet no flower so fair
With thee dear heart can be compared
For thy dear form so pure and sweet
Is full of love and truth and trust
You know dear heart that I am thine
And by God's help will be till end of time
For in thee and from thee our Souls do meet
And fills us with joy and bliss so sweet.
Though the darkness is so heavy
There are gleams of light
Visions of my darling's brightness
Gladdens now my sight
Though the shadows - shades and darkness
Makes my life so dull and drab

Soon will come my darling's sunshine
And my heart will then be glad.   14/7/18
There is love for me awaiting
Across the distant seas

Where gloom and darkness are unknown
When dear heart I am with thee
Just now we have to work and wait
In the joy that affords
But oh the richness of the days
When we win and reap our rich reward.
There is no Cross without a Crown
No test without a prize
And we shall find our Crown and Prize
When we gaze with our eyes
Those eyes which are windows of our Souls
And which reveal the secrets of our hearts
Just one look and then we shall know
That love, purity and happiness shall reign
For our Souls and hearts and minds and thoughts
Are as one when together - or apart. 28/7/18
And soon shall come our glorious Easter
When our lives again entwine
And clasped in arms with heart to heart
We can true heart thou art mine
And I feel that God will bless us
And will lead us on our way
So that life will ever hold for us
The Sunshine of a perfect Summer's day.   31/3/18
And straight before me I discern
A star so pure and true
It leads me ever upward darling mine

For that pure Star is you
And when the days are dark and drear
My star shines clear and bright
For my Star is the Soul of thy great Love
Which shines with heaven's pure light.   19/6/18
For though the days are lone and dark
And nights be lone and drear
Yet, I bring to them both love and light
By thoughts of thee - my dear
For no matter how drear and dark the day
Thou hast the power to shine
And add pure love and sweetness bright
To my life - for thou art mine - mine!   9/6/1

Placed in this order of verse by W.J.D.

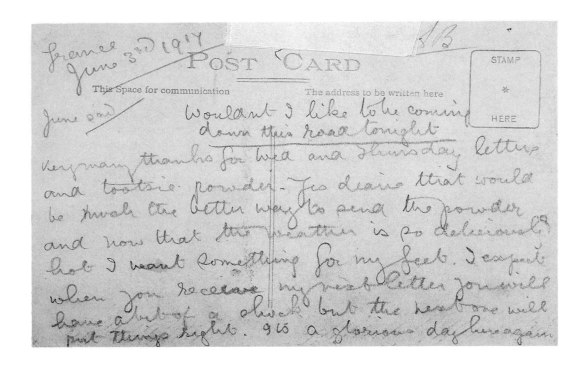

James Fielder Denman

the same year succeeded the Rev. Alan Green on the Horsham Rural Council and Board of Guardians. During the next ten years Bill's involvement in the social welfare of the community escalated. He, with one or two friends, founded the Crawley Labour Party in the early 1920s and he was both President and Chairman, until the passing in Parliament of the Trade Disputes Act. Though he remained a labour man for the rest of his life, he was unable to take any active position within the group. With the legacy of the war, we find him involved with promoting a permanent memorial for the village - something everyone could enjoy. This eventually brought The Recreation Ground, with the Memorial Gates. He was prime instigator in the formation of Crawley's British Legion branch which met at The Railway Hotel, until finally they achieved headquarters in Spencers Road in 1928.

During the next ten years, Bill's involvement in local duties snowballed until he rarely had an evening at home. Sometimes he managed to attend three different meetings at three different venues in a single evening! This as well as doing his full-time postal duties, and continuing with his writings. There were occasions when his Council duties were in conflict with decisions made in other capacities, and he found himself voting against himself in the interests of the whole community.

In those days everyone knew everyone else in the village, and everyone certainly knew him, and he knew the name of every person and where they lived. It was not really necessary to put the number of the house, or even street name on letters; they were always delivered to the correct address.

Amongst many of his activities he was a member of Crawley Water Committee and the Crawley Drainage (before their extinction) Management Committee of Crawley and Ifield Co-operative Society, Crawley Town Band, and Crawley. Rusper and Worth Fire Protection Committee, and Crawley League of Nations Union. When he stood for election to West Sussex County Council, he was unopposed, and in this capacity he served on the Education Committee.

A committed churchgoer, he became appointed to the Crawley and Ifield Parochial Committee, and a sidesman at St. John's Church. In fulfilling these duties, he elected to be responsible for raising the flag on the church tower. To do this, it necessitated in climbing on the parapet of the tower. One day, when after some considerable time he had not returned home for lunch, his wife went to the front garden gate to see if he was coming up the roadway. She saw him all right, only not coming along the road but hanging over the side of the tower, clutching the rope hidden from view at the front of the church. Alerting the police three doors away, he was rescued, but he had been suspended on the slim rope for nearly half an hour. The accident had been caused by the force of the wind buffeting him.

In 1932 Bill became a Justice of the Peace, the first Crawley-born person to be accorded this honour. When serving on "the bench", he preferred to work with juvenile cases. By this time, his home had become a citizens' "Advice Bureau", unofficially,

HORSHAM RURAL DISTRICT COUNCIL.

IFIELD PARISH.

19, STATION ROAD,
CRAWLEY.

Dear Sir (or Madam),

On Monday next you will be asked to elect three persons to represent Ifield Parish on the Horsham Rural District Council, and I again offer my Services to you.

I have been one of the Members for Ifield for seven years, and during that time have done my best to forward many things for the benefit of the Parish, especially in regard to Housing, Footpaths, Lighting, etc.

Within a few weeks will be started one of the greatest improvements that the District has ever had—the cutting off of the corner at Snell Hatch, the filling in of the ditches in front of the Council Houses and Mayfield Terrace, Footpaths made on either side and the road widened. This scheme, initiated by myself, has taken four years to get through. At the moment there is before the Horsham Rural Council a resolution (moved by myself), passed at the Annual Parish Meeting, for a scheme of House-building to let for a rental that a working man can afford to pay, and of no cost to local ratepayers.

I have been a Member of the Water Committee since its inception; also a Member of the Drainage and Lighting Committees for Ifield for nine years.

Being born in the Parish and having spent practically all my life here, I am fully conversant with the needs of the District.

I appeal for your support in the belief that I can be of service to my native place.

Yours faithfully,

W. J. DENMAN.

Printed by P. Standing, 6, High Street, Crawley, and Published by W. J. Denman, 19, Station Road, Crawley.

Opening of Rectreation Ground 1923, with Mrs Moses Nightingale

Sir John Drughorn planting 1938 Coronation Tree

GENEROUS GIFT TO CRAWLEY

SIR J. DRUGHORN PRESENTS IFIELD GREEN

At the monthly meeting of the Crawley Parish Council on Tuesday a letter was read from Sir John F. Drughorn, Bart., in which he offered to dedicate and present Ifield Green to the Parish Council as an open space for all time, subject to the water main which runs through the ground and the electric light cables being undisturbed unless the Horsham Rural Council should take over these services.

Ifield Green is many acres in extent and is well known to Sussex cricketers as cricket has been played upon it since 1802. The Green was awarded to the Lords of the Manor of Ifield in 1855 (under the Enclosure Act), and it is as Lord of the Manor that Sir John has made this splendid gift to the parish.

In 1937 Sir John and a few friends made a very fine hard playing ground on the Green for the children of Ifield School, as they had only the roadway to play in.

On the proposition of Mr. W. J. Denman, J.P., seconded by Mr. R. M Crowe, the gift was accepted with grateful thanks.

The White Hart 1943

THE NEW SUSSEX MAGISTRATES

—————

A SKETCH OF THEIR CAREERS

December 1932

WESTERN DIVISION
MR. W. J. DENMAN, CRAWLEY.

Residents of Crawley have been elevated to the Bench, but Mr. William J. Denman, of 19 Station-road, Crawley, is the first local born man to receive that honour in his own county. Mr. Denman, who was born at Crawley on 30th December, 1877, vies with Dr. S. P. Matthews, J.P., and Mr. Ernest Stanford as a leader of Crawley activities, and he certainly has a remarkably long list of public service records. In private life he is a postman. He entered the Post Office on 5th November, 1894, and has been head postman of Crawley for the past eight years. In the early days of his postal service, it was his duty to meet the four horse coaches running between London and Brighton.

However, his career of public service commenced at an even earlier date, for as almost a schoolboy, Mr. Denman was Assistant Hon. Secretary of the Crawley Football Club, and held the full responsibilities of the Hon. Secretaryships of the town Football and Cricket Clubs at 16 years of age. For 40 years he has played cricket, and was on the football field for 38 years. In the Crawley Horticultural Society shows, Mr. Denman has been a keen exhibitor, and his entries secured him numerous awards and trophies, including three R.H.S. Banksian medals. His prowess as an athlete was well known, but nowadays Mr. Denman has to be content with organizing sports events. He served during the war in the 1st Essex Regiment as a corporal.

Other Activities.

Almost immediately after the war, Mr. Denman was elected to the Horsham Rural District Council and the old Board of Guardians and the Ifield Parish Council. He is now Chairman of the Crawley F.C., Crawley C.C., and of the Bonfire Society. He helped to form the Crawley Charity Cup football competition, while he is a member of Drainage and Water Committees; a member of the Committee of Management of the flourishing Crawley Co-operative Society; and a long-standing sidesman at Crawley Parish Church. In 1920 and 1931, Mr. Denman organized the Christmas Fund for local unemployed, and this year he is Hon. Secretary of the Crawley and Ifield Council Welfare Committee. Mr. Denman is a Council School Manager, and is a frequent writer upon sports subjects and Crawley's entertaining history. For many years he has been a contributor to the *Sussex Daily News*.

He was President and Chairman of the Crawley Labour Party until the passing in Parliament of the Trades Disputes Bill.

*Mr. Chalk of The Limes, Brighton Road,
Clerk to Crawley and Ifield Parish Council.*

CRAWLEY COMMENTS.

Crawley and Ifield have confidence in its Rural Council members, it seems, all the retiring members being re-elected on Monday. Seventy-two per cent. of Crawley voted, the largest total for some years. Mr. W. J. Denman recorded 495 votes, the highest total a Crawley man has ever obtained in a like election.

A DANGEROUS DOG. — When leaving the Crawley cricket ground on Monday evening Mr. W. J. Denman, postman, who had been practising at the nets, was attacked by a terrier dog and bitten on both legs. On the left leg a wound was inflicted below the knee, and on the other leg above the knee. Blood was drawn from each bite, and Mr. Denman had to have both wounds medically treated.

RURAL COUNCIL ELECTION.—Polling for the election of representatives of Crawley and Ifield on the Horsham Rural Council took place on Monday. There was little excitement and just before 9 p.m. it was announced that all the retiring members had been re-elected. Mr. Ernest Stanford, Crawley secured a majority of 112 over the opposing member, Mr. J. F. G. Hopkins Mr. W. J. Denman topped the poll for Ifield with 495 votes. The results, in full, were as follows:—Crawley (one member), Mr. Ernest Stanford, 146; not elected, Mr James Francis Gordon Hopkins, 34; Ifield (three), Mr. William James Denman, 495; Mrs. Gertrude Hilda Courage, 474; Mr. Louis Edmund Hassells Yates, 431; not elected, Mr. Stanley Henry De La Mare, 246; Mr. William Gatland, 147.

Wayside Notes "Wayfarer"

TWO events of last week have a direct interest with old Crawley. First, there was the golden wedding of Mr. and Mrs. J. Izard. Mrs. Izard was the daughter of Mr. and Mrs. John Court, a tinsmith, etc., of Crawley. The Courts lived in the Upper Square, their house being directly opposite the church approach. There were about six steps up to the front door and stone banisters, and the choir boys of those days used to find great fun in sliding down these banisters. On the opposite of the Square were workshops, entrance to which was obtained by going up wide wooden steps, something like granary steps, and the workshops looked like the galleries one sees illustrated in the works of Charles Dickens. In those days there was no promenade as we know it to-day. Mr. Fred Russell's emporium was the only trading concern, but he dealt in everything possible. The changes from those days can be seen by the number of businesses (10) in that block and the fact that such things as outside steps are things of the past. Just where the wooden steps went up became one of Crawley's first banks (Messrs. Henty's).

THEN the death of Mr. George Parker brings back memories of Miller's, the saddlers, of Crawley, for George's father was one of the band who worked for Millers, whose establishment is no more after serving the whole district with saddling and sporting equipment from 1770 to 1939. The shop and house were pulled down, much to the regret of all who take an interest in old buildings, and modern business premises took their place. Millers had a very wide circle of clients, including patronage by Royalty—King George IV., King William and Queen Victoria. So well established was Miller's that though other firms set up as rivals they gradually dwindled away. Mr. Parker, sen., Mr. Golding, Mr. W. Duck, Mr. Westaway and Mr. Arthur Penfold were on the staff of Millers within my memory, but only Mr. Penfold is now with us. The coming of tractors and the decline in horses, of course, led to such businesses being unwanted. But, strangely enough, the machine age brought no extra trade to the black-

smiths, as Crawley always had two, and, at one time, three, but now only one remains.

* * *

DURING this week falls the anniversary of two notable events in Crawley which occurred 60 years ago. One was the placing in the church of the new reredos and Communion table carved in oak and chestnut woods, chiefly from the old gallery and belfry fittings. This was the handiwork of the Rector of that time, and the work occupied 12 months. The wood weighed nearly a ton. The five panels were so beautifully carved that no frontal was required for the table, but an embroidered velvet super-frontal was worked by Mrs. J. Barrett-Lennard, wife of the Rector.

THE other event was an onslaught on the Post Office by Mr. Scaramanga, of Crawley Down. He pointed out that the electric telegraph took many hours to deliver a message. One given in at a post office in London in the morning reached Crawley Down at 8 p.m.; one from Redhill took eight hours; and another from Horley 4½ hours. There was only one delivery of letters daily. Letters posted in East Grinstead for Crawley Down 3½ miles away took two days in transit; and a letter posted on a Friday was delivered on Monday. The parcel post was even worse. He suggested that what was needed was a man with a tricycle instead of expecting a man to walk from Crawley to Worth, with another man walking from Worth to Crawley Down. The reason of the telegraph taking so long was that all telegrams for Crawley Down had to go to Tunbridge Wells before being transmitted to Crawley; and telegrams from Crawley Down had to be sent first to Crawley and then to London before being transmitted to Redhill or Horley. There was at that time no post office at Crawley Down. The outcome was that a horse and cart visited the Crawley Down district and Worth and post offices were opened at Crawley Down, Turners Hill, Copthorne and Copthorne Bank. Pound Hill already had a post office. Mr. Scaramanga certainly rendered the district good service in this respect.

Wayside Notes By "Wayfarer"

MY note of last week as to the 60 years of work by Mr. "Ted" Mills at Messrs. J. Cheal & Sons' nurseries has brought reminders that he is one of quite a small crowd who have served (and are serving) the firm for that length of time. Here is a list of these fine old horticulturists: Messrs. W. Orton, R. H. Holton, W. E. Mills, E. Parsons, A. Tyler and A. Tyrell. Mr. C. Streeter has 57 years, Messrs. W. Tullett and T. Sageman over 50 years, and Mr. H. Rofe 45 years. The doyen is Mr. W. Orton, who joined the nursery staff in 1873 when he was 16 years of age. He has an interesting history. He was born at Colgate in January, 1859. His schooling lasted three years—at Horsham—the family having moved to the Bishopric at that place. At the age of nine years he became a shepherd's boy at the historic Rusper nunnery. Evidently that place was richer in history rather than in coin, for all the shepherd's boy received for a full day's work was sixpence. Considering the long walk from the Bishopric to Rusper which had to be undertaken it meant a very long day indeed. He had two years of this and then had work at Plummers Plain and at Tilgate before entering Cheal's Nursery.

THE large chestnut tree on the Middle Green was planted by him and he has told me that when he planted it he advised the Misses Smith not to have it just at that spot because on the south side is a large boulder which would "unbalance the growth." Mr. Orton, despite his 84 years, is a familiar figure about the town. Mr. Holton was one of the pioneers of the Crawley and District Gardeners' Society and was for several years its hon. secretary.

* * *

IN 1937 Messrs. Cheal entertained the men who had served with them over 50 years, and in addition to the names mentioned here we find those of the late Messrs. E. Middlecote and C. W. Chantler. Mr. Middlecote was well known throughout the South of England as he was one of the representatives of the firm at all the big shows. He was for many years the hon. secretary of the Charlwood and Lowfield Heath Horticultural Society and frequently acted as judge at local shows. Mr. Chantler was a noted bandmaster, a rôle he filled for both the Crawley Town and West Crawley bands. His two sons were also gifted in the same way. Turners Hill and Worth, Copthorne and West Crawley bands all winning prizes under their tuition. It seems that not only is digging good for victory, but for a long and healthy life.

Crawley in 1934

1934 has marked great changes in the town, oth in regard to its growth and its amenities, ind the augmenting of its public services. On ll sides changes have been seen, and perhaps he greatest of all was that caused by the demoli-ion of the George Hotel Annexe, which for early 200 years had stood, and formed, the oundary between the Middle and Lower Square. t will not be possible, however, to judge of the eal effect until spring, when the long line of rees—memorial and otherwise—burst into leaf, or then the whole will be seen with the view f the Surrey Hills beyond. The northern end f the town is being rapidly developed until soon here will be houses linking up Crawley with Iorley just as Three Bridges and Ifield are now onnected. Although the southern end of the own has not developed so rapidly there have een several houses of the "better" class erected. The old Crawley Athletic Football Club's ground s covered with houses and, if present intentions re carried out, the whole of Goffs Park Road vill be built on. The old Crawley Football Club's ground is already covered with "resi-lences" possessing lovely gardens. Crawley "Rural" at Pease Pottage is rapidly being leveloped and soon, if plans mature, there will e an estate of several hundred houses up there. 934 has marked a big advance in the growth of he town.

With the increase in population comes the ecessity for increases in the water supply and the ewerage service. It is therefore good to record hat after three years of continued work and vorry the Water Committee have succeeded in ecuring a good additional supply by the com-letion of the new borehole. Therefore, so far s can be foreseen, the water supply of the own is assured for some years despite the con-inued expansion of building. For the first time he million gallons per week has been exceeded. When looking back over the past six years the teady progressive work carried out by the com-nittee can be seen. No longer is water cut off o many hours a day, as in the past, but for five ears there has been a continuous supply. What vill happen if the new Water Bill promoted by he West Sussex County Council is sanctioned loes not come under this review of 1934.

Equally hard has been the work (though per-aps not so worrying) of the Drainage Com-nittee, but with the up-to-date equipment of he recently completed farm there should be no urther worry for at least twenty years. True, omplaints are made of "smells," but similar grumbling obtains everywhere and is not common o Crawley.

There have been great changes in the Church ife of the district. As is now well known, the oining of the livings of Crawley and West Crawley has been dissolved during the year so hat Crawley reverts to its Rector, while West Crawley will have its Vicar. The result has een a great addition to Crawley parish, which iow takes the whole of the east side of the main London-Brighton road from the Surrey boundary o the East Sussex boundary. The Rev. H. A. K. Baynes has therefore received a very big ncrease in the number of his parishioners. The Rev. E. M. Sidebotham received a hearty welcome rom old friends when he was inducted as priest-n-charge of West Crawley St. Peter. The Rev. E. M. Sidebotham lived at Ifield for some years revious to his ordination and was thus assured f a whole host of friends. At Ifield the sudden nd much lamented death of the Rev. B. B. Ford caused yet another change, the Rev. G. R. Barnett being inducted to the living. The Rev.G. R. Barnett has quickly made himself opular. He spent many years abroad (in New Zealand) engaged in church work and was then ttached to Brighton Parish Church, so that he as had a wide and valuable experience. Another ewcomer to the district is Captain Kirby, of the Church Army, who has aroused so much fervour or Church life at his services in the Montefiore nstitute, Three Bridges, that a church is being uilt there. Captain Kirby is very popular at Crawley and he is in great request at gatherings n the district. At the Crawley Monastery nother large wing was opened during the year nd the Friary is now more than twice the size t was a few years ago. There has been no ddition to the Baptist Church, but the Congrega-ionalists had the pleasure of seeing the fruition f years of effort by the opening of their new Sunday School. There have been changes in the ersonnel of the Salvation Army.

THE SCHOOLS.

The big changes in school life was the resigna-ion of Mrs. F. Dancy, after nearly 30 years at he Crawley Council School, and the coming of Ir. Maisel Jones to the West Green Schools.

Airries and helpers served tea.

CHURCH FINANCE. — According to published statement of accounts, the inco for the two Crawley churches for last y amounted to £927. 16s. 7d. The Dup. envelopes brought in £742. 1s. 9d.; Ea offerings amounted to £43; the garden realised £32. 12s. 9d.; and the harvest fest appeal produced £109. 2s. 1d. Of this s £231. 18s. 8d. was allocated to each chu £317. 13s. 10d. went toward the Clergy Fu and £43 was the Rector's Easter gift. In nection with Crawley Parish Church deficit of £29. 19s. 2d. was reduced to 6s. 7d. St. Peter's Church accounts show t the 1938 deficit has been reduced to 17s. 11d. The organist and choir of Parish Church involved an expenditure £44. 14s. 3d., and at St. Peter's Church item amounted to £66. 15s. 4d.

b

d

e

D

GOLDEN WEDDING.—On Friday Mr. a Mrs. E. Pearce, of Rose Cottage, Malthouse Road, celebrated their golden wedding. Both are well known and highly esteemed in the town.

BLACK-OUT FINE.—At Horsham Petty Sessions on Friday Miss Jones, of Ifield Nurseries, was fined £2 for displaying an un-obscured light at her shop in High Street, Crawley.

Wayside Notes

A walk through the fields in the neighbour-hood of Crawley reveals how great is the increase in magpies in this district. At one time it was a rare thing to see these birds flying about, but at Ewhurst Woods, Hut Lane and the surrounding fields they are really plentiful and make quite a splash of colour. Another bird which has greatly increased is that bugbear of gamekeepers—the jay. These birds usually keep to the woods, but in the fields mentioned they are now quite common. Bird lovers will note with pleasure the great increase in the num-ber of goldfinches. There is plenty of food for them in some of the fields at the Tush-more entrance to the Crawley by-pass road.

• • •

For the first time for many years (17) the long field through which runs the footpath from Crawley Church to Black Dog Farm is being ploughed again. Time was, of course, when the meadow at the back of Crawley Rectory—the Railly Field—was under corn, and then came Snakes Lane plot and what is now known as the long field but formerly the "five acres," and Little Cobbles and all the fields that way to Punch Copse were all used for growing corn.

• • •

Now "Ploughman" has an outlook on life which, if generally followed, would lead to a quieter world. In conversation he said: "I be 74 years old, and four years ago I came down here to live, as I thought it was time I had a good rest, as I have worked hard ever since I was a nipper. Well, then, four years ago when I came here it was harvest time, and my son-in-law says 'Going to give a hand, dad?' I did, and I have been working here ever since and feel better for it. I looks at it like this, sir—74 years is a long time in one way, and not very long when you look the other way. So I thinks—what difference does it make how you fills up the time from your coming to your going, as long as it's some-thing useful?"

• • •

The day usually observed as August Bank Holiday was a curious day at Crawley as the shops remained open, but very little trade was done. Now all who work in shops will have to get down to the long four months of work between now and Christmas. Parties of lads did some useful work during the morning of Bank Holiday as they went round the lanes and byways collecting scrap metal, and many truckloads were gathered together. There is a great quantity of scrap lying about, and as the country is badly in need of this, it behoves all who can do so to get it collected.

• • •

While talking to a musician on Saturday—one who has travelled extensively on the Continent—he informed me that Germany and Austria have always been keen on securing all the scrap possible. There are receptacles for paper, others for bones and others for tins, &c. The tins, he assured me, were used for making the cheap toys which formerly came to England.

WAYFARER.

CRAWLEY'S INDUSTRIES.

To the Editor.

Sir: Through the medium of your interesting and always newsy columns, may I, have the privilege of expressing my appreciation of the response and kind interest of Mr. W. J. Denman anent inquiry respecting the old Crawley names of "Clappers" and "Magazine."

"Bee Taking" by W. J. D. is a memory-stirring item. "The Cobbles," what a magnifi-cent field that used to be; large, shapely, always cultivated in such excellent manner; what crops of grains and roots of various kind. How strong the temptation to help oneself when the peas were in pod and toothsome. On several occasions the writer formed one of a gang of some half a dozen boys, weed pullers, under the direction of old Charles Court. To this day I have never engaged in anything that to appearances was more effective, to go into the young growth of grain where the weeds were flowering in their yellow blossoms and then to leave the field with its whole surface of uninterrupted green gave one a feeling akin to that of the village blacksmith, "Something attempted, something done, has gained a night's repose." Charles Court, with three boys on each side of him, would set the pace, and the example we were to follow. The old man and the boys, each taking as wide a space as he could reach, would cover quite a sward across the field and then back again until the day's work was ended or the job finished. It was a backaching kind of task, for which we received sixpence a day. As I remember it now I seem to see old Mr. Court, his back naturally bent from many years of labour, the better fitted for just such humble service. Invariably, the day would not pass until one of the boys, not necessarily the same one each time, would throw, not viciously, but with roguish fun, a handful of small stones which would fall upon the back of our leader. His quick response, however, was never speedy enough to catch sight of the real culprit, who was apt just then to be the most industrious worker. The scolding was of short duration, for time was flying and there was much to do, and a dozen busy hands were idle while stopping to listen to a "lecture."

It is gratifying to know that the name "Black Dog Lane" is still retained. I have thought at times by certain references that "Woolborough" had been adopted in its place. Woolborough is undoubtedly more euphonious, but there are those to whom Black Dog has an association strong and abiding. What fun and real thrills were had in catching lizards in the gravel pits on the right hand side of Black Dog Lane; some of them in our boyish estimation were miniature crocodiles. They were the finlike tail variety with yellow speckled bellies.

Reference to Jack and Joe brings vividly to mind the family of Boxer Johnson. How we would hang around the Johnson premises at the pig-killing time, looking on, and counting it a great compliment if called upon in the slightest degree to assist. It was the day after one of these special favours when we were given a pork pie all hot, just out of the oven, to take home for our consumption.

Some years after, when the writer's family lived in the centre of the town, there were few sights more interesting and typical of the John-son family than that of Boxer Johnson with Jack and Joe seated on their donkey cart, their legs dangling. They are coming home from work at the close of day down the easy grade of Main Street, the donkey going at full gallop, to the amazement and wonder of a stranger, but to the understanding and admiration of those who knew the character and industry of the family.

Yours truly,

JAMES BRISTOW.

Warwick, N.Y., May 26th, 1930.

because no such institution existed in those days. Any problem was given every care to resolve; nothing was considered trivial.

By the 1930s, Bill was also the local reporter for the Sussex and Surrey Courier, The Sussex Daily News, West Sussex County Times, West Sussex Gazette, The Evening Argus, and the Evening Standard, as well as sending items to national papers which he considered of interest. His sports column continued under the name of Onlooker, and his Weekly Diary reports under the name of Wayfarer, an inherited title from previous subscribers, as well as straight articles using his own name.

On 31st. December 1937, William Denman retired from the postal service after 43 years two months. He had served under the direction of six postmasters and had been head postman since 1924. The only difference this made to his life was to give more time to devote to public duties and his writing. At the time of his retirement, he was still very involved with sport in the area being chairman of both the Football and Cricket and The Rifle Clubs, vice-chairman of the British Legion Benevolent Committee, Committee of Crawley Harriers, Crawley Gardeners Association, Crawley and Ifield Old Boys Association. Also one of the Managers of the Council Schools.

Around this time, Bill's wife became very ill, and finally had an operation for cancer in the Crawley Cottage Hospital. While she was convalescing with her friends at Brighton, Bill contracted whooping cough at the age of 60 years! This played havoc with his public life for some time, as he would cough in any smoky atmosphere ending with a whoop!

The outbreak of the Second World War in 1939 sees both of Bill's sons in the army. James was the first to depart at the age of 18 years, having joined the Territorial Army at the end of July, and was drafted two days prior to the declaration. George went later, serving in Iraq, Iran and Italy. Meanwhile, Bill carried on with town problems. The Parish Council members were mostly "elder statesmen", and so could continue to oversee the town's welfare. The old Post Office in Robinson Road became the A.R.P. centre, reinforced with sandbags. Schools had air raid shelters built in the playgrounds. Similar facilities for the public were erected in the middle square, and in the market field along Ifield Road. Ration books and identity cards were issued from The Ministry of Food Office above Dean's shop in the High Street, while Mr. Gadson's garage and adjoining empty Imperial Cinema were requisitioned by the R.E.M.E. for the duration of war. They also built a depot north of Pope Mead (same site as M.F.I.), Gatwick aerodrome became a Spitfire base, and Canadian soldiers occupied Tilgate Mansion.

The village continued with its daily life as near normal as possible. The people coped with the blitz and the nightly drone of aeroplanes. Absorbed and welcomed evacuees in their midst. Supported the war effort fund raising activities from fetes to concerts. The Punch Bowl became a Y.M.C.A., well patronised by the forces stationed in the area. The cinema remained open in the evenings. All around the village, the fields

Mr. W. J. Denman

FUNERAL AT CRAWLEY

The funeral of Mr. William James Denman, of 19, Station-road, Crawley, whose death, at the age of 67, brought over 50 years of varied public service in his native town to a close, took place on Saturday morning. The service in St. John's Church, Crawley, was followed by interment in the churchyard in the grave of his wife, who died 12 months ago. The Rector (the Rev. A. Douglas Wing) officiated, the choir attending and Mr. Vernon Blount presiding at the organ. Four members of the Horsham division of the Sussex Constabulary — Sergts. Winton, Bulbeck, Scotcher and Peters— acted as bearers. Police formed a guard of honour at the entrance to the church, including Supt. W. H. Wright (also representing Mr. R. P. Wilson, assistant chief constable of West Sussex), Inspector N. Longley (special constabulary) and a detachment of regular, war reserve and special constables.

RECTOR'S TRIBUTE.

In a striking tribute to Mr. Denman, the Rector said the presence of the police, the choir boys and other representatives was an act of sympathy with the members of the family who were left. Tracing deceased's life from a boy and his interest in local affairs, the Rector said he loved the old church, he loved the old village, and it did seem rather sad just at that time that so many of his particular generation seemed no longer able to stand the strain through which civilisation had been passing. For the last few months he was very sad and very lonely. A few months ago, the Rector said, they buried another of their public men in that parish—Dr. Sidney Matthews. The speaker said he felt it was a work of mercy on Almighty God's part that after Dr. Matthews died, Mr. Denman was given those few months to take the leadership of the civic life of that village, that Dr. Matthews had held for so many years.

Concluding, the Rector said: "For Mr. Denman we may say, 'Thank God.' May this country go on producing men who are prepared to give themselves to the public service as he did."

MAGISTRATES' TRIBUTE.

Before the business at Horsham Magistrates' Court on Friday last week was proceeded with, Mr. E. E. Lawrence (chairman) referred to the death of Mr. Denman, whose co-operation, he said, they had received as a magistrate for 12 years. Mr. Denman was a man of great human sympathy, and they learnt to respect his judgment. He would be greatly missed. Supt. W. H. Wright, on behalf of the police, associated himself with the Chairman's remarks.

PARISH COUNCIL SYMPATHY.

At the meeting of Crawley Parish Council on Tuesday Mr. R. M. Crowe (vice-chairman) referred in feeling terms to the death of Mr. Denman, who had so recently been elected chairman of that Council after many years of very active service for the welfare of the town. Mr. Ernest Stanford added a tribute to Mr. Denman's many public services, and the Clerk (Mr. W. L. Small) was asked to express the Council's condolences to the relatives.

11 – 5 – 45.

...gate,

On behalf of the Staff & Scholars of the C.E. School, I wish to convey to you, & to those near & dear to you, our deepest sympathy in your great loss.

We are all conscious of the honour that such a loyal & respected son of Crawley was once a pupil in this school. In his life of service to his fellow men he has set a standard difficult to equal & impossible to surpass.

We would like to express our personal regret (apart from our public work together) at your Dad's leaving you all. We had hoped he would have been able to enjoy some of the honour of being old & seeing the fruits of his work, in the more peaceful days to come.

May we express our appreciation of the fact that in all the work he did & honours he enjoyed never altered him, he is still "Billy Denman" now as he was years ago.

Our sympathy to you all.

Ely. H. C. Carman

were once again ploughed and golden with corn. To the northwest were the herds of dairy cows. Primroses and bluebells continued to bloom in season at the Hawthe.

During May 1944 Helen Denman died after a long and painful illness. In the last two years of her life, Bill had kept a nighty vigil as she needed constant attention. It was a blow from which Bill never recovered. The only thing which now kept him going was his work for the town. In the same year, his friend and long standing colleague, Dr. Sidney Matthews also passed away, another blow.

Gradually his own health deteriorated, but he refused to give in. In April 1945, he fought another Council election. This was the first time party politics had entered the fray at local level. Although a staunch labour man, he did not approve of party politics at this level, believing the good of the community of paramount importance. He stood as an Independent, and topped the poll, with a large majority. At the first meeting of the "new" Council in early May, a meeting which he did not attend, he was returned as Chairman.

May 8th. 1945 saw the end of the War in Europe. Bill insisted that all the bunting used in the 1937 Coronation be found and the house decorated, only for it to be removed 24 hours later. William James Denman died early in the morning, on the 9th. May, of lung cancer.

On his retirement, Mr. Denman said, "No working man in Sussex could have had a finer life than I have had - full of sport and interesting events, and everyone has been really good to me."

He was laid to rest with his wife in St. John's churchyard on Saturday 12th. May. The police lined the route to the church and stopped all traffic from entering the High Street. Flowers were largely unobtainable during this time. The shops closed early for lunch. People stood silently along "The Street" to pay their respects - a brief moment when Crawley remembered its own.

At the time of his death, Mr. Denman had not found the time to achieve his ambition of writing a book about his beloved Crawley. He started it in 1927 and added various chapters in the 1930s, but it lay unfinished amongst his many papers. Written to guide the visitor on an afternoon stroll along the High Street and adjacent areas, it is a typical way of depicting the village of his era. Much of his knowledge went unrecorded, but, lest these things be forgotten and hopefully in fulfilment of his dream, for my grandfather, I present the following.

Historical Crawley

W J Denman
1927

The visitor to Sussex has many approaches open to him, but none more picturesque or more appropriate than the old London-Brighton road, for Crawley is undoubtedly a fitting introduction to the "*fair land beside the sea*", giving as it does a vista of the great forest and the hills beyond towards which the visitor is advancing.

Crawley lies at the bottom of the beautiful basin formed by the South Downs-North Downs and Surrey hills. On three sides of it one sees the lovely rolling Downs with monuments and chalk hills shining on the horizon. Eastward and Southeast one gets wonderful forest scenery. Trees, trees, trees, higher yet even higher they rise, and the whole forms a wonderful picture of beauty.

Sussex is entered one and a half miles north of Crawley. Once over the boundary, one leaves behind the flat uninteresting country, and experiences a gradual rise after County Oak is passed. Trees guard the road on either side, and hills and horizon are enshrouded in an entrancing blue.

Here is the Manor House, the old home of the famous Sussex family of Robinson. A few yards further on is "Jordans" with which the names of Fox and Penn are associated, and from here one gets a first glimpse of Crawley nestling at the foot of forest and hill.

A sweep round the winding road brings the visitor into Crawley High Street and here the lover of the picturesque will find much that is delightful. The broad street with its village

LONDON ROAD, CRAWLEY.

greens and the long line of memorial trees with the ancient elm in their midst; on either side beautiful houses of timber and plaster, centuries old, and then under the sign of Saint George and the Dragon which hangs right across the road. This is The George Hotel, the famous old coaching house. Adjoining The George is another old house of plaster, while immediately opposite is the Ancient Priors House, one of the most interesting to be found in the long run between London and Brighton.

For some hundred yards one sees houses of very old build and appearance, though the hand of the *"improver"* has been heavy. The level of the High Street rises gradually, and when the Half Moon Inn is reached, the great forest ridge lies in full view of the traveller and the road winds upwards and onwards to Handcross.

Let us return to Crawley. It will be noticed that the town inspires the very old joke: Why is Crawley the longest town in the world? Because it stretches from the Sun to the Moon! Crawley has a traditional reputation for smuggling, for sport and for trees. The love of trees is evidenced by the fact that all historical incidents - coronations, royal deaths, jubilees etc. - are commemorated by the planting of a tree; for example:

1   The Oak on the lowest green near The Cottage was planted as an acorn in 1887 in Mr. Smith's garden and transplanted to its present site in 1897 to commemorate the Diamond Jubilee of Queen Victoria.

2   The Copper Beech near the Oak was planted in honour of the present King's wedding.

3   The American Elm opposite Tyler's house was planted in 1901 in memory of King Edward's accession.

4   Copper Beech opposite Denman's and the Chestnut close by were both to commemorate King Edward's coronation.

5   The large Oak on the uppermost green, just above the brewery, was planted in 1887 by the late Lord de Blaquire in memory of Queen Victoria's Diamond Jubilee.

6   The Oak opposite the brewery was planted on June 22 1911, the coronation of King George V.

History tells us that Crawley was formerly just a clearing in the forest and we learn that as late as the beginning of the last century, a row of trees grew right down the High Street to the Ancient Elm and here the crows used to build their nests. It is interesting to note here that Crawley is a corruption of Crowlieu "the place of the Crow". The trees have long since disappeared (except the Elm) to make way for buildings and the great increase in road traffic which opened up the London-Brighton route when the First Gentleman in Europe discovered Brighton in 1783.

This began a new era for villages along the famous road and Crawley grew from a hamlet to its present size. The hand of the despoiler has swept away many beautiful buildings, yet several are left to us in this year of Grace 1927.

CRAWLEY GREEN.   1653.

Know all Men by these presents that I Richard Smith of Crawley in the County of Sussex Innholder am

... held and firmly bound to Thomas Friend of Hurstperpoint in the said County Tallow Chandler in the Sum of four Hundred Pounds ——— of good and lawfull Money of Great Britain to be paid to the said Thomas ——— or his certain Attorney Executors Administrators or Assigns ffor which payment to be well and faithfully made I bind myself my Heirs Executors and Administrators ——— firmly by these presents Sealed with my Seal Dated the Twenty second day of July ——— in the nineteenth year of the Reign of our Sovereign Lord George the Third by the grace of God of Great Britain ffrance and Ireland King Defender of the faith And in the year of our Lord One Thousand Seven hundred and Seventy Nine ./ ———

The Condition of this Obligation is such That if the above bounden Richard Smith ——— his heirs Executors Administrators or Assigns do and shall well and truly pay or cause to be paid unto the above named Thomas Friend his ——— Executors Administrators or Assigns the Sum of Two hundred Pounds of good and lawful money of Great Britain together with lawful Interest for the same on or upon the twenty second day of January now next Ensuing and which will be in the year of our Lord One Thousand Seven hundred and Eighty without any Deduction or abatement out of the same for Taxes or otherwise and without fraud or further delay

according to and in full performance and discharge of the proviso or Condition mentioned in one Indenture of Mortgage bearing date ——— with these presents made or mentioned to be made Between the above Bounden Richard Smith of the one part and the above named Thomas Friend of the other part ———

And so also well and truly observe perform fulfill and keep all and singular the Covenants Grants Articles Conditions and Agreements whatsoever which on his and their parts and behalfes are or ought to be Observed performed fulfilled and kept Comprized and mentioned in the said recited Indenture ——— And that in all things according to the true intent and meaning thereof and of the parties to the same Then this Obligation to be void or else to remain in full force

Sealed and Delivered
(being first duly Stampt)
In the presence of ...

Jn. Cook

Charles Griffith

Richd Wood

Richard Smith

The Rising Sun

At the extreme end of Crawley High Street going toward London is a house which to the observant would be at once noted as a house with a character. Its wide spacious windows, its imposing porch, and its mellowness stamp it as a house "with a past". A large brass plate bears the inscription "North House School."

The well known scholastic establishment is a house with a history, having been the venue of many exciting scenes, and from the middle of the 17th century onward to 1860 it was undoubtedly one of the busiest places on the London to Brighton Road. The house was the Rising Sun Inn, in later years becoming known as the "Old Sun." In the middle "seventees" long before the Prince Regent made his trip to Brighton, 7th September 1783, the "Old Sun" was a noted hostelry and it continued to be so for another 80 years. Its origin cannot be determined, but it is worthy of note that it was old nearly 200 years ago. Here were established the "Postboys" who were chiefly responsible for the horsing of the coaches which became so popular during the dates mentioned.

The last of the old Postboys in Crawley, Mr. Harry Holder who died in 1897, used to retail stories of exacting rides and incidents in their mode of living. Mr. Holder with the remainder of the "Boys" used to live in the outbuildings attached to the old "Sun" for they had to be ready at any hour of the day or night to take up their duties. "We used to live in the lofts, eight of us." Here, too, the horses for "posting" were stabled, the "George" Hotel having but room for the coaching horses. The Postboys' uniform, Mr.

Holder recalled with pride, was short blue velvet tunic (braided for high days) white buckskin breeches, top boots with overhanging tassels and a **huntsman's** cap.

About 25 yards below the "Sun" was the old "Tollgate" and here the horses were changed on private vehicles and the two extra "leaders" put on the coaches which were conveyed to Pease Pottage where the Crawley horses were unhitched and others put on. At the most popular time of coaching no fewer than 60 coaches per day passed up and down, and this meant 120 horses to provide (though naturally many of the horses made several trips per day) and private vehicles had to be horsed, the scenes of activity can be imagined. Mr. Holder said it was no enviable task to take a family "out in the country" in those days particularly after nightfall as of course there was no lighting, and the roads were more or less like farmways. He was the means on one occasion of helping to the "crowning of a romance" when he horsed a conveyance containing a young lady who was eloping with her lover. The old Postboy used to chuckle when recalling this adventure, saying the young lady was being pressed to marry for money and her lover was refused admittance to her presence. Holder got well away with them after making arrangements with postboys along the road, and by making a good start and then a detour, he followed the pursuing father (who had been told by the postboys "a couple just passed through") and so reached London in safety.

Returning to the mid 1700s one finds the Sun was the haunt of smugglers then so active throughout Sussex, East Sussex in particular. It is recalled on many occasions the Revenue Officers raided this house but never succeeded in finding any contraband. During this period the parents of old Mrs. Russell (she later lived in the "old" White Harte) were members of the Hawkhurst gang from Copthorne area. Old Mrs. Russell was a cook for her parents prior to her marriage. On one occasion when she cooked for the gang they stole many pounds of sausages which were hung from the kitchen ceilings. On their next visit the ceiling was once again hung with sausages, but this time their skins were filled with chopped turnips, liver and offal, which led to no end of jesting at those who tried to eat them. On another occasion dinner was prepared for over 40 persons. A sparrow pie was brought in - the carver being in the secret took off a fine cut, when out rushed several dozen live sparrows which had been seated in bran, flying about the room knocking the lights out and producing pandemonium.

Once the landlady defeated the Revenue Officers by her own efforts. The Officers had learned that contraband goods were in the house and having made certain that only females were in the house made a raid. The landlady however was equal to the occasion. She seized the fireirons and placed herself across the stairs defying all who attempted to go up, demanding to see the search warrant which alone made the raid lawful. The whole household of course were in league with the smugglers and whilst the parley at the stairs was going on, the maids had handed out the contraband from the bedroom windows to the stablemen below, who quickly dashed through the buildings and hid the goods in the ditches in the adjoining meadow (now Victoria Hall Meadow). By the time the warrant had been secured and produced, the word was passed "all

P.A.

North House School on the left

Mr. Conlan and pupils

NORTH HOUSE SCHOOL,
CRAWLEY, SUSSEX.

PRESENTATION TO MR. J. O. CONLAN.

At the annual entertainment held at North House School, immediately prior to the breaking-up for the Christmas holiday, Mr. J. O. Conlan, who has just completed 25 years as head master, was presented with a purse of gold from the past and present students of the school.

The presentation was made by the Rector of Crawley (the Rev. H. L. Barrett-Lennard), who remarked that the occasion was a very auspicious one. He could remember the school under two former heads—the late Mr. Rowse and Mr. Coles—and now they were met to recognise the 25th anniversary of Mr. Conlan, an event which the scholars, past and present, desired to mark by the presentation to him of a purse of gold, as a token of their affection and goodwill, and as an appreciation of the good service he had rendered them. Two gentlemen had been mainly instrumental in raising the needful for this gift, viz., Messrs. W. H. Waller and C. W. Lovett, and he (Mr. Lennard) was acting as the mouthpiece of those who had subscribed. A large number of boys must have passed through Mr. Conlan's hands during the last 25 years, and his influence had undeniably been a good one. Those whose names were on the list hailed from all parts of the world, including Canada, India, South Africa, Australia, South America, and even the United States of America, so that this gift came not only from all parts of the British Empire, but also from the whole English-speaking world. It was not only from John Bull, but also from Cousin Jonathan, or Uncle Sam, as he was sometimes called. In conclusion, he wished Mr. Conlan many more years' success in his work, and asked his acceptance of the purse of gold as an indication of the past and present scholars' regard and esteem for him (applause).

Mr. Conlan was greeted with rounds of applause. Addressing the lads as " My dear boys," he said he felt his position very keenly, and he greatly appreciated the honour and the kindness they had bestowed on him by presenting him with such a handsome gift. They could rest assured he should never forget their kind thoughts on that occasion. He was very proud and thankful to think that he had been spared to occupy his position for 25 years, during which period 250 boys had been under his care, snd he was very happy to say that the majority of them were doing well in the battle of life. He thanked Mr. Lennard for the kind things he said about him, and for presenting the gift on behalf of the past and present students, and he also warmly thanked Mr. Waller (his first pupil) and Mr. Lovett for their kindness in raising the testimonial.—Reprinted from the *Sussex and Surrey Courier.*

clear" and the Officers searched but in vain. There was an underground passage constructed so that the exit came out in a nearby field to aid the smugglers' escape.

Another subterfuge of the smugglers was carried out in the plantation immediately opposite the house. The smugglers had a very clever hiding place for the contraband, the simplicity of its construction evidently misleading the preventive officers. From the forest were brought many "brakes" (fern) to be used in the stables and piggeries of the "Sun". The smugglers had a large wooden framework made and the stack was built around this, but the centre was filled up with a cleverly made bundle of brakes which fitted the entrance to a nicety. The stack was cut away in the ordinary way so that the framework was not exposed and here the contraband goods were concealed. These unlawfully secured goods were disposed of in an ingenious way. The landlady had a daughter (old Mrs. Russell) who was the recognised "Belle" of the place. She made occasional trips to London "dressed in the latest fashion" by chaise with posthorses, having a load of "luggage" with the fair lady's named painted on them. The trunks contained contraband goods which were conveyed to certain houses in London. Here the goods were quickly spread among customers and the "Belle's" little holiday was over. While smuggling was also associated with the Old White Hart, the families of both places being connected, the point of transporting of the booty was usually the "Sun."

In 1833 or '34 Crawley and Horsham Foxhounds were formed, and for several years the hounds were kennelled at the "Rising Sun", this being an ideal place. With the coming of the railways, the stabling for coach horses and post horses was becoming unwanted. Mr. Lee Steere who started the foxhounds pack decided the Sun with its commodious stabling accommodation was then available. The stables ran the entire length of the courtyard and the hounds were kennelled in the "loose boxes" at the south end of the courtyard. The hounds were moved to Warninglid when Mr. E. Stanford became Master. Though the Hunt was removed from Crawley it has had much to do with the town since. It was during the Mastership of Mr. Charles Bethune that the famous huntsman Jack Press was engaged to manage the pack. Mr. Press had a daughter who married Mr. Edward Dean who kept a dairy and general shop, but afterward secured the licence of the Rising Sun Inn, and founded the present "Sun Inn" some 250 yards further north and on the opposite side of the road.

When the old inn closed, after some time it was used as a family home and changed its name to North House. It was occupied by Dr. T.H. Martin, whose name was synonymous with Crawley for many years. He married a daughter of Mark Lemon, and Mrs. Martin took a leading part in the social life of the place. Dr. Martin became the first Justice of the Peace for the district. The Martin children performed many little theatricals. Charles Dickens was a great friend of their grandfather Mark Lemon and a frequent visitor. He helped the children write several little plays.

In later years the North House became that well known scholastic establishment. A large brass plate bears the inscription **North House School J.O. Conlan**. This house is the "alma mater" of thousands of boys many of whom hold responsible positions in our great Empire.

It will be seen that the Old Sun Inn has a high place in the history of Crawley. Now its inhabitants are taught respect and obey the laws of the realm, but even so, doubtless in their thoughts the young scholars will dwell with delight on thoughts of the "Smugglers" and "Post Boys."

After the closure of North House School, the premises were altered once again. There was a notable find last December (1926) at the "Olde Sunne". The ancient house was being turned into flats. As will be understood, in the old house, were huge fireplaces, and these had to be pulled out. The builders (Messrs Parsons) noticed that when smashing up two of the hearthstones, there were letters and figures on the reverse side. The other was carefully prised up and proved to be a tombstone in memoriam of a man and a girl who was buried before the Reformation. Undoubtedly, alterations presumably at Crawley Church had led to the tombstone being taken away and used as firehearths. The whole of the inscriptions and figures were in Latin. It reads:

D.E.   HAC

PAROCHIAL VIXIE PACES I M

TO R.E.M. DIE OCTORBRIE

DOMNI 1668 RECTIONEM

SANCTUS

M.O.R.

BAR   BARA

OB   H.T.   24 - T. BRIS

8

(The first stone should read "Here lieth - of this Parish, who died 8th of October in the Year of Our Lord 1668. - The Lord giveth salvation to his saints - Barbara who died on 24th September 1668.")

This building was in the occupation of John Heaver in 1767. He was an apothecary and surgeon. John Heaver died in 1769, and all his property, apart from his medicines which he left to his wife Ann, became the property of his father William Heaver, a miller of Ifield, who lived with his son.

"William Heaver, a messuage, a garden, orchard and lands in Crawley, in occupation of the testator, and his said father."

William Heaver died in 1773, and from his will we find that he had divided the land holding thus: "to his wife Mary, a piece of land ten rods in length and the same in breadth to be taken from the south end of his orchard in Crawley, together with a dwelling house and all the buildings which he shall erect thereon. To his daughter Mary, who was married to Richard

Smith, a victualler, a messuage, garden and the remainder of the orchard, and the land now in the occupation of the said Richard."

This now shows how two substantial houses very close together acquired the same name, and known as The Rising Sun Inn. There is no mention of this name being used to describe the house prior to this date.

In 1793 both properties were sold to Edward Lee, victualler. The original building owned by Richard Smith being held jointly with William Ellis of Horsham, a mortgage being raised from Henry Wood of Chestham in Henfield, sold subject to paying quit rent to the Lord of the Manor. After Edward's death in 1798, the Inn became the property of his widow Susannah Lee.

Susannah leased it on a yearly tenancy to James Lee of Crawley, inn holder, to commence from 24th. June and to run for one year, and so from year to year during her lifetime.

During 1801 Susannah Lee was able to complete the repayment of the principal sum, and interest owing to Henry Wood.

James Lee was given notice to quit in 1801, and the property was leased to Faulkner Best, inn holder, on the same terms as the previous tenant.

In 1817, it was leased to George Lee, inn holder, on the same terms, and a Covenant "to keep the property in repair and to paint the front of the inn during the first year, and the rest of the property in the course of two years afterwards, and to keep the same open as an Inn and conduct the Business thereof in such a regular and proper manner in every respect that the Licence of the same shall not in any wise be legally forfeited or refused, or pay to Susannah Lee £200 as liquidated damages."

In 1826 James Newman became the innkeeper.

Susannah died in January 1826. According to her husband's will all his property was to be sold and monies raised divided between his children, though the children had the right to purchase. All declined, so the Rising Sun Inn buildings were sold at auction on 26 April 1826, at the Kings Head, Horsham for £1,800. Purchased by James Newman on behalf of Joseph Johnson Innkeeper of Ifield, who also owned The George Hotel.

In later years Joseph Johnson sold his properties to Mrs. Montifiore and in 1841, the licensee was Jane Bartley, a widow who was a publican. But it appears at this time that the buildings were operating as separate entities, for a distinction is drawn between The Sun Inn and the Sun Hotel in the census. Perhaps this had always been so, in as much as one establishment provided accommodation only, and the other licensed for drinks.

The Sun Hotel was a conglomerate of buildings including what had originally been the cottage of The Parish Poor. In 1841 one housed George Elphick and family, a butcher, another a group of servants, another a painter and his family.

By 1851 the hotel section was rented to Jack Press, the huntsman though the public house continued to flourish next door with Jane Bartley.

Robert Gates leased this property in 1858 and lived there with his large family. But the public house building became a private home. By 1871 Mr. Rouse had rented what had previously been the public house for his Grammar School, moving from Gravesend Cottage, Worth Lane.

When Robert Gates's family grew up and left home, he himself moved to a small cottage at the rear of The Rising Sun Inn, and in the 1870's he rented the building to Dr. Timothy Martin, who remained there until the mid 1890's. Robert Gates died in 1881.

After Dr. Martin moved to The Gables along the Brighton Road, the school moved into the house, the accommodation being more commodious, the old school building becoming tea rooms.

After the retirement of Mr. Conlan, headmaster, in the early 1920's North House School ceased, and once again the building was converted, this time to Northgate Laundry.

Meanwhile, Edward Dean who had married Mary Press built a new inn on the opposite side of the road, and in the first instant called it The Rising Sun (Census 1871), but ten years later it was known as The Sun, and remains so until this day.

Crawley Tollgates

Crawley was favoured with three Tollgates and a "Tollbar", the difference being that the "gates" had residential attendants whilst the "bar" was locked from 9 p.m. to 6 a.m. during which hours there was of course no means of using the road. Crawley was very differently situated then in regard to roads. The only egress from the town on the westside was Smalls Lane, and though the traffic from the east could come via Three Bridges Lane, it had to pass either of the Tollgates on the main road, or if going westward, was trapped at Goffs Hill. It will be seen that the gates were placed in such a way that no one could escape. The only other road from the east was Tushmore Lane, but here the "Tollbar" operated.

The north Tollgate was placed just where is now the entrance to the town meadow (more popularly known as the "Fair Field"). The little four roomed cottage was placed in such a way that traffic could be observed in either direction. A little wooden porch with windows and a seat enabled the gatekeeper to look after his or her charge without using the cottage. The toll was 6d. (2½p.) for a vehicle and horse, 3d. for a horse alone and 1d. for attendant, 1d. for adult persons, ½d. for children, 4½d. for ten sheep or pigs. This gate was a particularly busy one, as all the southward traffic passed through, much of it en route for Chichester and Shoreham ports. The last attendant was most appropriately named Agate (Mrs.). She was a member of the well known Robinson family, her sister being responsible for building of the "Servants Home" and the "British School" at Crawley, - now the "Crawley Cottage Hospital" and "Crawley Council School".

Mrs. Agate (according to a friend who knew the old lady) used to wear a coal scuttle bonnet and of course a crinoline, being officially employed she could afford to be fashionable.

The Misses Smith "The Tree" house, have a splendid print of the scene with the Gates across the road. Mr. W. Mitchell (father of Mr. C.J. Mitchell the well known Crawley Post Office family) once jumped the Gates with a tankard of beer in each hand. In 1924 when Crawley Fairs were abolished from the streets, the town meadow was fitted with suitable sanitary arrangements, and in carrying out this work it was necessary to dig near where the gate used to swing. The workmen found the bottom of the gatepost, a very large one, too, and in splendid condition, evidently real Sussex oak.

At the southern end of the town, just where Goffs Park Road is now, stood the South Tollgate and the last keeper of this was a retired ostler named Jones, who came from the Pease Pottage-Handcross district. The cottage was much like the northern one except the porch had no seats. The keeper was a somewhat singular gentleman for he had a large box on one side of his front door, and a large basket on the other. In these he used to sleep never going to a proper bed. He was, presumably, a very pious man, as he was always reading his Bible, and he confessed he had read it through and through but oldtime coachmen have informed me that when disturbed at night he used words that one never saw in the Bible. Jones was a very short thickset man, and owing to the continual disturbance of his rest at night time, he had a code of signals for the local coachmen and fly drivers. The George Hotel drivers used a certain signal, as did the "Old Sun" drivers and the "Old White Hart" drivers. Dr. Smith (The Tree House) had one of his own and, as he was the only doctor for miles, he was frequently out at night. Jones used to make marks on his box or basket and next day or at the weekend there was a square-up.

The West Gate was at the top of Goffs Hill, and placed between "Springfield" and "Goffs Manor". This was a round house, quite different to the others, and the last keeper was Mr. James Charman. Mr. J.T. Charman who is happily still with us was the last child to be born there, and that was 75 years ago. This road was a busy one, as it had all the west bound traffic to deal with, but otherwise it was exactly the same as the other places. There is one thing worthy of note, and that is that each of these cottages was a wayside cottage, that is neither was enclosed but stood on "common-land". At each place were large ponds for watering the horses.

The sites on which the cottages stood have long been acquired and the ponds. The one at the Southgate is now the water garden at Upton House, and the West Gate one serves a like purpose at Goffs Manor. At the North Gate the pond has been filled in and is now enclosed within the bricked wall in front of North House School - freeholds in every sense of the word.

I would like to add a word of thanks to Messrs G. Holman, G. Parsons, James Charman and J.T. Charman for much information in regard to these old tollgates.

P.A.

Mr Funnell's daughter, the last occupant of the cottage.

Note: This article appears to have sparked some controversy in the local press as to the truth of the contents, for I have found the following reply to some correspondence).

CRAWLEY TOLLGATES

Sir,

The notes in Current Topics referring to Crawley Tollgates were read by me with very great interest. As one who has spent practically the whole of my life in collecting the history of the town, I would like to give reasons why we are certain there were not only two tollgates on the main London - Brighton road, but that there was another at Goffs Hill (on the Horsham Road) and a Toll-bar in Tushmore-Lane.

Let us take the North Gate (which the writer of the note agrees was there). The last keeper of this gate was one James Funnell, who was not only the keeper of the Paygate but also the Vestry roadman; as assistant (if necessary) to the sexton and also Assistant Waywarden.

The South Gate was kept by a man names Jones (I have never learned his initials) a retired coachman who came from the Handcross district. It is reported of him that he had standing in his porch (all tollgate houses had porches) a huge cradle-like arrangement that he used to shift around with the wind.

The Goff Hill paygate was last kept by a Mrs. James Charman, whose son, John, was born about the time this gate was closed. The tollbar in Tushmore-Lane was also looked after by a family named Charman. The "bar" was locked at dusk and opened an hour after sunrise.

My authority for these are the old coachman who used the South Gate (one Mr. George Holman is still alive). The George Hotel at Crawley was the recognised centre for all big social events, and the "gentry" coming into Crawley from the south, south-east and south-west of the town would go nowhere near the North Gate, so but for the South Gate would have used the turnpike without paying fees.

Over 50 years I used to converse with an old friend Mr. Harry Holder, the last of the Crawley Postboys. He used to show me his uniform of a short red coat (then much faded), a blue huntsman's cap, buckskin breeches and top boots. He told me that one of the biggest difficulties they had to contend with was the South Gate, as old Jones was a "hern of a disagreeableman". What we had to do was blow a horn if we had passed through the North Gate, but whistle if we had not, and then he would book us and the account was squared up by the boss. Other old coachmen have told me that at night as they approached the South Gate they shouted out "George", "Railway", "White Hart" or "Old Inn" these being the recognised livery stables.

Now, Sir, either there was a South Gate or the old coachmen were confirmed perverters of the truth and must have been in league for a number of years as I was but 12 when. Mr. Holder told me about it, and up until six years ago old coachmen have told me the same story. Each has described the South Gate Cottage as an "end-to-end" cottage with a porch stuck on the road end, and a pond right opposite. The cottage went with the paygate, but the pond is still there.

Whether the South Gate (why South Gate unless there was also a North Gate?) appears on road books or not, I feel sure that the old coachmen can be accepted as authorities.

Yours etc

W.J. Denman

19, Station Road, Crawley

(Author's note) When checking before submitting for publication using data unobtainable in 1927 I find:

William and Mary Stoner (wife toll keeper) North Gate in 1851 Census.

James Charman and wife toll keeper South Gate in 1851 Census

The 1840 tithe maps show all of the Tollgates marked including the bar of Tushmore Lane.

So while names are correct in the article, the periods of time particularly with North and South Gates seem confused.

"THE TRUSTEES OF THE BRIGHTON CUCKFIELD AND WEST GRINSTEAD TURNPIKE ROADS TO THE REVD. MATTHEW HUGHES GEORGE BUCKLE.

We George Blaker of Pangdean of the Parish of Pyecombe in the County of Sussex, Gentleman, James Wood of Ockley in the Parish of Keymer in the said County Gentleman and Sir Walter Wyndham Burrell of Cuckfield in the said County Baronet, M.P., three of the Trustees acting in the execution of the Brighton Cuckfield and West Grinstead Turnpike Roads Act 1854 in consideration of the sum of one hundred and fifteen pounds to us paid by The Reverend Matthew Hughes George Buckle of Elsingham Vicarage in the County of Northumberland, Clerk Do hereby grant and release unto the said Matthew Hughes George Buckle his heirs and assigns ALL THAT messuage or dwelling house lately used as a Toll house and known as Crawley North Gate with the outbuildings garden and land thereunto belonging containing in the whole by estimation Thirty seven rods or thereabouts situate in the parish of Ifield in the said County of Sussex with all the rights and members and appurtenances thereunto belonging and all our right title and interest to and in the same and every part thereof TO HOLD the said hereditaments and premises unto the said Matthew Hughes George Buckle his heirs and assigns To the use of the said Matthew Hughes George Buckle his heirs and assigns for ever by virtue and according to the true intent and meaning of an Act passed in the Fourth Year of the Reign of King George the Fourth intituted "An Act to explain and amend an Act passed in the second year of the Reign of His present Majesty to amend the General Laws now in being for regulating Turnpike Roads in that part of Great Britain called England" AND it is hereby declared that if the said Matthew Hughes George Buckle shall leave a Widow she shall not be entitled to dower out of the premises IN WITNESS whereof we have hereunto set our hands and seals this thirtieth day of December One Thousand eight hundred and seventy six.

Signed, sealed and delivered by the) Geo. Blaker   (L.S.))

above named George Blaker, James   ) James Wood   (L.S.)

Wood and Sir Walter Wyndham Burrell) W.W. Burrell   (L.S.)

in the presence of————————————)]

Edward Waugh

Solr. Cuckfield."

THE TRUSTEES OF THE BRIGHTON CUCKFIELD AND WEST GRINSTEAD TURNPIKE ROADS TO MR. JOHN WRIGHT.

Trustees acting in the execution of the Brighton Cuckfield and West Grinstead Turnpike Roads Act 1854 in consideration of the sum of Twenty Pounds to us paid by John Wright of Crawley in the said County Farmer Do hereby grant and release unto the said John Wright his heirs and assigns ALL THAT piece of land lately forming part of the site of a Dwellinghouse used as a Toll House known as Crawley South Toll House with the outbuildings and land thereunto belonging containing by estimation four rods or thereabouts situate in the Parish of Ifield in the County of Sussex.

County Hall, Lewes

8th January, 1877

Intolled in my Office with the Records of the County of Sussex this day, pursuant to 3 Geo. IV Cap.126, sec.86; and 4 Geo. IV Cap. 95.

W. K. S. LANGRIDGE

Clerk of the Peace for the County of Sussex

(by permission West Sussex County Record Office Chichester)

The Ancient Elm

A monarch of the past stands out prominently on the northern village green - The Ancient Elm.

Within living memory great oaks and elms covered the space on which the Railway Station is built, and right down to Three Bridges Road. (A sawmill stood where now is Sadlers Chemist shop, this being used to saw up the trees when building of the railway commenced. The sawmill was afterward situated where Mr. M. Nightingales wharves and yards now reside.) Of all the trees none can compare with the famous Elm.

Title of 'ancient' no one can dispute for it is upwards of 600 years old. The thousands who have examined this great tree have little knowledge of its history. Dr. T.H. Martin J.P. - the 'father' of Crawley we know today - was passionately attached to the Tree, and through his labours and research we have learnt much about the ancient elm's history.

The tree is the common Elm, Ulmus Capmastris. At its full height experts estimated it to be 140 feet, but fierce storms had torn terrible wounds as can be seen from a print by J.G. Strutt in 1824, the whole of its upper limbs and trunk had been torn away. The picture shows the trunk at this time measured about 25 feet high with branches of huge proportions spreading out. The base is huge in size and on the south side is a gothic doorway which gained admittance to the hollow trunk, which at ground level was 35 feet circumference inside. The whole mass of roots and bole outside measured 53 feet at a level of 3 feet from the ground (measured by Dr. Martin and Mr. Marcus Woodward.)

In 1883 this ancient monarch received another terrible wound when in the September of that year a terrific storm swept the South of England. Our friend not only lost many of its branches but also had a large proportion of its side torn away. It was feared that this would be its death blow, but in its fight for existence the old tree threw out fresh limbs which are now quite 50 feet high and of good substance.

The tree figures in that famous Sussex novel *Rodney Stone*, Sir Arthur Conan Doyle having a most interesting cameo of the tree as seen on the night "Young Jim" was abducted.

The history of the village is bound up with the tree, for it was around its great trunk that villagers used to assemble for their local Parliament and to discuss public affairs.

Inside the trunk was quite a large chamber, and many strange things took place within those living walls. A young woman used this ancient chamber for the accouchement chamber. This gave Crawley mothers another version of the "Gooseberry Tree" as the provider of new babies. For some generations the Doctors Smith had lived

By J.G. Strutt 1824 —
Copied by M.F. Matthews 1926

at "The House", this gave the name of "Doctors Tree" to the elm, and it was from there he filled his black bag when presenting Crawley with a new inhabitant. Naturally such a romantic place proved a most fitting rendezvous for lovers.

Another time many years ago the villagers were scared because ghosts had made a home in the tree. The ghosts proved to be owls whose tenancy was quickly terminated.

On another occasion a family of wayfarers were accommodated in this ancient trunk because no alternative lodgings could be found. It is recorded that they lived there for many weeks.

In the olden days, when "Reviews" were so popular with the old Volunteers, Crawley was one of the garrison towns and soldiers were billeted in the Elm when other accommodation could not be found suitable for soldiers.

To the youngsters of Crawley a tea party inside the old tree was the height of ambition, for it was here that Sunday School prize giving took place, and the writer has on many occasions been one of a dozen to enjoy tea within the precincts of the ancient trunk, the huge boulder like roots being used as seats.

In 1823 a Madame de Genlis who was touring these parts visited this tree and her impressions found place in the *London Literary Gazette* of May 24th. 1823 are recorded as follows.

"Madame de Genlis speaks of the Elm of great size at Crawley in the hollow of which a poor woman gave birth to an infant and where she afterwards resided for a time.

The tree is of great curiosity, it is still standing in the village of Crawley, but as the Parish is not willing to be burdened with all the young elms that might be brought from the trunk of this singular tree, the Lord of the Manor has very wisely put up a door to the entrance of this lying-in hospital which is kept locked up except upon particular occasions when the inhabitants meet to enjoy their pipe and tell old tales in the cavity of this elm that is capable of containing a party of more than one dozen.

The interior of this tree is paved with bricks and in other respects made comfortable for those whom it holds."

This monument of nature has been lovingly tended by the Smith family who live in the house hardby called "The Tree".

The family took up residence there in 1798 when Dr. Robert Smith went there with his bride.

His son succeeded him and both generations have lavished care and loving tenderness on the great tree. The paving stones were put in by Dr. Smith hoping to stop the rot and decay, but without success. He also planted a young elm inside the trunk in the hope that it would grow up a support to the old tree, but this, again, proved unsuccessful.

The family have taken great pride in their old friend and to their care the healthy state of the monarch is due.

Miss Mary Smith has had the rustic fence renewed and also planted ferns, periwinkles and other plants at the base.

A strange incident occurred when Miss Nelly Smith was on a visit to Ireland some years ago.

She had occasion to go into a small stationers and there saw several photographs of Crawley's Ancient Elm. The stationer had no idea how he became possessed of them. Miss Smith brought several home with her.

At the present time the tree is a decaying monarch and its doorway is a thing of the past. The limbs which are growing vigorously favour the northwest portion. Though decaying rapidly, one can easily trace the great size of the tree when in its full strength and beauty.

'The Tree'

One would be quite safe in saying that no house has had more influence on the life of Crawley and district that "The Tree", that spacious rambling residence in the High-street, Crawley, and adjoining the famous elm. The age of the house is quite unknown, but we find that in 1731 it is referred to in a medical book, and it is undoubtedly a very old place, the rooms being very spacious with huge oak beams, large chimney corners and with huge flagstones for the flooring in the kitchen, larder and dairy. The south end is gabled and is by far the widest part of the house. Throughout the whole building the oak beams provide an interesting feature. The roof is of slab, and the whole front of the house is covered with wisteria. The house was, apparently, at one time a farmhouse, as a print shows ricks standing below the house and a farm building with the old "Tollgates" across the roadway. It is interesting to note that there are but stepping stones for a footway, and the only tree near the house is the Crawley elm.

It is from 1778 that the house has been occupied by the "Smith" family, when Robert Smith, who (after serving apprenticeship under John Dungate, one of three brothers and the first to commence practice in Crawley) was married and took his bride to "The Tree". This Robert Smith was a remarkable man, and, of course, much in request socially and professionally throughout a wide area. He was brilliant conversationalist, a hunting and shooting man, and "hail fellow well met" with everybody. All his journeys had to be done on horseback, though it was during his residence at "The Tree" that the coaching era started. He saw the commencement (1802) of the postal system as we know it, as Crawley was made the Head Office for miles around, Cuckfield, Crawley and Croydon being the recognised Head Offices between Brighton and London. He also saw the Prince Regent's ride to Brighton, which commenced the great trek to "Dr. Brighton". Robert Smith was followed by his son Thomas Smith, who succeeded to the practice (and "The Tree") in 1825. His life was indeed a full one, the increasing traffic with consequent casualties making his services and his surgery at "The Tree" of the greatest importance. In 1853 there came to him as a pupil one John Leach, who was destined to reach great heights, though not in the profession intended (a medical one), but as an artist. "His bedroom walls were covered with horses and caricatures of the family and friends, and he was often teased because his horses had bannister brooms for tails." (Dr. Martin's Memoirs). He became John Leach of *Punch*, and unfortunately his bedroom walls were papered over so that his earlier works are hidden. Another who

Dr T. Smith   *H.F.*

was to become the most beloved man of his time in Crawley, the late Dr. T.H. Martin, also came to "The Tree" with Dr. Thomas Smith, and it is interesting to note that, when in later years Dr. Martin married Miss Lemon (daughter of Mark Lemon of *Punch*), John Leach was a witness and signed the register in Crawley Church in 1862.

It was this Thomas Smith who planted the row of lime trees which run right along in front of the house in line with the famous elm. He was married in 1838, and his family has during that long period filled a conspicuous part in the life of Crawley. The family consisted of six girls and one boy, but it was the "Ladies of the Tree" who took such an active part in the everyday life of the town. They had a library for the Sunday School, were teachers there, members of Crawley Church choir and generous supporters of the church. In all charitable works they were to the fore, and many a young Crawleyite was clothed in its first garments from the "Dorcas" box from "The Tree". It was they who tended and protected the ancient elm, and it was to them that the various memorial trees which grace the village greens were planted. One of their last public acts (as Ladies of the Manor) was handing over the control of the village greens to the local councils. The family has now dwindled down, death taking away all but two of them, but their memories will not be erased from Crawley whilst their living memorials - the trees - are in being. This old house is hallowed with happy memories of gatherings in their young days by older Crawley residents.

It would not do to fail to mention that the one time surgery has served as a school room, a Bible classroom and a relief room. With the late Dr. Martin one would like to see the old walls stripped of their paper to see what is hidden beneath.

From out leaded panel windows bright eyes have seen Crawley spring from a straggling place and a handful of houses to a real live place with its thousands passing up and down the Brighton to London road. Happy indeed are the memories that cling around "The Tree".

The Tree
Crawley

Sir,
    We the Misses Smith as Ladies of the Manor having seen the motions to be brought before Crawley & Ifield Parochial Committee on Tuesday 26th. day of August 1924 we raise no objection to the schemes contained in the Resolution.

Faithfully yours

Isabella Smith
Eleanor Smith
Catherine A. Smith

To
    Mr. W. Denman

The Tree
Crawley
Jan 21st 1925

Dear Sir,
    We regret that we did not give an answer to your former letter. Will you please tell the Crawley Parish Council that my sisters and I are willing to give them power over the Crawley Greens that they may be kept clean and tidy, as we think it will be a great improvement to the Village.

Yours faithfully

Eleanor S Smith

The Tree
Crawley
Jan 29th 1934

Dear Sir,
    In reply to your letter, my aunt wishes me to say that, provided it does not necessitate cutting down The Tree she will agree to the proposal to ease the South Green by 3 feet for a length of 5 or six yards.

Yours truly

Ina Easby

Letters from the Misses Smith giving responsibility to Crawley Parish Council for future management of the Greens, which they did not own as it was 'Common' land.

A Bit of Old Crawley.

The Old Tudor Cottage

Standing on the east side of Crawley High Street is a beautiful specimen of the "timber and plaster" house known as the Old Tudor Cottage. This is however incorrect as the "Old Tudor Cottage" was a lovely old cottage which stood on the site of the now Rectory Lodge, but was pulled down in the early 1880s to make way for the Lodge. The old cottage was much like the one under notice, though smaller, and was undoubtedly the cottage of one who worked at "The Tree" when that was a farmhouse. An examination of the ground shows that there was a pathway at the end of the garden. As however the present building has been known for years and appears in various guide books as "The Old Tudor Cottage," it is not now worthwhile calling it anything else.

The proper name is "The Mychells" and it was the farmhouse of Mychells Farm. The house is quite a large one with dairy, large kitchen etc. and throughout has beautiful timbers. The floors of the bedrooms are composed of wide oak and mellowed with age. It is a treat for the lovers of the antique. The external appearance is most pleasing, the great beams running across the front of the house and others outside from side to side to support the overhanging room, which is quaint and serves the purpose of shelter in stormy weather. All the windows are small and, of course, of lead mouldings. High up under the eaves of the "great" bedroom is a small window set in large beams and surmounted by a small plate depicting a very warlike figure with lance or pike in hand attacking or keeping at bay some object in the background. The one word "Protector" appears on this and its origin is unknown, though it lends colour to the legend that Oliver Cromwell stayed for quite a considerable period at this house. There is no documentary

P.A.   P.A.

proof of this, but there again is no reason why it should not be true, and as the "Protector" is over the "great" (or Nest) bedroom window one has all the necessary proof. This is a joke as "Protector" was really a Fire Insurance. This room, too, was another in which Queen Anne slept! The extreme ends of the house are of boards, and the foundations are of stone laid in small slabs and the whole of the wood is wooden penned at the joints. The beautiful old Horsham Stone roofing was sold many years ago, and the tiled roof certainly looks out of place on such a lovely old foundation.

Standing as it does within view of the London to Brighton road, it forms an object of interest to hundreds of people who stop and examine the ancient building. For up to thirty years ago, the building had farm buildings alongside and behind it, stables, granaries, barns etc., it being the largest dairy retail farm in the district. At this time the occupants were Mr. Ephraim Knight and Mr. Stephen Tyler, both haulage contractors and dairymen, Tyler living in the farmhouse. The old thatched buildings proved a worthy and appropriate setting for the delightful old house. It was a sight to see the herd of cows come out the yard right across the High Street and away to pastures, though in these days of motor traffic one hardly knows what would happen, though one suspects "it would be bad for the coo."

In the aftermath of the Great War, the house had got into a somewhat dilapidated state, till purchased by Mr. and Mrs. Charles Messer, who restored it and brought out much of its hidden beauties.

The house was sold to a gentleman in the catering trade who re-named it "Ye Olde Punch Bowle." He had the whole of the old plaster taken out to show up the wonderful timbering and built a "Tudor" kitchen at the north end. He had the old minstrels gallery freed and made as great a change inside as out. Thus it became a restaurant, and was not licensed to serve liquor except as a private club in the late 1930's.

In the 1940s the lovely old place opened as a Y.M.C.A. since when it has been the centre of great activities. The opening of such a place has proved how great was the need for such a hostel. Large numbers of Forces make use of the facilities offered and on certain nights, when dances, concerts or debates take place, friends are admitted by invitation.

It is interesting to recall that the Mychells Farm and Crosskeys Farm occupied all the land which lies between Priors Farm and Black Dog Farm, the former being halfway to Three Bridges and the latter on Woolborough Road. A lane ran right through the farmyard and around through Crawley Recreation Ground and up "Mill Lane" (Malthouse) which led to Brook Log where the iron mill used to be. Those wishing to get into the Brighton Road took a right hand turn and came out at Hogs Hill Farm. But if one wanted to go northward when leaving Crawley High Street one went up the lane

P.A.

A SIDE VIEW, YE OLDE PUNCH BOWLE.

and turned across "Railway Field", now Rectory Meadows, and out by Tushmore Lane. All these devious ways were caused by a desire to avoid the "tolls", for Tollgates stood at both entrances to Crawley.

It should be added that these outhouses and surroundings attract artists every summer. A delightful residence as well as a beautiful building of Tudor Days.

In an effort to find out why this house was known as "The Mychells" originally, and if there is in fact a valid answer, records show the following:

A first mention is made of a Thomas Mychell in 1532, in a will mentioned in the section connected with the Ancient Priors. But I cannot establish any link between Mychell and ownership of that particular building known as the Chantry House in those days. Unless, the land had been given many years before to Rusper Priory, because in the Valor Ecclesiasticus A.D. 1535 a mention is made of some possessions belonging to Rusper Priory were leased by indenture to a Thomas Mychell.

Thomas appears to have been a wealthy man for the Chantry records 30 January 1526 accord him, two closes called Moresland containing 10 acres, rent 12s. A 15 acre farm in Waneham called Warrensham 28s 8d. From the "Victorian Sussex History" we learn that Worth Forests and estates were in 1546 bestowed upon Thomas Seymour, Lord High Admiral. In less than eighteen months his property was seized by the Crown. Consequent upon this an inventory was made which shows Thomas Mitchell (gent) ranger, who had the herbage and pannage of the said forest and parks by patent throughout his life. In 1545, Thomas had actually bought the Manor of Worth.

> "Thomas Mychell of the Parish of Worthe, gentilman, died 6 June 1551, will proven 5 November 1551." *Perogative Court of Canterbury. Bucke F.O. 31.* He was buried in the chancel of Worth Church by his wife. "I give and bequeathe to the high aulter of Worthe ten shillinges."
>
> "I give and bequeathe to the churche wardens of the Parishe of Worthe to the use and profit of the said church xx's (20s) yf in chaunie there to be buried."

As well as lands already mentioned Thomas also owned Childingly Manor in West Hoathly, and tenements in Hodelygh.

All his property was inherited by a nephew, Edward Mitchell, as Thomas was childless.

Claims were made by various people against sections of his property, and in the Feet of Fines of 1570 Easter Term - George Blundell was the Plaintiff, petitioning for the Manors of Childingly and Woolborough, and tenements in

Coockfeld, Westhothy, Worth and Crawley - but they were settled upon Thomas Mychell and his heirs.

However, Edward Mitchell had in 1553 sold to John More:

> "Where myne uncle Thomas Michell by his last will willed unto me the manor of Worthe wt all other his landes and tenements called Crabbe haselwicke Mylle and Mylle landes" paying to his executors yearly £10 "and where also I had of the graunte of John Apeslye Esquyer the survivor of the executours" "one lease" of a parcell of ground called Allen of Warwicks all of which I sold unto John More Esquyer my executor John Apeslye shall take yearly £9 out of my lands at East Grinstead & 33s/4d rent for Allen of Warwicks and £6 3 4 for the manor of Redstone towards the performance of my uncles will until it be performed -"

John More also held fealty and rent of 6/11 Tynsley, and lands in Ifield, Rusper and Worth.

In 1589 these lands were owned by Edward More, whom had inherited from his father.

After a space of 200 years the house is once again traceable. The following information is by courtesy of the Messer family.

<u>23 Feb 1789</u> Robert Hall of Ifield Sussex made his will. He owned land in the Parishes of Ifield (Sussex) Oxted (Surrey) Crawley (Sussex) and Worth (Sussex).

<u>1792</u> Robert Hall died - leaving his son Richard as heir.

By the terms of the will Richard became tenant for life of the Crawley and Worth properties - the rest of the property was for Richard's children, no provision was made for the property if Richard did not have any children.

<u>6 Feb 1822</u> Richard Hall made his will.

<u>8 April 1824</u> He made a codicil to his will.

<u>12 Nov 1825</u> Richard Hall died without issue: his wife Sarah having predeceased him.

This means that the property should have returned to his Father's estate, but as his father was already dead, it was Richard's to do as he liked with. In his will he did not dispose of the said property but left a life interest only to Sarah Medgley with the remainder in fee to his kinsman Michael Harmes of Cuckfield Sussex (son of Michael Harmes of Bolney Sussex, yeoman.)

Michael Harmes died just before Richard Hall; consequently, there was an intestacy after the determination of Sarah Medgley's life interest.

Sarah Medgley became the wife of William Blaker Caffin in 1835 and she lived until 1 April, 1900.

The position being that Sarah Caffin was entitled to life to the Crawley and Worth estates.

1848

24 Jan 1848. John Daycock filed a bill in the Chancery for an enquiry to ascertain the heirs or co-heirs of Richard Hall. He also asked that considerable quantities of oak and other timber trees should be felled and sold.

2 Nov. Vice-Chancellor Wigram ordered a Master of the Court to answer the enquiries.

June 1850. The Master of the Court (Doweswell) reported that John Daycock and George Donaldson were the co-heirs of Richard Hall.

July 1850. The Vice-Chancellor Knight Bruce ordered that the Master's report be confirmed.

Feb 1851. The Master of the Court (Humphrey) reported in favour of a sale of the timber and appointed an auctioneer to sell it.

Nov 1851. The same Master reported who were the purchasers of the timber.

19 April 1852. The proceeds of the sale of timber (£808) were paid into the Court.

29 April 1852. After paying the cost of the Chancery proceedings only £240.14.0 was left of the proceeds of the sale of the timber and this was invested in 3% annuities.

4 Aug 1852. George Donaldson offered for sale by auction his half share of the Crawley and Worth properties expectant upon the death of Sarah Caffin. John Daycock bid for it and was declared the purchaser at £590.

By this transaction John Daycock became the owner of the entirety of the Crawley and Worth properties subject to the expectation of the death of Sarah Caffin.

Oct 1892. John Daycock died before the conveyance to him of George Donaldson's share was complete.

Jan 1853. John Daycock's will proved.

By his will he gave his interests in his Crawley and Worth properties for life to his sister Mary Ann Daycock, then to Charlotte Nichols for her life.

From later documents it is shown that the Crawley and Worth (freehold) properties were described in 1901 as:

1) *Mitchells Farm containing 70 acres in the parishes of Crawley and Worth let to John Wright on lease expiring Michaelmas 1901 at a rent of £100.*

2) *Part of Black Dog Farm containing about 43 acres in the Parish of Worth let to the same tenant on lease expiring Michaelmas 1901 at a rent of £44.*

3) *Part of Black Dog Farm containing about 8 acres 2 rods 7 perches in the Parish of Crawley let to Horsham Rural District Council for sewage purposes on 21 years lease expiring Michaelmas 1908 at a rent of £25.*

An auction sale of 1919 shows lot 4 the property upon the plan attached to these notes and colour blue and pink.

The property remained in the possession of the Nichols family until 1919 at which period Mr. Alan Dobie became the owner.

In the same year he sold the part marked blue (Rectory Field) on the plan to Mr. Barrett-Lennard and in 1928 the part coloured pink, with the cottages, to Mrs. E.C. Messer.

At the beginning of the century the Old White Harte was apartments. Elsie Mitchell (Denman) and her husband with their children occupied the first floor, between 1904-12.
The young lady looking from the upstairs window is Ellie, their second daughter. While below, with their mother, are the two Misses Chantler, Ethel and Alice. Their father owned the Brewery Shades, and adjoining shop.

The Ancient Priests House

It will be seen that the house now called "The Ancient Priors' House" has been given its original name and I do this to avoid any controversy. There is no evidence that a priory or friary ever existed in Crawley. All writers on church matters rather ridicule the idea, and Mr. Salymann, a great authority on priory matters and who wrote the *Victorian County History of Sussex* does not mention a priory or friary and without one or the other there could be no prior. We know beyond doubt that the house is of great antiquity, a rich casket of beauty and interest, and with a wonderful history.

What is the age of the house? Its age is unknown, but it was the Priests' House.

The house is first mentioned about 1250 when all the churches in this district were under the authority of the Benedictine Nuns of Rusper, and the Priests occupied the House. Later it became the Chantry House. In his little booklet "Old Catholic Churches of Crawley and Neighbourhood" Father Aselm O.S.F.C. gives a copy of the following will, which readers will find remarkably interesting. (The spelling is modernised.)

> "In the name of God, Amen. The last day of September, in the year of our Lord, 1532, I, Nicholas Wordsworth, Chantry Priest of Crawley, being whole of mind and perfect remembrance, make my will and testament in manner and form following:- First I bequeath my soul to Almighty God, our Lady, St Mary and to all the Company of Heaven, and my body to be buried on the south side of the steeple in Crawley Churchyard. Also, I give and bequeath to Sir William Knotton, Curate of Worth, my large gown, my best doublet, and all the hangings in the great chamber, all my books, a chest, a table, a chair, and my quilts, and a pair of andirons for a chimney.
>
> Item:- To Mr. Vicar of Ifield, my second gown; to Sir Richard, of Cappele (Capel) my third gown; and to Sir Henry Trowbeke my old gown.
>
> Item:- I give to Oliver's children (*brother's son*) all my brass and pewter, a little cupboard, a cup, a pair of sheets, two shirts and a vest.
>
> Item:- To Richard Cop a pair of sheets.
>
> Item:- To Thomas Juster a coverlet.
>
> Item:- I give to William, Mr. F. Ffenner's son a feather bed and a bolster.
>
> Item:- To Edward Ffenner a long settle and to Mrs. Ffenner a cupboard.
>
> Item:- I give to my brother-in-law, that did marry my sister, a little chalice, a vestment and a superalter.
>
> Item:- I will my house shall be sold, which I did buy of Mr. Thomas Mychele, and four marks of the same money to go to Mr. Ffenner, which I owe him for my board, and the rest thereof to be divided between my brothers.

Item:- To Hethe's wife a pair of sheets.

The rest of goods I give to Thomas Dawes, whom I make my executor of this my last will and testament.

I will Sir William Knotton, aforesaid and Thomas Dawes, to receive and gather up all my debts and to see them disposed of for my soul's health and all Christian Souls according to their discretion, these being witness Sir William Knotton, Priest, Thomas Dawes, Harman widow, good wife, Hethe and others"

There is no mention made when the Chantry House was abolished as a Chantry but probably Henry VIII did away with this as in other cases.

In his interesting address in Crawley Church in January 1896, the late Rev. J. Barrett Lennard said:

"The old house near here, "The Old White Hart", one hundred years ago (1796), the resort and refuge of smugglers and all sorts of ruffians, was once a church house. The roof of it, inside is almost identical with the roof of this church, and I believe about the time when our tower was built (1480) the Old White Hart formed part of a monastic or church house.

Tradition has it that there is a subterranean passage between the house and the Church, but none has been found."

No one knows when this fine building became the "Ye Whyte Harte". In February 1882 Mr. F. Russell communicates the following information in response to an article in the previous month's local paper.

He states that his mother was born in that house, and that he himself first saw daylight in it. His grandfather and grandmother lived there a great number of years. At that time the house was the farmhouse of the old White Hart Farm. At the time the Rev. Fowler held the Crawley living, he (Mr. Russell) recollects Mr. Fowler showing the old house, the old staircase, the Smugglers' room, the carving over the fireplaces, and the large oak entrance door, to the late Mark Anthony Lower, President of Sussex archaeological Society, who had much to say on its antiquity. That the house was an hotel is beyond question, and its large spacious rooms, beautiful oak staircases and oak panelling would make it a real old time Hostelry, quite on a level with the famous 'George Hotel' on the other side of the road.

A few years ago a coin was dug up in the garden which proved to be a half farthing "token" date about 1662, bearing on one side an Irish Harp with "Ralph Patrick, Crawley, Sussex" running around the edge (even as we see on our currency today). On the reverse side was just R.P. engraved. According to the church register in 1659 a daughter Judith, of a Ralph Patrick was christened, followed by Patrick in 1666 and Henry in 1667. In 1692 Ralph Patrick was churchwarden and he was buried on 18th September 1693.

Ralph Patricke, Senior, followed by his son, Patricke owned a livery stables almost opposite to The Rising Sun Inn. It was here he had his cottage, barns and stables while his horses were in meadows to the west, a little along Small's Lane.

> "John Guillam of Slaugham to Ralph Patrick 1667, a house and 2 acres, and close and barn, adjoining the King's Highway from Slaugham to Reigate, bounded on east side to a lane leading from the West green, and on the west by a parcel of land called Kites, to the north by lands of Walter Burstow, land of James Willow south." (G.L.R.O. Acc. 2017)

So Ralph Patricke had no connection with the Old White Hart.

This house has also been " a Farm House", and a more delightful one it would be hard to imagine. Fifty years ago there were farm buildings, horse pond etc. in the grounds. The cart horses and granary stood where now is St John's Lodge.

It was a favourite haunt of the Copthorne gang of smugglers, and had its secret chamber in which many of my readers have had the pleasure of standing. This was situated over the dairy of the house. The entrance to this secret chamber was the long passage leading from the kitchen to the dairy. As is usual in such old buildings, long hooks hung down, and those who knew the secret would push one of these toward the right and then upward, which released a spring and a trap door swung back. The room was cunningly placed between two bedrooms and from these it was impossible to tell there was a secret chamber adjoining. The huge kitchen fireplace, too, had a hiding place behind it, which easily concealed a couple of men. It seems a most ridiculous thing that a house which is really a "show" house should have had these places destroyed, for surely in these days the rooms would have been of the greatest interest. After its decline as a hostelry it was divided into tenements let out to families. In 1881 after renovations it opened as a temperance hotel - at this time owned by Hon: Mrs. Lytton, managed by Mrs Gates. Crawley folks remember it as a general store. Old Mrs Russell, mother of a famous Crawley historian (who kept a barbers shop within this building) also had a shop there. At this time a large half circle window with leaden mouldings faced the north room, and was the shop window.

IFIELD PARISH CHURCH RESTORATION. — The building of the tower of Ifield Parish Church is rapidly progressing. The large west arch is completed, and promises to present a noble feature. The three light window at the west end is finished, and the amount of light which will be admitted will be a great improvement upon the somewhat dull appearance the church has of late presented. The re-roofing of the nave and also of the chancel has been completed, the nave and chancel still retain the old Horsham stone, the two aisles are roofed with red tile, which will soon tone down to a good brown colour. The casing over the porch has been removed, so that the old porch is again brought to light, and the builder awaits the architect's instructions as to what is best to be done with it. The two bells will soon be raised to their proper place in the tower. We shall hope soon to be able to chronicle that the whole work of restoration is completed. The subscriptions received now amount to £968 7s 6d, which includes the following items :—Mr H. O. Blaker, £2 2s ; General Hayland, £1 ; General Alexander, £1 ; Misses Clarke's card, £10 12s ; Miss J. King's card, £1 10s.

YE OLD WHYTE HART HOTEL, CRAWLEY.—Mr Head (East Grinstead), on behalf of Mrs Gates, the landlady of Ye Old Whyte Hart Hotel, Crawley, applied for a full license for that house, and after sustaining his argument was opposed by Mr J. K. Nye, on behalf of the owner of the White Hart Inn (Mr Nightingale), and by Mr Evett, on behalf of the landlord of the George Hotel (Mr J. Mitchell). — It was stated by the opposing solicitors that there were already four licensed houses in the immediate vicinity—ample for a town stated to be of only 420 inhabitants, and 89 inhabited houses. — Application eventually granted.

P.A.

1930

THE ANCIENT PRIORS HOUSE, CRAWLEY.

The Old Kitchen-Ancient Prior's House-Crawley Sussex

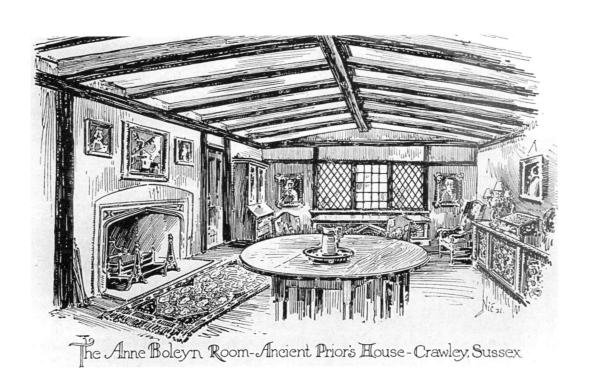

The Anne Boleyn Room-Ancient Prior's House-Crawley, Sussex

P.A.

Entrance Hall

South staircase

The Queen Elizabeth Bedchamber - Ancient Prior's House - Crawley, Sussex.

Recently Mr. Parkhurst (who now owns this lovely building) has had the place renovated and has restored as nearly as possible, the front to its original design. In doing so he has earned the thanks of all lovers of old buildings, and particularly for sweeping away the ugly square bow windows which someone had built into the overhanging upper rooms. The interior has been carefully treated so that the full beauty of the glorious oak can be seen. The owner has gone to considerable expense in preserving the fabric of the old building and has revealed delightful inglenooks, chimney corners and many oak beams which for years had been hidden by brickwork and plaster. One could write pages of the contents of these lovely rooms, but one must refrain. Needless to say such a wonderful old house has had thousands of visitors. The late Lord Kitchener was not an infrequent visitor.

Whether the house was erected "in the time of Stephen" or not is a matter of controversy, but I trust those who read these notes will agree that the "Ancient Priests House" is one worthy of the name of "historical" and from present appearances the building will be here another 500 years hence.

We are now in the heart of the Manor of Crawley, that narrow strip of land which extends from Three Bridges Road, down the centre of the High street to the Sun Hotel and lies east of this line for a depth of approximately 500 feet.

To try to establish the age of the few remaining buildings is difficult, due to lack of information as to the exact buildings referred to in the reference books.

The Penguin Guide to Sussex 1939 gives: "The Ancient Priors has as its kernel a 12th century house restored and enlarged in 1440 of which date are two fireplaces." Work was also done on this building in 1881.

However, if we assume that this house and the church are linked, and are therefore of similar age, ownership of the Manor of Crawley gives some indication of age.

The first recorded owner individually named was Thomas de Poynees, a Knight, who was awarded for service to Earl de Warrene, 10 Knights' fees, at Poynings in 1180. By 1202 the family also held the Manor of Crawley. It remained in the family until the late 1400's when it was in the possession of Alianore who married Sir Henry Percy.

That a chapel was well established by the middle of 13th century is shown in the Chichester Chartulary of 1267.

"I, Luke, son of Thomas de Poyninges, for the salvation of my father and mother, grant in almoin to the Chapel of St John Baptist of Crawle for the keep of Thomas de la Brewere, Chaplain, and his successors a house in Crawle and 71s. 5d. rent, as follows: from Warin Canterell 9d, Osbert the Clerk 9d, G. de Wolberong 18d, R. beg (sic) 3s.6d, W. Austery 2s 6d, W Terishe 10d, R. Smale 12d, W ? AdSy (sic) 12d, Nicholas White 18d, half at Candlemas and half at Michaelmas, from lands they hold of me in Crawle, together with their homage, reliefs and escheats. Also from William David 20s, Richard Hoges 5s, W Noybur 2s. 6d, John Noyke 2s 6d, W. Brogsmeglle 7s, W Newsmith (Novofabro) 6s 8d, J. Feld 6s saving to me their homages, reliefs, escheats and suits of Court. Also pannage for 6 swine in my wood of Crawle and three four-ox cartloads of wood."

In 1545 the Manor of Crawley was granted to Edward Shirley, who sold the Manor to Walter Covert in 1632. His son Thomas settled the Manor and Patronage of Crawley in jointure on his wife Diana, daughter of Lord George Goring and Thomas's brother John Covert of Slaugham, by indenture agreed to levy a fine and suffer recovery (inter alia) of all that Manor of Crawley and the advowson of the church, and the Inn in Crawley called The George. Recovery was executed in Easter Term 1649.

In 1671 this advowson was settled on Anne daughter of Sir Walter Covert upon her marriage to Sir James Morton. Dame Anne Morton sold the Manor of Crawley to Leonard Gale. Leonard Gale was survived by three daughters:

Sarah married Samuel Blunt of Horsham.

Elizabeth married Henry Humphrey of Lewes.

Phillipa married James Clitherow of Brentford.

Upon the division of Mr. Gale's estate, the Crawley Manor share fell to Mrs. Clitherow (1750), whose son James Clitherow succeeded to the Lordship, thence to Colonel Clitherow in 1834.

From 1750 we are able to trace easily the ownership of the main buildings as the Manor began to dissolve.

The Manor House and The George Inn, and probably also the Manor rights were acquired by Mrs. H.F. Montefiore. She died in 1915 and the Manor House was then bought by Monsier Jacques Mend de Costa, but no manor rights could be shown to have been conveyed to him. After his death in 1934, Sir Francis Montefiore repurchased the estate. After his death, all the manor which he possessed was bought by Mrs. Brown, all manor rights having lapsed.

The Ancient Priors House was mortgaged to John Davy Brett for £3,500 in 1832; he later sold the property to Francis Croftswell of Kings Lynn.

> "All that messuage or tenement with yard and garden, and land thereto belonging situate in the parishes of Worth, Ifield and Crawley - known by the name of the Old White Hart Farm, 66 acres, 3 rods and 13 perches now in the tenure or occupation of Richard Easton. 11th May 1837."

In 1881 this was refurbished and opened as a Temperance Hotel, the mortgage later being redeemed. It remained in the Blunt family until 1916 when it was sold by auction, and bought by Mr. Parkhurst.

The church patronage remained with the Clitherow family.

I can find no evidence which substantiates Mr. Fred Russell's claims as to any connections between the families occupying the Rising Sun Inn with The Whyte Harte. Smuggling undoubtedly existed, but the part his mother played is open to question. Louisa Russell was living in this building prior to 1840. She was christened Louisa Chart Boswell and illegitimate, her mother being Ann Boswell, who married William Chart when Louisa was three years old, so he appears to be Louisa's father. Mr. Chart ran livery stables in the Crosskeys area. Louisa herself was married at fourteen years of age and a widow at the age of thirty-four. Her husband ran a hairdressing business in one section of the old Whyte Harte, carried on by her sons. When the children no longer lived with her, Mrs. Russell changed the business into a Toy Shop. When at the age of 80 years Mrs. Russell "retired", the Toy Shop was taken over by Mrs. Ruth Coates and it was still in business in 1891.

This means that the renovations mentioned in 1881 changing this back into a Hotel, can only relate to part of the whole building as we know it today. Between 1840 and 1900 it is always recorded as housing two families.

From other evidence regarding secret rooms, and "escape routes" and their positions, which overlap with what became Burgess Shop, coupled with the fact this shop has deep cellars which have (had) passages under the square, I conclude that at one time, the shop which was built in the late 1600's was part of the same structure, and operated as two separate entities, the section on the south side being associated with smuggling.

1886. A water colour by Albert Bowers who was born at Twineham in 1839,
and came to Crawley as a small child. A shoemaker by trade, and a fireman.
The Bowers family have a long association with the Fire Brigade.

Crawley Church

"St John the Baptist Church is one of periods and therefore very difficult to determine even approximately its age", so said a writer some years ago. Just now this can be easily proved as the creepers on the wall of the Church have been thinned out and a most astonishing variety of materials in the wall is revealed. Stone that has been shaped up, rough stones, slabs of iron, stone and flint and pieces of various kinds of stone can be seen pieced together with very rough lumps of daub and plaster. Much of the stone is extremely weather beaten and looks to be crumbling. The wall of the old vestry (now alas turned into a stoke hole) looks centuries older than any other portion. Midway between this vestry and the tower, has been filled up either a very low window or door, as there are pieces of timber built round it. Parts of this wall have been plastered over. This part of the church has not been touched in centuries.

The earliest records mention 1257, but relate to an already existing chapel, so that the age of the building cannot be traced, nor the builders, and one can only surmise its original shape. The late Rev. Barrett Lennard made exhaustive researches and once said that he was satisfied that the original church or chapel was quite small probably built of wood and with a shingled spire standing in a clearing in the forest. When we read that in 1731 Crawley consisted of but twenty houses one wonders how many inhabitants there were 800 years ago.

To fix the approximate date of Crawley Church perhaps the most reliable guide is Sir W. Burrell's MSS in the British Museum which state that the first Vicar of Crawley was Walter de Marmetop, Chaplin to Richard de Colwick, Bishop of Chichester. The bishop is called Richard de la Wick by Dugdale in his Monasticon. A marginal note on the MSS states "this Bishop of St Richard." He was consecrated to the See of

Chichester in 1245 and died in 1253. This must mean that there was already a church in 1253. In the taxation roll of Pope Nicholas in 1291, Crawley is mentioned as a Chapel of Slaugham.

The history of our Church is linked up with that of the De Warrenes, the Poynings and the families that find their head in the great house of Norfolk. The first de Warrene and then the Poynings, passed from the former to the latter. It is recorded in 1202 Michael gave to King John a good Norway Goshawk for license to hold a market on their Manor of Crawley. We next find mention of our Church in connection with the Poynings in 1370 when the proof of age of Thomas de Ponynges, chivaler, son and heir of Michael de Ponynges, chivaler deceased, taken at Crawley on Monday after the feast of St Mark the Evangelist 1370, when deponents say he was born at Slaugham 19th April 1323 and was baptised into the church of St Mary's there. This Thomas was in the expedition to Flanders 1373 and he died there some years later. He died without issue, and by his will the manors of Slaugham, Crawley and Poynings passed to his wife and thence to Richard Poynings. This Richard Poynings became Patron of Crawley, but he died with the ill-fated expedition to Castile under John of Gaunt. He was followed by his son Robert and it is recorded that this Robert became in 1415, Patron of St John the Baptist Church at Crawley.

It will be noted that though we have Patrons of Crawley, this is the first time that we have directly had it recorded "St John the Baptist Church."

This Robert Poynings was killed in battle at Orleans, and was succeeded by his grand daughter and it was through this Lady that the connection with the house of Norfolk was made, and also the Percies and the Coverts.

It has been necessary to give these details because with the next 50 years one reads of the "fine freestone tower of the fifteenth century date." Though there is a lengthy break in the history of the Church, we find that William Blast was buried in the nave in 1438 as the inscription on his tomb shows: "Here lies William Blast, who died 27th February in the year of our Lord 1438, on whose soul may God have mercy. Amen."

Bishop Bedes Register 1398 - 1415 says the Parish Church of Crawley was old, a free chapel or Perpetual Chantry of St John Baptist in the Parish of Slaugham.

We find in the Valor Ecclesiasticus of 1525 an entry under the deanery of Lewes "Slaugham cum capella Crawley" a benefice of which Thomas Catesby was then the Rector and which was the annual value of £10.19s.2d.

So far it is fairly proved that the Church of Crawley was originally only a Chapel of the mother Church of Slaugham and even when the commissioners at the close of Henry VIII's reign reported that "the ould chappell of Crawley with above one hundred houselyng people" might now be reckoned a Parish Church, the old custom of appointing a priest to the Rectory of Crawley and Slaugham continued for another 200 years. A will of 1532 of Chantry Priest of Crawley Nicholas Wordsworth (see Ancient Priors) gives further evidence. The chief duties of the Chantry Priest being apparently the celebration of "Obits" or Obituary Masses for souls of the departed.

An unknown writer in a paper written many years ago says: "If part of the rude imagery, long ago built up into the west front of the tower, came from the first fabric, it was probably standing even in pre-Norman times. The figures are said to represent the Holy Trinity."

Another of the great mysteries attached to our Church. The Dean and Chapter Muniments at Chichester Cathedral of 1536 give Slaugham St Mary cum Capella de Crawley and also Capella de Shelley cum Crawley. In what way did Shelley become attached to Crawley and why? Is it too far fetched to suggest that the great iron works which took Slaugham, Shelley and Crawley within its folds also had much to do with these churches or chapels? The population must have consisted of a majority of iron workers, and it should be remembered that this Rape had long been looked after from a religious point of view since 1066. Where did the church on Shelley plain stand? We know that a portion of that estate is still in Crawley Parish miles away from our little town. It is known that the "Chappell of Shelley near Crawley with David Kirk

*1884 The gateway on the right and footpath lead past the monastery wall
to the crossing over the railway line at East Park.*

incumbent" stood near where is now Shelley Plain Farm. But there is nothing to prove or disprove whether Shelley Church or Shelley Chappel were one and the same building. It has also been stated that certain fields on the Buchan Hill Estate carried a charge for the upkeep of the Broadwood tomb in the chancel, the Broadwood family being formerly of Holmbush Faygate.

To deal with the actual building, Mr. Andre F.S.A. made an official visit in 1878 on behalf of the Sussex A.S. and he writes "The tower is of the 15th century. *(In 1460 money was given by Richard Jay of Crawley for the church steeple; if not completed in his lifetime his executors were directed to complete the work.)* It has a west doorway, with traceried heads to the panels. North of the doorway is a recess for the holy water stoup now mutilated. Over the doorway are some flat panels and on the inside of the side windows of the tower are placed some canopies. The tower arch is a good bold segmented one, continuously moulded and of perpendicular date. The tower so far as can be discovered was rebuilt in 1500, when the Church was remodelled, but after many years this had to be redone again and in 1804 the tower was completely restored. The Church suffered restoration in 1845 when the chancel was shortened (It has since been lengthened again). There are two light windows, one on each side of the chancel which may be Decorated (14th century) date. The chancel has two pews for stalls of which the fronts seem to be made of old Rood Screen and consist of linen fold pattern

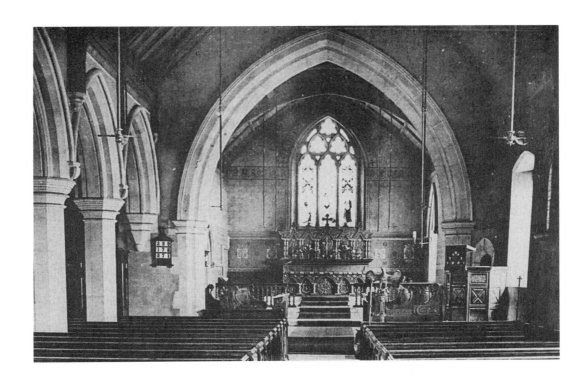

in panels. These stalls have elbowed seats and a high flat backing which is I presume Jacobean. The pulpit retains one or two small but good panels of 17th century date. The roof beams are in a wonderful state of preservation." The huge roughly-hewn tie beams (3 in number) which span the nave are a great feature of the roof. The centre beam has a quaint inscription in old English the lettering being gilded: "Man ye wele bewar, for worldly good maketh man blynde. Bewar befor whate comyth behinde."

The Church has many beautiful memorial windows, the majority in memory of the ancestors of present day Crawley families; and others are to the patron of the Living (Mr. Stracey Clitherow), Rev. J. Barrett-Lennard, Bishop Durnford, Mark Lemon, John Penfold (of "Forge"), the Leach family and the Blake family. The beautiful east window is a memorial to the Redford family, and another magnificent window was placed a few years ago to the memory of the late Mr. John Goddard. Perhaps the most beautiful of all is not seen by the majority of visitors to the Church, as it is in the Vestry. It shows the Ascension, the Sermon on the Mount, and the Anointing with Oil.

The coming to Crawley in 1876 of Rev. John Barrett-Lennard opened a new era in the life of the Church, which grew under his guidance and energy from a most disreputable condition into the fine building we have now. Prior to his arrival the Church was in a disgraceful state, neglect and ruin marked it for their own. The stone windows were so rotten and worn that they were nearly falling out. The woodwork in the pews was so affected by dry rot that one could put one's foot through the seat. The walls were damp and the church had a most unpleasant and unwholesome smell. The bells were cracked and broken, and the belfrey unsafe. The clerk used to stand under the archway when he tolled the bell for a funeral, for fear the bell would fall on him. Everywhere there was neglect and squalor, only the noble tower remained. Even a hundred years of neglect could not spoil that.

During the time the Rev. J. Barrett-Lennard was Rector all this was altered. The Chancel was rebuilt and restored to its original length. The north Aisle was added. The old choir gallery at the west end was demolished. The belfrey was put into a safe condition, and a peal of eight bells installed. Incidentally, it is worthy of note that within the ringing chambers are a number of certificates which testify that the Crawley Band of change-ringers established many world records and the whole of that band were in the employ of Mr. James Longley, who took a keen interest in the Church. The old harmonium was replaced by a beautiful organ, and the mixed choir by a male choir, with cassocks and surplices. The old gallery was utilised by this indefatigable worker who carved and turned out the beautiful chancel now. His final achievement was the throwing open to the high road of the approach to the Church by the purchase and demolition of cottages which hid the fine old building. The pulpit contains a carved text, the work of his hands "Be Brief."

To commemorate the Diamond Jubilee of Queen Victoria, a clock was erected in the tower. Paid for by public subscription, it did not in fact reach its destination until 1901, so marked the occasion of the Queen's death as well.

The Church just now is in splendid condition. One cannot but wonder how those huge unfinished beams reached their resting places. How the noble tower was erected, when we remember 800 years ago the whole of this district was one vast forest. The many visitors to the Church testify to its beauty, and each year sees even greater numbers visiting what has appropriately been called "A shrine to God erected to His Glory amidst the great forest."

Cameo

REVEREND JOHN BARRETT-LENNARD

Rector of Crawley 1876 - 1898

No other word than "reigned" could describe the Rev. John Barrett-Lennard of Crawley for he made the place his kingdom, and he has left behind many monuments to testify to his strenuous services to the town. Some of his actions might seem incredible today. He was a man of short stature, strongly built, absolutely fearless, a firm believer in the muscular Christianity, and a typical Englishman - whatever he set out to accomplish he carried out though it might take years to complete. Anything that he considered unjust or cruel he attacked both in the Press and from the pulpit.

He stated: "When I came here in 1876 the Church and churchyard were in an absolutely disreputable condition. The church was dirty and neglected; in 'God's' acre the grass and weeds were waist high. Sheep were grazing among the graves and chicken were running all over the place, and the church completely shut in. I ask you - do you think our forefathers who built this noble church to the glory of God would let it be shut in on a piece of ground not much larger than a sheet or a table cloth? I am certain they would not, and I am equally certain that land on which some of the houses, chicken-houses and dirty-looking sheds are built were stolen from the church. I want to get some of that land back to open up the church so that those who pass through our town can see, what all must agree, is Crawley's greatest treasure."

His first big work commenced in 1879, when the North aisle was added, and the seating in Crawley Church was completely re-modelled. The altar was raised, the old gallery taken down, and the wood of oak and chestnut used to make a new reredos and communion table, choir stalls and Rector's chair. Most of the carving Barrett-Lennard did himself, taking more than 12 months over the task. The wood weighed nearly a ton.

P.A.

Above - The family outside the Rectory.

Below - At the entrance to the new Vestry.

P.A.

The five panels were so beautifully carved that no frontal was required for the table, but an embroidered velvet super-frontal was worked by Mrs. T. Barrett-Lennard.

His next task was the bells. Thanks to his persistent work, the peal of bells that we now have was hung and a band of ringers was formed, he himself being a member.

After a few years he launched the scheme of opening of the view of the Church and providing a proper approach to it. At that time the only approach to the Church was by the Church Walk. It was in connection with the Diamond Jubilee that he launched his scheme. The scheme was to purchase the old cottages in the High Street and pull them down, and purchase the gardens in Three Bridges Road, the estimated cost being £1,800 (the North aisle and other things, 1879-81, cost £4,000.) But only two cottages were demolished and the scheme cost £1,200. The Church approach as we know it today was opened on the first Wednesday in July 1898. Shortly before the opening ceremony a terrific thunderstorm passed over the town and the church tower was struck by lightning, but happily without serious injury.

Throughout his time at Crawley "the Rev. J.B." as he was familiarly called, was extremely popular with all the classes. He mixed with all and sundry, and at public functions he was in great request as a speaker. This was the era of public dinners, a time of which it has been written: "Dinner followed dinner. Every excuse possible was made to have a dinner and smoking concert." The Rev. J.B. attended all such gatherings and often responded to the toast: "The Bishop of the Diocese, the Clergy and Ministers of all Denominations." He was a staunch Conservative and used to flay his liberal opponents, but at one of these meetings he got flayed in return and gracefully retired from a Press dual tacitly admitting defeat.

One thing the reverend gentleman did at practically every vestry meeting was to propose, immediately after the meeting had assembled, an adjournment to the White Hart where it was "warmer and more commodious."

One would have thought that the reverend gentleman, popular with everyone backing him in his many ventures, would have hesitated to launch a fierce attack on some who made him an honoured guest. However, there had been a coursing meeting in a meadow near the Sun Inn, and this aroused the ire of Mr. Lennard. From his pulpit he made a slashing attack on the promoters of the coursing and sent a letter to the local newspaper.

Another time, when gypsies were camped on the greens, one Sunday morning there was a line of washing strung across the green. No one dared to complain. Nothing withstanding, the reverend marched up to the clothes line, removed the pegs and clothes and handed them to the astounded gypsy woman, telling her it was the Sabbath, and marched off again. They were not rehung.

The Reverend John Barrett-Lennard died towards the end of 1898 and is buried near the south wall in the churchyard, and was later succeeded to the living by his son Rev. Herbert Lorraine Barrett-Lennard.

Long before the Crawley Football Club was formed (and that is over 40 years ago) and before the game had caught on to any extent in Sussex, the Rev. Lennard bought footballs and had all the boys who cared to join in from the West Green Schools, the choir boys of both Crawley and St. Mary Magdalene (now the Parish Room) up in the park to learn the game. He had as helpers Dr. Chignall (who was assistant to Dr. Martin), Mr. Ransome (North House School) and Mr. F. H. Leary (organist and choirmaster, St. Mary Magdalene). The Rev. Bristow will surely recollect these names? Never shall I forget my initiation into football there, looking on (of course I was quite a small boy) and wondering why it was that such a huge "pumpkin" ball went about so easily. I was assailed thus. Now, Willie, why aren't you playing? Please, sir, I don't know how; I have never seen a football before. The rev. gentleman (who was in shorts, sweater, &c.) fetched the ball and placed it about six yards from me and said—now run and kick hard. I did so, and oh my relief when I found that my foot was still attached to my leg. Among the boys then playing, but who made their mark in Crawley football, were R. G. Morley, Frank Baldock — Chantler (I forget the initial, but he was "Taters" to everyone), Tom, Jack and Charlie Messer and my brother Jack.

And does not the Rev. James Bristow recall the Rev. Lennard's prowess with the gloves? My eldest brother Tom was pretty good at this game and when home on leave from the Royal Marines often had a bout up in the "carving" room, and he considered Mr. Lennard "hot." Did he not subdue that great bully, Fred Easton, a navvy who used to terrorise smaller men, and above all surely Mr. Bristow will remember the occasion when gipsies had encamped in the High Street, opposite his mother's house, for a week before the fair and on the Sunday had the week's laundry flying on the lines. The Rev. Lennard demanded that this laundry should be removed during Sunday, but was only met with abuse, so he promptly removed the lot himself, carefully depositing the whole in one waggon. No wonder that he endeared himself to all, for he took a keen interest in everything for the good of the parish and was the embodiment of the term, "A Muscular Christian."

Yours faithfully,

W. J. DENMAN.

19, Station Road, Crawley.
20th January, 1930.

I left the dusty high-road, and my way

Was through deep meadows, shot with copses fair

A choir of thrushes poured its roundelay

From every hedge and thicket there.

Mild, moon faced kine looked on, where in the grass

All heaped with flowers I lay, from noon till eve.

And hares unwitting close to me did pass,

And still the birds sang, and could not grieve.

Wilfred Blunt from *A Day in Sussex*

The Hawthe

Within a few minutes walk of Crawley High Street is the "Hawthe", a beautiful wood several acres in extent, and one of the beauty spots of the neighbourhood. At the moment it is carpeted with primroses which will be followed by bluebells. The starry brightness of the first and the waves of the blue made by the latter make the place a veritable sylvan retreat. From the south side one gets a glorious view of the Forest Ridge and the Downs, probably one of the finest in the county.

It is however with the past that we deal, and here is a fitting subject to hand. The Hawthe was in the long ago the centre of the great iron industry, and all the western end of the wood is dotted about with pits from which the iron was dug. Some of these are quite deep, while others go down a few feet. All of them are gradually being filled with leaves which have fallen since the iron industry found its new home in the north of England. These little pits are beautifully fashioned and naturally are objects of great interest to visitors.

Standing on the south side one can see how easily the ore could be transported down to the furnaces below, as the ground shelves steeply down to the spot where now stands Furnace Farm with its cottages built of ironstone. From here directly south-east lies Cinderbanks which name of course bespeaks its origin.

It is quite easy to visualise the scene when our forefathers worked in the Hawthe, and recall the time when forest covered the whole of the area where now stands Crawley. The great families of Gale and Black were associated with the place, being ironmasters, and members of the Black Family reposing in the aisle of Crawley Church

The date on the tomb is 1435. The Gale family it is stated lived at Crabbett Park and owned a great part of Crawley including the Old Priests House. (In all probability

they may also have lived in it as in 1671 and '73 a son and a daughter of Leonard Gale were baptised at St. Johns Church). Tradition asserts that the timbers of which all these ancient houses are built, and also of The George Hotel, came from the adjoining forest.

In an article written many years ago it was stated that "the great tie beams of Crawley Church - huge in size but rudely fashioned - came from the land around the spot." Unfortunately, no actual proof exists (or at least none has come to light) to verify this, though there is no reason why it should not be so. From the same source we learn that all the old "firebacks" in the neighbourhood were fashioned at "The Forge" (Tinsley) from iron dug and smelted at Tilgate. The iron fencing round St Paul's Cathedral was also dug and fashioned in this neighbourhood, and it should be remembered that practically all really old ironworks came from Sussex.

It is said that when the iron industry was first established here, great was the trouble over the cutting down of good oak trees for charcoal and the digging of ore-holes into which people and cattle fell o'nights. But in spite of internal troubles the forest did magnificent work in supplying timber for the ships and steel for the guns and pikes wherewith to chase the enemies of Britain from our shores, until the rise of the northern iron industry and the deforestation of the county put an end to the Sussex iron trade.

For a long time Sussex remained largely impassable to wheeled traffic. "Sussex roads" and Sussex mud were bywords of scorn, and many are the tales of woe on the part of would-be travellers of those days; but we should be grateful all the same for the badness of those roads for they have to a great extent preserved for us the amenities of this beautiful county.

The Hawthe is open to visitors, or rather part of it, thanks to the kindness of the owner of Tilgate (C.C.A. Nix Esq.) though there are public footpaths which run along the south side and also from north to south through the wood. Needless to say it is a favourite spot and well worthy of a visit. Strangely enough, one frequently meets visitors with guide-books of Sussex who are seeking the ancient ironworks and who know more of the history of the Hawthe than do the majority of local people. So long as the history of our ironworks exists will the Hawthe be remembered, and so form an interesting page of Historical Crawley.

1880   The first two Post Offices   *courtesy of R. Carmen*

The Postal History of Crawley

The coming of "fast" coaches marked an important era in the postal service as by the new means of transport "in bulk" the postal messenger service was gradually superseded. It was in 1810 that a direct service was established between London and Brighton and in consequence, Reigate, Crawley and Cuckfield were raised to the exalted status of head offices. It is interesting to note that during the passing of years Crawley is the only office to retain its status as Redhill and Reigate are now combined, whilst Cuckfield has long been absorbed by Haywards Heath. The fast mail coaches, 48 in number, passed up and down the famous London to Brighton Road. The Crawley Post Office was then at the corner of the White Hart Hotel. At this period the Postmasters were responsible for the horsing of the coaches in their respective districts, and the Postmaster of Crawley experienced little difficulty in meeting his obligations, as there were plenty of horses at the George Hotel and the Old Sun Inn (now North House School) where stood the posting horses and postboys.

It was in 1812 that the nightmail coaches started, and at Crawley the changing place was The White Hart, because not only was it a recognised posting house but the post office was on the premises.

The original Crawley Post Office of 1810 occupies a portion (the most northerly) of the White Hart, and the old lettering by which it could be identified might be seen on the walls of the building, though painted out many years ago now. When Mr. William Mitchell succeeded as postmaster, he built the little house on the north side and continuous to the White Hart. It was a quaint little building hardly in keeping with its exalted status, for it was the centre of a great network of social service on behalf of the community. It presented much the same appearance as it does now, except that one of the panes of glass in the window on the left hand side of the front door, had been replaced by a little door to open and shut. Through this small opening letters of importance were sometimes handed in or out and communication held with the presiding official who did not encourage people to go inside to hinder them in their arduous duties. Mr. and Mrs. Mitchell alone did the whole of the business of the Post Office for many years - she poor lady suffered from bad headaches, and little wonder with such work to do and so much of it. The area covered was a tremendous one extending beyond Charlwood nearly to Newdigate, right round Hookwood and Horse Hills to the borders of Reigate, Horley, Smallfields, Burstow, Copthorne, Crawley Down and Turners Hill to Staplefield and Slaugham, and nearly to Faygate and, of course, all places within the ring. This great area naturally entailed a tremendous amount of work, even though only postal matters were dealt with. The outlying places had deliveries on alternate days and there are still living people who remember letter carrier Amos Sayers, who used to push a truck round Charlwood on three days and round Hookwood and Horley on the other three days. This truck deserves a word to itself as it resembles nothing else on earth except a bedstead on wheels with the axle about three inches above the bed of the truck and, being of iron, made an unearthly row when in use. It will be noted that "letter carrier" was the official designation of the uniformed staff, but the public made "postman" more popular and the department agreed. Mr. Sayers was the first "postman" in the south to wear six stripes. The truck was in turn discarded for horses and "mounted" (i.e. horses and carts) postmen used to go out to Horley, Crawley and Staplefield.

The first head Postmaster was Mr. James Swift, who held office from 1810 to the 24th April, 1838. He was the great uncle of Mr. C.J. Mitchell. Mr. Swift was succeeded by Mr. William Mitchell, father of C.J. Mitchell, and he was Postmaster from 25th April, 1838, to the November of 1875. Not only was he Postmaster, but he and his family did nearly the whole of the business attached to the office. Mr. Mitchell used to deliver letters, riding his horse out to remote parts. He was a noted athlete and it is recorded that one night when the coaches were snowed up he walked all the way to Brighton carrying his mail bags. On his retirement a Mr. Henry Gatcombe was appointed Postmaster, but in name only, as he was immediately given a post elsewhere, and Mr. C.J. Mitchell, who had been assistant Postmaster since 1864, was appointed head Postmaster on the 27th January, 1876, and he continued in office till the 4th August, 1908. It will be seen the Mitchell family were connected with the Postmastership of Crawley for 98 years.

James Bristow worked at the Post Office for four years commencing 1874. He recalls his

> "principal work being the Black Corner route in the morning and
> the Ifield route for the evening, with now and then the mid-day mail to
> Three Bridges and Pound Hill. "It is quite possible that I am wrong in my
> judgment, but I have often thought as a boy of from 12 to 16 years of age
> my daily stint was as much and more than the task that many of the men

Post Office on the right. 1883 - 1895

Staff 1894 - W.J.D. front row 2nd left

courtesy of H. Frost

are doing to-day, and we had no horse nor car to aid, but did it all on shank's pony. And then between times there were telegraphic messages to deliver. One instance as follows. It was a dark night and Tilgate Forest Lodge, Mr. John Nix's place, was the destination. Failing to find anyone to go along with me I struck out alone. The carriage drive from the turnpike at Broadfield was as dark as pitch; one could find the way by steering from the light of the stars above the trees. How welcome the servants' hall with its warmth and the piece of something to eat while waiting for the reply message. On the return journey, rather than face the dark forest road, the way through the park was chosen; all went fairly well until reaching "Cobbler's Pit." Then the reputed tree where the cobbler enacted the deed that I had often pointed out with glee to someone seemed an awful spectre to face and pass, and I recall distinctly how the sound of my footsteps seemed to echo as I made my way in the darkness across the bridge with its loose wooden floor. A little later I was passing Calf Hovel Pond, and over the railway track, then with Ambrose Webley's timberyard on one side and the high monastery wall on the other was soon through the churchyard and back to the post office."

"It was about that same time, perhaps about the year 1876, that I went as a boy on several trips to mind the horse for Mr. Charles Mitchell. He and his sister were securing signatures from prominent persons to a document for the purpose of transfer of the postmastership from Mr. William Mitchell to his son. One of these trips was in the Worth district, Three Bridges, Worth Park, Crabbet Park, etc. We reached home quite late that day, Mr. Mitchell drove up into the yard at the post office adjoining the White Hart Inn. Then I was told to take the horse to the stable at the station hotel. Probably it was due to my lack of skill, or just as likely to the desire of the horse to get to the stable; anyway, in coming out of the yard that night the horse turned so swift and sharp that the axle caught one of the posts which with the iron rails were planted along in front of the property. The sound of the breaking post made such a racket that the horse bolted and was entirely out of control until reaching the station, where it quietly settled down."

It was during Mr. Mitchell's tenure of office that the great changes in the postal service took place. Telegraphs, parcel post, telephones all being inaugurated. The work now became so great that the office could not cope with it and it was decided to move into larger premises.

NOTES OF THE WEEK.

I learn that the premises recently occupied by Mr Albert Smith, at the corner of High Street and New Road, Crawley, have been purchased by the Postmaster of Crawley, Mr C. J. Mitchell. They are now undergoing extensive alterations with the object of the front being fitted out as a commodious and convenient post office, suited to the requirements of this thriving district, and the other portion will be occupied as a private residence. The present post office is a very unpretentious little place, utterly inadequate to the growing importance of such a populous district, and I congratulate the residents of the town on their prospect of shortly possessing a post office where the increasing postal business of the district can be transacted with far greater convenience than at present.

*   *   *   *   *

By-the-bye, would it be amiss to suggest that with increased postal accommodation the inhabitants of Crawley and Ifield would feel grateful if there was also in improvement in the postal deliveries? If the genial and obliging Postmaster of Crawley could see his way clear to accelerate the delivery of the second and third mails he would confer a boon on his fellow townsmen.

In 1883 the Head Post Office was transferred to the corner of Post Office Road on the site now occupied by Mr. Banks, clothier. It was with great regret the old office (of which Mr. Mitchell had a very fine photograph) was vacated. The new home was a queerly fashioned one, as the sorting office was shaped like a triangle and was shut off from public view by a sort of folding screen. The public counter also served as a retiring room for the telegraph messengers, and a narrow slip at the side was screened from the public and used for telegraphic purposes. There was no provision for the storage of parcel baskets or truck (the same noted vehicle) so these were stacked in the roadway outside the office (one wonders what Sergt. Capelin and his staff would say to this?). The building certainly did not lead one to suppose it was H.M.'s Post Office. On one occasion two "Fair" ladies, resplendent in their finery, embellished with clothes pegs, wire articles and customery baby slung across their shoulders, marched in and demanded "two halves of mild and bitter, please!"

In 1907 Horley was separated from Crawley and took Charlwood, Smallfields and Burstow with it, but the work continued to grow so much that in 1895 a move was made to the present office, which was at least six times the size of the High Street office. It is of interest to point out what a great outcry there was because the office had been removed from the High Street to "such a ridiculous position in a cul de sac." The Crawley Parish Council (which had lately been created) made an attempt to stop the transference, but in vain. Now one hears complaints because the new office is built on the best site in the town. During Mr. Mitchell's regime one saw the passing of the horsed coach for the motor coach and bicycles brought into use.

The retirement of Mr. C.J. Mitchell snapped a long link of family service. He was succeeded by Mr. J. Carey, who reigned from 14th September, 1908, to 16th October, 1914. He was followed by Mr. F.W. Weskett, who came on the 1st January, 1915, and was afterward promoted to Matlock on 4th April, 1920. The present chief (Mr. D.F. Clarke) came on the 8th April, 1920, and he will have the honour of presiding over the first Crown Office when the new office is opened on the 29th inst. The three offices hitherto used have all been rented places, but the new one is the property of the Crown. Though Handcross and district has been transferred to Haywards Heath the continual growth of Crawley and district has made the provision of a new office a necessity.

Crawley enjoys facilities that few towns of its size possess, in fact, they are equal to places like Redhill, Horsham and East Grinstead with their much greater population. In the lighting area there are three deliveries of letters and five collections. In the rural areas two deliveries and two collections take place. Telephone facilities have been extended to all rural areas. A few figures of the growth of work will be of interest. In 1919 the number of telephone calls was 189,000; in 1927 upwards of 500,000. In 1927

Left - Right. Camborne, A. Groom, C. Merriken, W.J. Denman,
R. Turner, H. Tester, Packham, Wildish, H. Hearsey,
J. Charman, A. Gibbs, Randall, Phipps.

3½ millions of letters etc. were dealt with, and upwards of 100,000 parcels. With the continual growth in the population these figures will be beaten.

Although one always refers to the Post Office it is, in these days, something of a misnomer - the National Business Office, being a better designation, for in addition to its proper business, the following are among the multifarious duties now performed:- Dog, game, wireless, gun, motor, male servant and Armorial Bearings Licences; old age and widows, and Disabled Service Men's Pensions; Life Assurance, Endowment Assurance, Life Annuities, National Savings, Inland Revenue Stamps, Agreements, the Great Savings Bank, Money Orders, Postal Orders, etc. These are some of the duties "covered" by His Majesty's Post Office.

New Post Office: Crawley (June 1928)

The new Post Office at Crawley will be opened within a few days and the occasion will mark a memorable step in the history of the town. It occupies one of the finest sites in the High Street, immediately facing the Westminster Bank, but by its height and spaciousness it dwarfs its immediate surroundings. The building is four stories high in front and is centrally heated throughout. Beneath the pavements and northern corner of the building are large cable rooms and the usual engines connected with the heating. The Public Office is a handsome room with up-to-date fittings. Two stamp machines are fitted in the outer wall near the posting box, so that stamps can be obtained at any hour. The counters for the writing of telegrams are of the latest design, and the same can be said of the telephone kiosk. The telegraph messengers' room is at the north end of the office. The Sorting Office is a spacious one with large skylights with special fittings for ventilating purposes. Here the staff will be able to carry out their duties with greater ease and comfort. Special fittings for lighting up the individual benches will make for speed in preparation. All the latest fittings and "gadgets" have been introduced into this room. The dining room and kitchen are adjacent. The remainder of the ground floor is occupied with the engineering departments' various tools and instruments, together with lavatories, garage, cycle sheds, etc. On the next floor are the Postmaster's room, the telephonists' retiring room, the telegraph room, the telephone room, offices for inspector and linesmen, and various store rooms. The caretaker's rooms are on an upper floor. The yard provides ample room for the storage of vehicles and cycles, and in future all branches of the G.P.O. will be under one roof. The whole is electrically lighted. This is the fourth Post Office used in Crawley since 1810.

So far as is known there will be no ceremonial opening, but the doors will be thrown open for business in the ordinary way.

The site of the post office in the early 1920s. Willetts shop acquired Taylors Auctioneers.

William Denman with his son George, on the day of Will's retirement in 1937.

DAMAGE IN INLAND TOWN

One of the half-dozen raiders which took advantage of the low cloud and fanned out after crossing the S.E. coast caused extensive damage in an inland town on Tuesday morning, dropping a stick of H.E.'s across the residential and shopping area, while travelling at high speed at roof top level. Fortunately there were very few casualties. Had the lone raider been half-an-hour later the children would have been in the Church of England School, where the playground is now a deep crater; evacuees would have been in the classroom of the Baptist Church, which is now a shell; and more civil servants and business people would have been in an office which was badly damaged. The entire raid was over within a few seconds.

With little warning, except for the swish of the H.E.'s as they were released, the bombs demolished the Baptist Church, wrecked two houses and damaged two others behind the Station, where most of the casualties occurred. A bank and several shops and houses also suffered. One bomb fell in the middle of the Church of England School playground, where the youngest kiddies' classrooms and three homes were almost completely destroyed. The Boy Scouts' Hut and Salvation Army Citadel—whose flag of Blood and Fire still flutters high in the breeze—was also damaged. Doors and windows were blown in and the explosions caused havoc among roofs.

In one office, where the main clock stopped on 8.30 a.m., the staff were just preparing to open when the bomb clattered through the building. Although there were about 15 employees, only one, Mr. Hall, was seriously injured. Girls at the main counter soon recovered from shock and minor injuries, and were able to carry on at temporary premises. Their colleagues in another department also suffered from shock. Mr. W. Thomas, who was dressing at home at the time, paid tribute to the entire staff on the heroic way they carried on in spite of their nerve-wracking experiences

Working about the school at the time when the raider swooped was the caretaker, Mrs. Rice. She was thrown along a passage way by the effect of the blast and was heavily struck by the debris, but she suffered no more than from shock, cuts and bruises.

The town's Civil Defence Services were all out in double-quick time and, strongly supported by the military, they worked extremely hard throughout the day, digging and clearing like Trojans here and giving a helping hand there. They had no envious task, particularly in one street, which had to be roped off, but it was not long before things were back to normal. Business people who had suffered improvised and carried on. And at least one of them still retained his sense of humour by chalking up a notice "Open (Very Much) as Usual."

courtesy of W. Charman

W.C.

Telephone exchange back in action within one hour, bombed section behind the curtain.

Temporary postbox at corner of Station Road

W.C.

Crawley Hospital

History of the Institution

The Crawley and Ifield Cottage Hospital was established in 1896. Previously the building had been used for many years as a training school for servants. It was built mainly through the exertions and instrumentality of the late Mrs. Sarah Robinson of Manor House, Crawley, who was indefatigable in collecting funds for this purpose, and also for the erection of the British School lately pulled down and replaced by the County Council School. In 1896, for various reasons, amongst others the departure for Canada of the matron (Mrs. Long), the servants' home was broken up and it became a question with the trustees, who consisted entirely of the Robinson family, what should be done with the building.

At this stage it was suggested by Dr. Martin to Mrs. Robinson that there was an excellent opportunity of starting a cottage hospital for the neighbourhood. In this she readily acquiesced, she and her family becoming warm supporters for the cause. Funds for equipment were collected and in furtherance of this object the late Mr. Samuel Burgess worked very keenly and successfully. A committee of management was formed consisting of Dr. Martin (chairman), Mr. S.C. Burgess (secretary), Miss Robinson, Miss Pearson, Mrs. Martin, the Rev. J. McAuslane, Mr. T. Lee, Mr. W. Gatland, Miss Davidson and the medical men of the town. Later they were joined by Mr. F. Luscombe, Mr. Binyon, the Rev. H.L. Martley and Mr. Thomson.

Willing hands at once set to work to prepare the house for the reception of patients - cleaning, scrubbing and collecting bits of furniture. Among the most prominent of those engaged in these necessary operations were Mrs. C.J. Mitchell, Mrs. Martin, Miss Burgess, with others.

This was the modest beginning of the hospital, now become one of the best equipped institutions of its kind in the neighbourhood. With its growth came, of course, increased expenditure upon its maintenance, and at times special efforts have been made to raise funds. These spasmodic attempts, though they have been successful, have been a tax upon the committee as well as upon the more willing subscribers and donors. It is, therefore, very desirable that the number of subscribers should be increased and a larger endowment fund acquired.

The hospital was started with two wards - one for men and one for women - with two beds in each ward. One of the first patients was old Mr. Funnell, of Ifield; and his wife was matron, or, at any rate, the only person answering to such a description.

Crawley Cottage Hospital.

Another very early patient was a little girl - the first recorded accident due to a motor car. She was knocked down by one of the cars which passed through the town on the Emancipation Day run to Brighton to celebrate the legalising of motor cars running on the road without a man with a red flag walking in front. This girl, named Dyer, from Three Bridges, had a fractured skull. Happily, she recovered, and so is Mrs. Dench, of Mill Road, Three Bridges.

> "In 1897 Lucy Warren (mother of Daisy Warren) was the first private patient. She was operated on while lying on the kitchen table by Dr. Arbuthnot Lane (later Sir Arbuthnot Lane) assisted by Dr. Sidney Matthews. The window in the little bedroom was difficult to open, so Mr. Warren cut the glass out and put in perforated zinc for ventilation, and this remained for many years."

As the hospital became more widely known, its work increased, but its need and usefulness were never so strikingly emphasised as by the terrible "Vanguard" accident on Handcross Hill which took place on July 12th. 1906, ten persons losing their lives and 24 others being injured. Several were taken to the Cottage Hospital and had to be accommodated in improvised beds, some being placed on the floor of the committee room. The building had never been properly adapted to its new purpose - there was no operating theatre, nor sufficient lavatory, or bath accommodation, and the stairway was extremely inconvenient.

In 1907 the committee decided that the time had come when these defects should be remedied and the hospital enlarged. A subscription list was opened and realised £922 14s. 4d. To supplement this amount and to obtain enough money to carry out the reconstruction and enlargement of the hospital according to plans prepared by Mr. G. F. H. Banks it was decided to hold a bazaar. The late Mrs. John Goddard lent the grounds and gardens of The Elms, and on July 1st. 1908, the bazaar was opened by Princess Alexander of Teck. It proved a brilliant success, the profits being £555 5s. 11d. The preparations were on a very elaborate scale and entailed an enormous amount of work. An extract of a report of that memorable day reads: "Never before was Crawley so bedecked with bunting, nor did its ancient streets resound with cheers such as those which greeted the Princess during her progress through the town escorted by the local Yeomanry Troop. The royal visitor went to the Cottage Hospital, which had been renovated, and she expressed herself as greatly pleased with it. The nursing staff and medical officers were introduced to her, and before leaving she graciously gave her name to the new ward - the other two having been named the Joseph Robinson and the John Goddard wards. The Princess was accompanied from London by Col. and Lady Rawson, who were instrumental in procuring royal patronage for the bazaar."

That the history of Crawley Cottage Hospital has aroused interest has been evidenced by the sending to me by a very old friend, Mr. T. Hollman Lee of a notice issued after a preliminary meeting and I give the exact wording of it. It was sent to Mr. T. Lee, father of Mr. Thomas Hollman Lee, who was a member of the first committee formed:

At a meeting held in the British School on Wednesday, April 22nd. 1896, T.H. Martin, Esq., in the chair: -

It was resolved to establish a cottage hospital to be called the "Crawley and Ifield Cottage Hospital," and the following have been elected to form the executive committee to raise the necessary funds and carry out the arrangements: Mr. Joseph Robinson, the Rev. W. Loveband, the Rev. H. Mais, the Rev. J. McAuslane, the Rev. Edward Lee, Mr. Thos. Lee, Mr. Gatland, Mr. Tizard, Mr. M. Nightingale, Mr. Hibbs, T.W. Binyon, Esq., Mr. Chas. Longley, Mr. H. Gravely, Dr. Hitchin, Miss Robinson, Mrs. Loveband, Mrs. T. H. Martin, Mrs. Burgess, Miss Martin, Mrs. Trist, Miss Pierson, Mrs. Binyon, Mrs. C. Longley, Mrs. Gravely, Mrs. Arnold.

Hon. treasurer: E. Henty, Esq.

Hon. secretary: Mr. S.C. Burgess

The following medical gentlemen have kindly offered their assistance: T.H. Martin, Esq., S. Matthews, Esq., and W. Arnold, Esq.

The need of such an institution is urgently felt in this place, and the present is a peculiarly favourable opportunity for establishing one, for the trustees of the late Servants' Training Home have very kindly consented to allow the building to be used as a cottage hospital at quite a nominal rent. Although called the Crawley and Ifield Cottage Hospital, it will, of course, be available for the surrounding neighbourhood, such as Worth, Lowfield Heath, Peas Pottage, Handcross, etc. It is computed that about £200 will be necessary to start and maintain the hospital for the first year, and the committee trust they may rely upon your support and help. As they are anxious as soon as possible to commence operations, they venture to appeal to you for a donation towards the first year's expenses, and a subsequent annual subscription. As the building is too large to be at present utilised entirely as a cottage hospital, it is proposed to combine it with a convalescent home for the reception of about six females, and any subscriber to the amount of £2 2s. would have the privilege of nominating a convalescent patient, subject to the rules of similar institutions.

Mr. S.C. Burgess, Crawley, has been appointed hon. secretary, and will gratefully acknowledge the receipt of all amounts sent to him for the above purpose.

During the 1914-18 war Crawley Cottage Hospital was placed at the disposal of the Red cross Society, certain beds being retained for local patients. At this time the building was the scene of intense activity dealing with a number of casualties and its worth could not be too highly estimated. Gradually the place became more and more used as it is the centre of a wide district covering Lowfield Heath, Handcross, Ifield, Peas Pottage, the whole of Worth, and, of course, Crawley. Many additions were made, including an operating theatre with up-to-date equipment, more beds in the wards, and additional staffing.

In 1933 a wing was added at a cost of approximately £700. This included an X-ray room and equipment, two more staff rooms, a lift and other amenities. Each year

P.A.

View showing new extension built in 1933

Visit of the Duchess of Kent

P.A.

there has been a growth in the number of cases dealt with and last year the thousandth case was approached.

Throughout the history of the hospital certain private residents, with the medical men of the town, have run the hospital, but in 1938 a move was made to put the management on a wider and more definite basis and a general committee was formed.

It is hoped that Ifield Lodge will be opened in September as the Crawley and District Hospital.

Crawley folk are saying nice things about the Sites Sub-Committee of the Crawley and District Hospital in securing Ifield Lodge on such advantageous terms, for it would be impossible to find a better site for a hospital than Ifield Lodge, situate as it is off the road but approached by a nice drive and with the house standing amidst lovely trees and well-kept lawns and gardens. The spacious billiards room and lounges on the south side are ideal for wards and will require little alteration.

Ifield Lodge has had several notable tenants. It was a former home of the Rawson family who were followed by Lady Blackett-Holt and Mr. Holt. Lady Blackett was a well-known hunting woman and she had the large range of stables built where now is the Crawley Cake and Biscuit Factory. Then came Mr. E. Dunn, a very fine cricketer, who did splendid service for the Crawley Cricket Club.

Next came Mr. E. B. Lehmann, without question one of the most talented and generous men Crawley has ever had. He was a Cambridge Soccer Blue, the founder of the Crawley Harriers, a keen supporter of sport, a noted music and dramatic critic, a brilliant pianist, a prominent rosarian and a generous philanthropist. Mr. Dunn, with Mr. Lehmann, took the keenest interest in their poorer neighbours.

Mr. and Mrs. A Gordon who have lived at Ifield Lodge, for some years, have now gone to Oakwood (Horsham Road) but whilst at Ifield, they spent much money on making big improvements to the place.

Throughout the 43 years of its existence the hospital has had but two chairmen - the late Dr. T.H. Martin and the present chairman (Dr. Sidney Matthews). The trustees have included the following, all of whom have passed away: Mr. Francis Luscombe, Sir John H. Luscombe, Mr. J. Goddard and Mr. M. Nightingale. Mr. Gilbert Gardner and Mr. J. Goddard Jun., are happily still with us. The late Mr. S.C. Burgess was the first hon. secretary, and he was succeeded by the managers of the Westminster Bank until Mr. Penman retired from the Bank and Crawley. He was succeeded by Mr. A.G. Kale, who held office for several years until a very long illness caused his retirement in 1928. He was succeeded by the late Mr. Doveton, whose sudden death again brought a vacancy, and this was and is being filled by Mr. J.H. Sadler, who combines the duties of hon. radiologist with his secretarial duties. The whole of the medical profession give their services and have direct representation on the general committee. The list of matrons is: Mrs. Funnell, 1896; Mrs Chubbe, 1897; Miss Heriot and Miss Davison, 1908; Miss Humphries, 1910; Miss Howard, 1913; Miss Rolls, 1917; Miss Miller (present matron) since 1935.

courtesy of Mrs Richardson

Ifield Lodge

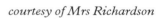

courtesy of Mrs Richardson

'The George Hotel'

The most famous house on the most famous road in the world is, perhaps, not too high a label for the George Hotel, Crawley, for the countless thousands who have traversed the London to Brighton road know this old hostelry with its quaint gallows sign swinging across the road. The house is exactly 29 miles 5 furlongs 4 yards from Big Ben, and the sign of the "George" is a landmark for the many contests that take place on this famous road.

Who would dream that this old house was such a casket of romance, of history, of mystery and sport, yet, could its quaint beams and plaster walls speak, they would a tale unfold that would delight the heart of the student of history.

What is age of the "George"? No one knows this, but records show that it was an inn in 1615, but how long before no one can tell. From its buildings it can be told that the house existed in 1500. Tradition tells us that all the oaken timbers which are such a delight to the antiquarian came from our local forests, and there is little doubt that tradition is right, for those versed in such matters say the Sussex oak is used throughout

the ancient building, and as Crawley stood within the great forest there is no reason why the great timbers should not be local oak.

I am not attempting to give a guide book description of the famous house, but lovers of beauty should not fail to pay a visit to the see the wonderful rooms, which are of enthralling interest, immediately one steps inside the door, for there is a large open fireplace with a huge Sussex iron fireback. Upon the stonework someone has carved 1615, but experts declare this to be 100 years later than the period which the fireplace and "back" represents. A scholar versed in languages, hieroglyphics, symbols and signs, could spend hours studying the works of visitors of decades ago. The old lounge and billiards room and the old coffee rooms, the "Den" and the public bar are all a mass of old timbers. The grand staircase leading to long oaken passage ways to the bedrooms is a real delight, the old timbers richly mellowed by time. The earlier history of the house is mystery, and it was not till 1696 that it became known to the outer world, though it is highly probable that two centuries had already passed over its head. (In 1635 Thomas Truncheon tapster at The George was buried in Crawley churchyard.) In that

year (1696) the road from Reigate was continued as far as Crawley, and horsemen found their way to the house. It was, however, the coming of the coaching era which followed the Prince Regent's trip to Brighton in 1783 that laid the foundations of the fortunes of "The George". From then right down to the coming of the railways this hostelry was the recognised changing place, no fewer than 60 coaches "up and down" changing horses here. One can easily visualise the stirring scenes, and it was from the "George" that Crawley gained its knowledge of the great outside world.

A very fine print (by Rowlandson) of 1789, depicts an auction sale of smugglers' horses, outside the George, and it is most interesting to note that the old sign swings across the road. The front of the house is, however, very different from that which we know; the overhanging windows are small, with leaden panes, and one extends much beyond the house, this being just about where the main entrance is now. The print shows the adjoining houses on the south side (Mr. Miller's) and also the upper square, though they appear to be but cottages. Rowlandson did not show the north side of the hotel, in its picturesque setting of wooden cottages. These were beautiful old dwellings and proved a most appropriate setting for the ancient hostelry.

Had a register been kept of the visitors to this ancient inn, it would now be worth a fabulous sum. We know that Queen Victoria visited the place when on her first visit to Brighton. "Granny Hole", who died some 30 years ago, (1899) aged nearly a hundred years, declared that she had seen three reigning monarchs of England enter the house. Queen Victoria's visit, due to a breakdown on the road, it is said is authenticated by the annals of the hotel. Tradition of course, credits Queen Elizabeth and Queen Anne with having slept at "the George", but, of course, all old houses make the same claim. Lord Nelson was a frequent visitor when his sister lived at Ashfold, Handcross. Lord Rodney (who lived at Ewhurst Place, Ifield) would assuredly have visited his colleagues. Charles Dickens, Mark Lemon (of *Punch* fame) and John Leech (the Cartoonist) all met at "The George" when Mark Lemon lived in Crawley. Sir Arthur Conan Doyle makes the inn one of his greatest features in his famous Sussex novel, "Rodney Stone", as it was here that Jim Belcher trained "Boy Jim", and it was from here that Boy Jim was kidnapped. Another writer who was a frequent visitor was "Richard Marsh".

To take the Sporting Associations of "The George". We know it was visited by the Prince Regent, whist the "Regency Bucks" and Corinthians made it a regular rendezvous. Of the famous coaching men we have the Duke of Beaufort, Lord Lonsdale, Chandos Pole, Stracey Clitheroe, gallant old Captain Carleton Blythe (happily still with us), Lord H. Thynne, Colonel Armitage, B.J. Angell, Captain Haworth, Cheyley and C. Lawrie. James Selby in his ever memorable race from London to Brighton and back for a bet of 10,000 guineas, the journey to be accomplished in eight hours had "The George" as his mid-way changing place. The "Old Times", "Quicksilver" and "Defiance" were three well known coaches. Mr. Vanderbilt, when running his coach, used the hotel for two summers for luncheon, and those who were present when the Americans visited the house will not soon forget their cries of admiration.

For some years mine host was Frank Carthew, a well-known Devonshire whip, and he had a vast number of sporting guests. In fact, hardly a week passed without some celebrity visiting the place. The George Hotel was also, at one time, a regular "house" for boxing men. Tom Sayers, John L. Sullivan, Frank Kelrain, Peter Jackson and Frank Slavin have all passed within its doors. "Pedlar" Palmer trained for his big fights (with a "camp", of course); and the great Hackenschmidt, Madrali (the terrible Turk), Peter Gatz, among others, have been guests. Crawley used to be a regular "Trotting" place, and naturally the George Hotel was Headquarters. All gatherings took place here and up to quite a short time ago it was the recognised place for all public meetings, dinners, etc. In fact Crawley grew up around the George Hotel.

Although much more could be written of this ancient place enough has been given to show that it is worthy of having "historical" connected with it. Though over 300 years old (probably over 400) there is every sign that a like period will find the Brighton-road crossed by the gallows sign of "The George Hotel".

February 1934

A Royal Rendezvous Crawley Landmark to Disappear

The impending demolition of the George Hotel Annexe will remove one of the most interesting buildings on the London - Brighton Road. Until the last few years it was always referred to as the private part of the George Hotel but a visiting official described it as an "annexe" and since then officials have always given it this name, except the locals who adhere to the old name.

Before

After

It is said that the building was originally erected as a soap and candle factory by a Mr. Mitchell, the then host of the George, whose descendents still occupy a prominent position in the town. It is understood that the factory was never used, as it became so sought after as a residence, that it became the private part of the Hotel.

It is known that Queen Victoria stayed within the building. King William also stayed there and the Hotel possesses a Royal coat-of-arms to mark that event.

With all its long and interesting history the annexe is to go and its site is to be used as a car park for visitors to the Hotel itself.

After demolition of the George Hotel annexe, when drainage and water pipes were being renewed, the builders, Cook's, found at a very great depth a tunnel, more than half way across the square towards the old Ancient Priors. Was this one of the legendary Smugglers' tunnels?

The picture used as an introduction for this chapter has been printed like this as opposed to the usual version deliberately: There is some artistic licence in the composition. By studying the roof structure and knowing from other sources there was no building adjacent to The George Inn on the South side during the life of Rowlandson, neither was the facade of The Old Whyte Harte on the opposite side of the road as depicted. Every Wednesday, auctions, usually horses or cows, held outside the Inn as least throughout the 18th and beginning of the 19th Century.

CRAWLEY SACRED HARMONIC
SOCIETY.

A
GRAND CONCERT
Will be given by the members of the above
Society, at the
ASSEMBLY ROOMS, GEORGE HOTEL,
CRAWLEY, on
TUESDAY and WEDNESDAY, APRIL 29th
and 30th, 1884,
When the Sacred Cantata,
"THE LION OF JUDAH"
Will be rendered by a FULL BAND and
CHORUS, under the conductorship of Mr O.
Snelling.
Doors open at 7:30, to commence at 8 o'clock.
Tickets, 1st night, 3s, 2s, 1s. Family tickets to
admit five persons, 12s 6d (to front seats only).
Tickets, 2nd night, 2s, 1s, 6d.
Tickets may be obtained of Messrs. Leach and
Weedon, where a plan of the room may be seen.
t660

THE GIANT AND THE MIDGET. — The largest
man and the smallest man in the world were in Crawley
on Sunday, Mr. C. E. Green having arranged for them
to visit his hotel and take luncheon together. Macknow,
the Russian giant, has been at the George Hotel on a
prior occasion, but it was the first visit of the Burmese
Midget, who was brought down from London in a motor
car by Paul Cinquavallie, the celebrated juggler. The
midget arrived first, and the little fellow was made much
of by the large gathering assembled to meet him. When
Macknow came on the scene, he having ridden in a motor
'bus, he became jealous of the attentions being paid to
his smaller friend and behaved in quite a surly manner.
He declined to partake of lunch and contented himself
with three cups of coffee. He also refused to be photo-
graphed with the midget, and in other ways displayed his
undoubted jealousy. Naturally these two extremes of
human nature attracted great attention and there was a
large concourse of people present. Macknow, the giant,
is 9-ft. 2½-in., and Swaun, the midget, is only 2-ft. 2-in.

CRAWLEY.

VOLUNTEER FIRE BRIGADE.—On Friday last the
annual general meeting of this brigade was held
at the George Hotel. The REV. J. B. Lennard
(the Rector), occupied the chair, and there was a
good attendance of members. The secretary
(Mr. Ernest Ockenden) presented the balance
sheet, which had been duly examined and signed
by the auditors, and showed a deficiency of
£53 19s. 3d. It was resolved that a circular containing the list of subscriptions, and a copy of
the balance sheet be sent to each subscriber.
The question of horses for the engines was freely
discussed, and also the desirability of obtaining
a further supply of hose, but the majority considered it advisable to clear off their present
liabilities before incurring fresh ones. A vote of
thanks to the Chairman brought the meeting to
a close.

CRAWLEY
BLACKBIRD MINSTRELS.

PROGRAMME of ::
:: ENTERTAINMENT

AT THE
GEORGE HOTEL, CRAWLEY,
ON WEDNESDAY, DECEMBER 2nd, 1908,
In aid of the Fund for purchasing a Fire Escape for
Crawley.

Doors Open at 7.30, Commence at 8 p.m.

Reserved Seats 2/-; Second Seats 1/-; Back Seats 6d.

Musical Director :   Interlocutor :
Mr. O. SNELLING.   Mr. F. KNIGHT.

P. Snelling, Printer, Crawley.

The "Old Crawley" Stage Coach

will run DAILY from

Monday July 19th to Monday August 2nd (Sunday excepted)

from

George Hotel, Crawley

Prices : **Day Tours £1. 1. 0.** (excluding Lunch)   **Half-Day Tours 10s. 6d.**
Box Seat extra.   Box Seat extra

Seats may be booked at the Misses Warren, 32 High Street, Crawley.   Phone No. 237

The Coaching Revival

July 1943 (an excerpt from the Fortnights Diary)

In view of the widespread interest taken in the revival of coaching at Crawley and the notable people who took part the Fortnight is worthy of a permanent record in the history of the town which has a long connection with coaching on the Brighton Road. We here will publish a day to day record of that hectic fortnight which was full of worries, enjoyment, and repayment for work well done. Thanks to the collaboration of Miss Daisy Warren, we are able to give full details.

Worries and anxieties

"The Crawley Coaching Fortnight had a successful opening on July 17th. The old Crawley Stage Coach owned by Mr. James Farmer, of Stumbleholme, Ifield, was brought out once more on to the road to raise money for Crawley Hospital."

Mr. Frank Ayling was organising Crawley Fair on Bank Holiday and he asked Mr. Farmer if he would lend his coach to help the effort. Mr. Farmer was delighted to do this, but he knew that the coach was only part of the affair; he had the coach and harness, but there must be horses, stables, grooms, and coachmen, Blacksmiths' forge, passengers and heaps of other things that did not meet the eye. He at once thought of Mr. Sidney Truett, the finest professional coachman in England and the owner of the "Old Berkley" Coach when it used to run from London to the "Old Ship" at Brighton, and from the Dorchester Hotel to Hampton Court. He was the coachman who drove it on its last journey from London to Brighton - before motor traffic made coaching impossible. But Mr. Sidney Truett had been living in retirement at Hassocks. He was 74; would he be able to put in the amount of hard work that would be necessary to run the "Old Crawley Coach" successfully?

Mr. Farmer telephoned his old friend and he promised to do his best, and so the matter stood.

The "Old Crawley" Coach Way Bill

From "GEORGE HOTEL," CRAWLEY

To *Lowfield Heath, Charlwood, Ifield*

Coachman *W. Jacob Farmer* *Monday July 26* 1943

SEATS	PASSENGERS		PAID	
BOX	Mr. & J. Denman		10	6
O.S. 1	Mr. A. Gafney		10	6
" 2	Mr. T. Gafney		10	6
N.S. 3	Mrs. W.J. Denman		10	6
" 4	Mr Sidney Truett		10	6
" 5	Mr Taylor		10	6
" 6	Mrs Taylor		10	6
O.S. 7	Master Taylor		10	6
" 8	Mr White		10	6
" 9	Mr White		10	6
" 10	Mrs Cicklewright		10	6
Guard	Mr Loder			
In 1				
" 2				
" 3				
" 4				
			£	

PLACES	TIMES	REMARKS	
Left CRAWLEY	11-30		
Arrived			
Left			
Arrived CRAWLEY			
Passengers	10		
Weather	Fine		Guard

Then things began to move. Mr. Truett and Mr. Farmer visited Messrs Carter Pattersons in London in search of a team of horses to hire for the occasion. None of these horses had been driven four-in-hand before, but four were chosen, a grey, a bay and two blacks to come to Crawley on July 14th. in readiness.

The coach was got out and cleaned and polished. Mr. Ayling saw about the stabling at the Railway Hotel, stabling being more difficult than garages in the present age, but Mr. Norman Longley soon had these converted to a four stall stable. The coachhouse was once more being used for what it was originally intended. The Host of the Railway Hotel even provided a harness room.

Mr. Truett brought with him an old London to York Waybill and this was copied to provide waybills for the passengers. He also had a timetable of "a great Sporting Event." This was brought up-to-date and copied with the local runs on it and the trains from Victoria etc. He then wrote to all his coaching friends enclosing a copy of the "Great Sporting Event" of the old Crawley Coach taking place from July 17th. to Bank Holiday.

Several more journeys had to be taken to London about horses. Some were out on film work, and would they be back in time? Letters to be written and driving to be arranged. The booking of the seats - that was another thing for who would undertake that? The staff of the George Hotel could not undertake the extra work, but it needed somewhere central. So, the Misses Warren offered to do their best, being quite inexperienced, but very interested in the event ever since Mr. James Farmer had mentioned that the coach might be running. But apart from asking if they might book seats on it, they had no idea of taking over £100 risked in this venture and it must be made to clear itself anyway. The advertisement for the hospital fair was worth a considerable sum, but they must not lose money.

Mr. Farmer sent a notice to the "Horse and Hound" announcing the event. Mr. Truett's friends, all coaching people came forward, letters were received by him booking seats and Box seats, also booking for driving the coach at three guineas (21 s.) for the day. He was kept very busy arranging these things and by the time he came to Crawley on Tuesday July 13th. with his whips and his coach horn, his coaching coats and grey top hat and everything relating to the correct procedure for driving a coach, he had the promise on bookings and donations due to him of £72. The thanks of the Crawley Hospital go out to these coaching people who gave just the start and confidence needed. But the people of Crawley must be made aware of it - the coach needed to be full everyday.

Crawley had been brought up on coaching traditions, at least the older generation, when part of the excitement of the day had been the arrival of the coach and watching the changing of the horses. But to travel by coach had seemed something beyond us, now Crawley was to run its own coach for a fortnight. For half a guinea we could experience the thrill of travelling behind horses on a coach, something we thought would never return to the Brighton Road. Or for a guinea we could travel further afield and join other passengers at lunch at some of the old coaching hostelries in the neighbourhood, although this was not included in the fare. Mr. Ayling had made arrangements with various hotels to accommodate the company on the different dates. Crawley must become coach minded - it must be a success. So the Misses Warren staged a small exhibition of old coaching prints, old coaching china and pictures of Mr. Alfred Vanderbilt with the "Venture" passing through Crawley. This aroused much interest and soon offers were arriving from everyone who possessed any pictures they thought would be of interest. As the exhibition grew so did the audience. From the first day there was such a friendly feeling about it all. "Holidays at Home," people travelled back 40-50 years in as many minutes and were once more in those peaceful days when Crawley was a village. People who felt they were back numbers suddenly became important explaining the photographs to the younger generation and the New Comers. This started on Monday night before the opening on the Saturday, and in less than a week we wanted to get the main bookings done.

Mr. W. Champkins came in with the "Waybills" programmes and bookings for ten seats he had obtained, and he explained the seating of the coach as we had not the faintest idea - apart from the Box seat, but we drew a plan so that there would be no mistake. Letters were written to anyone likely to take seats and everyone we met we asked and oh the joy of those first bookings! Those people who booked for the first few days on which the success of the whole venture depended. The opening day July 17th. there was not a booking apart from Mr. Truett's friends - nobody in Crawley wanted to go! Mr. Truett came in with his mail and the letters had to be answered.

Carter Paterson had to be telephoned about the horses, two that were chosen had not returned from film work so others had to be substituted. Horse boxes arrived at Three Bridges. We were part of the "Great Sporting Event." At last the horses were at Crawley, and two of them walked by the groom and accompanied by Mr. James Farmer and Mr. Sidney Truett went to fetch the coach. The great moment had arrived, the coach was on the road with the two wheelers, but the two headers were too big for the harness - so more telephoning - would the other two be back from filming in time to get here and be tried in the coach as these horses had never been driven four-in-hand before?

Then Thursday afternoon a message came through, the horses would be down the next day and we breathed again, but now we should need stabling for the other two horses as the railway could not take back the large horses that day. Mr. John Penfold was consulted once more and he suggested asking Rev. A.D. Wing for his stables at The Rectory and he willingly consented. The grey and the black headers arrived. There was very little time to try them out, but when that difficulty was over, we had everything except the passengers for the First Run.

Thursday night still not a booking. Mrs. Ayling said she would like to go. Miss Daisy Warren said she would make one but would stand out if the bookings came along. On Friday word came from our good friend Mr. Mellist (New York Times English Editor) that he had the promise of "The Times" to come and photograph the event. A

James Farmer driving - Sidney Truett on the box

fine achievement for a small place like Crawley. We still tried to get that coach filled by Saturday. Now we had three seats to spare and 3 guineas disappearing. Everything depended on the start. Mr. James Farmer was so busy with his hay making that he was unable to spare the time. We were so busy we hadn't time to worry much.

Letters were arriving from all parts of the country from readers of "The Horse and Hound" asking for further particulars. We answered them as time was short. Mr. Coop from Oldham wanted two days and hotel accommodation for his short holiday. He had travelled on the last coach from Dorchester to Hampton Court and he wanted to spend his short holiday on a coach again. The George Hotel was full but the Railway Hotel could take him, and so the answer was sent and he wired acceptance. Things were now looking up. We had written to several people suggesting that they booked the whole coach and chose their own private parties. Mrs. Lamb of Forest House, Pease Pottage - a good friend of the hospital - came forward and booked it for her little granddaughter's birthday party. Mr. Percy Nightingale, another good friend to everything connected with Crawley, booked it to take members of the Hazeldene Orchestra, also seats for his family another day, and the Misses Warren booked the whole coach on Wednesday 28th. July, for a Costume Drive, when their friends offered to book seats and start at 2 o' clock instead of 3.30 p.m. The coach was booked for the school children another afternoon.

Saturday morning arrived, waybills were ready and down the street comes the coach. It draws up with a flourish outside the George Hotel where the passengers wait. Mr. Sidney Truett having lost none of his skill in handling a team. Mr. James Farmer is on the brake, Mr. Harry Love is the guard and blows the posthorn. He, incidentally, spent his holiday on the Old Crawley Coach. He was on A.R.P. work in London, being on duty all Friday night and then came down for the opening run. Not only that, he had his only week's holiday the following week, and then the following week worked all nights and came down Tuesday, Thursday and Saturday, sleeping on the other three days. That was the sort of spirit that made the venture such a success. He had been guard on Mr. Bertram Mills' coach and was delighted to meet his old friend Mr. Impey (98, Ifield Road) who had worked with him in the "good old days," as a passenger.

The stepladder is brought out, and up go the passengers. Mrs. Lionel Herbert is on the box seat, this lady having owned and driven her own coach in the good old days of coaching. Mr. Geoff Hollebone was on the brake (Mr. Farmer having to return to Stumbleholm for hay making.) Other passengers being James Hopkins, Bill Thomas, Mr. Loader, Mrs. Frank Ayling, Miss Daisy Warren, A.V. Thorpe and Mr. D. MacArthur, and finally Mrs. Cross was persuaded to take the remaining seat.

Mr. Frank Ayling, Mr. Mellist and "The Times" photographer were busy, and then the brake was released, the groom and guard running with the leaders and off we go. The groom stumbling inside the coach and the guard climbing on to his seat and then holding on to the leather straps between the seats he plays one of his various tunes on the coachhorn. Now something is happening in Crawley that is not taking place anywhere else in the world at the present time. A four-in-hand coach is being run.

Everyone on the coach is expressing regret at the absence of the owner, but as it is the fourth year of war and the growing and harvesting of crops is so important, and it is a fine day, they admired him for putting duty before pleasure.

Off down the London Road goes the coach. How many years I wonder since one travelled that way before? Then we are on the by-pass road, an uncomfortable surface for horses. Mr. Sidney Truett shows in spite of 74 years he still deserves his title of the greatest professional coachman in England, managing his team with ease and skill. The horses seemed to know they were part of a great sport event, and meant to show off as though accustomed to this kind of thing all their lives, and may be they had inherited a feeling for coaching.

Well, Monday opened very auspiciously. There was an announcement in "The Times", the "Old Crawley Coach" had certainly arrived. There was a photograph in "The Daily Mirror" with Mr. Harry Love running behind, he having turned the horses on their way to the Lower Square...

For the remainder of the fortnight the coach was fully booked with people journeying from all over the country, just to ride on the coach. Coming from as far apart as Cornwall, Oldham and two American gentlemen on leave in London.

Cameo

CAPTAIN CARLTON V. BLYTHE

What glorious sporting history is bound up with the name of Carlton V. Blythe, which was indeed a name to conjure with in the "spacious" days of British sport," and in connection with coaching his name will live in history as one of the finest whips that ever tooled a coach and four over the Queen's highways. His name will ever be linked with the famous "Defiance" coach which in 1879 created a wonderful record, as on three days of the week it ran from Oxford, through London to Cambridge, and on Saturdays even extended to Cheltenham, making 112 miles in 12 hours on five days and 160 miles in 16 hours on the Saturday, a record without parallel in the history of the road. The "Defiance" in 1880 came on the London-Brighton Road, taking the Lewes, Uckfield, Tunbridge Wells and Sevenoaks route. The coach is illustrated in the Duke of Beaufort's "Badminton," which contains many eulogistic references to Captain Carlton V. Blythe. The following speaks for itself:- "Thank you very much for your letter of the 11th inst. (April, 1919), and I am glad to hear that old Carlton Blythe is pretty well. He was always the kindest of hosts and a splendid coachman, a good and loyal friend, and I always had the greatest admiration for him and his energy was unsurpassed. Give him my best love and respects. - Believe me, yours truly, "Lonsdale.'"

Captain Blythe was one of those on the coach when James Selby made the memorable drive from London to Brighton and back in eight hours. It was at Ascot that a bet of £5,000 to £500 was laid against the feat being accomplished. The race took place on the 18th July, 1888, the start being from Hatchett's Hotel to the Ship Hotel,

Brighton, and back. The start was at 10 a.m. and the feat was accomplished by 5.50, so the bet was won with 10 minutes to spare.

Captain Blythe had the honour of sharing the coaching tour made in France by His Majesty King Edward (then Prince of Wales). Though famous as a coaching man, Captain Blythe had all the sporting activities of "a man about Town." He was a member of the famous Pelican Club, the National Sporting Club and the Corinthian. A story typical of him is taken from *Sporting Tit-Bits*: "Captain Blythe is the hero of a great story that is told of him. Once he was in Heath's, the hat shop in St. James' Street, where his hat was being ironed. A certain Archbishop of Canterbury entered and, taking the bareheaded Captain Blythe for a shopman, handed him his shovel hat and said, 'Have you got a hat like this?' 'No, I haven't,' answered Blythe, to the surprise and horror of the Archbishop, 'and if I had I'm damned if I'd put the pesky thing on my head.'"

Since living at Crawley, at Tilgate Forest Lodge, Captain Blythe has endeared himself to all in his immediate neighbourhood. He has been strenuously working to secure a footpath alongside the London-Brighton Road at Pease Pottage. He has placed the matter before the Ministry of Transport and the East Sussex County Council, and has been assured that such a footpath will be made. None will forget his "snappy" lines in *The Times*:-

> "Council awake; and cease to snore,
>
> A path provide, or sleep no more."

An hour spent with this genial English gentleman is indeed a time to be treasured, for he is a fountain of sport of the Victorian period. By the way, Captain Blythe invariably wears a red, white and blue ribbon in his buttonhole, and at the mention of the Royal Family he never fails to raise his hat.

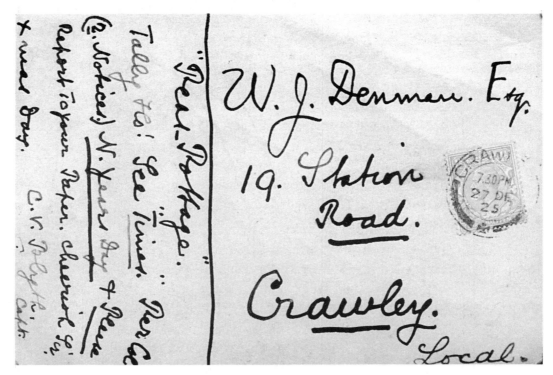

PEASE POTTAGE " DEATH TRAP ".

To all users of the famous ' Brighton Road,' the efforts of Captain Carlton V. Blyth, the famous old Coaching Man, to secure the provision of a footpath between Crawley and Pease Pottage will meet with unanimous approval.

Captain Blyth lives Mid-way between Crawley and Handcross and is therefore right in the midst of what is locally termed the Pease Pottage "Death Trap."

Last Easter Week no fewer than 7 serious accidents occurred on this stretch of road. With the promise of thousands of additional cars this summer the position of residents can be imagined when it is stated that at the recent census taken in August by the Ministry of Transport, lasting over one week, with 12 hours to the day no fewer than 150 Cars passed per hour, (16,000 in the week.)

Captain Blyth has had prepared the enclosed photograph showing a very dangerous point where three roads converge on to the Main Road, which is 18 ft. in width. Throughout the whole length of road there is a wide strip of waste land, which is under the jurisdiction of the East Sussex County Council, so that the expense of making the path would be very low. That Council refuse to take steps despite resolutions from all local Councils and petitions from inhabitants. All users of the road should send direct to the Ministry of Transport :-

Captain Carlton V. Blyth,

Pease Pottage,

CRAWLEY.

will give any particulars required.

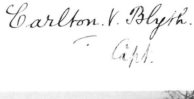

PEAS POTTAGE
— DEATH TRAP —

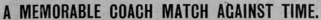

Crawley.

The Old Saddlers' Shop

In the many books which mention Crawley one reads of the George Hotel, The Ancient Priests House, The Old Tudor Cottage etc. but so far as can be ascertained, never yet has been mentioned the Saddlers' Shop which adjoins The George Hotel. That this building is as old as The George itself there is no possible shadow of a doubt, for the earliest print obtainable (1516) shows the hotel and the shop (though there is no indication of its being a shop) side by side with a small cottage standing in the square.

The building is worthy of thorough examination, its timber being rich and mellowed, and as the exterior has always been well preserved the building presents a neat appearance. The roof is of Horsham slabs and the most inexperienced observer can see that the place is old. It has never been ascertained as to whether at one time the house was a part of The George Hotel, but certainly the grandfather of the present owners was proprietor of the George Hotel (*this must have been held by licence*) and the Old Saddlers Shop. It will probably cause surprise to the public to learn that some 75 - 80 years ago (1855) there used to be a "drive" in between the hotel and the Saddlers Shop. A building connecting the cottage and the hotel was built and used as a decorators shop.

The Saddlers Shop is the home of the "Miller" family, though when they first came to reside there is not known, but sufficient for our readers is the fact that it was upwards of 200 years ago. The business stationery states that the business was "established in 1777," but when searching for data for this article an old ledger was found dealing with accounts in 1721! So that for once the usual methodical Nat Miller did not get his figures right, for obviously accounts could not be owing to a firm that did not come into existence until 56 years later.

A few years ago alterations were being made to the inner side of the roof and some most interesting discoveries were made. A find of great value was a gold and enamel snuff box, the inscription showing it belonged to a Captain, but owing to the fancy flourishes of the writing it would be a matter of great difficulty to find out the surname. Papers, coins and books were also found. The present "Nat" is naturally proud of the many things that have come down from his ancestors.

The Mr. Nat Miller mentioned as the grandfather, was a man of an extraordinary character. Not only was he a saddler by trade, but he was also a farrier (as those who had a good knowledge of animals were always called by old folks) and was much in request when sickness occurred. (His old instruments are carefully preserved.) He was also a hunting man and has left a collection of silver mounted hoofs etc. A breeder of dogs, he won many cups and other trophies. He was also the first Secretary of the Crawley Prosecuting Society, and has left behind a collection of window bills offering rewards for the detention of offenders. (These I hope to give on another occasion.) He was probably the most prominent man in this district, and his books show that he was a beautiful penman. He left many things for his grandson, and one thing in particular is very striking, a collection of "Cats eyes" for buttons. For these Mr. Miller has had innumerable offers, and large sums have been proffered for the gold and enamel snuff box.

Mr. Milton Miller succeeded to the business and to him must be credited the alterations which led to the large show shop, at the south end of the house after the death of widow Hards and old Mrs. Russell (Fred Russell's grandmother) who lived at the corner cottage alongside Ifield Lane until nearly one hundred years of age.

Like his father, Mr. Milton Miller was a great lover of animals and bred ponies and dogs. He was also Honorary Secretary to the Prosecuting Society, and his books are a model of neatness.

The old shop has served the whole district for quite two centuries and naturally in the days of horses "Millers" was a house of call for everybody. In his books, Mr. Miller has the names of royalty and half of the peerage, the Corinthians and bucks of other days, and in the coaching era was responsible for the upkeep of the harness and equipment generally.

Mr. Miller specialised in fighting dogs and was the breeder of the famous "Rattler", a dog that was never beaten, and eventually fought a young tiger at Crabbet Park. Rattler killed the tiger, but was himself badly mauled about and never fully recovered. From the story told to me by men concerned in the fight (This was when dog fighting was looked upon as a sport and quite fashionable.) It would appear that the Squire of Crabbet had betted that he could place in the pit a dog that would face and defeat anything on four legs, of its own weight. The Squire sought Mr. Miller and Rattler was selected to uphold the honour of Crabbet. He was a pure white dog with cropped ears, and Mr. Miller has splendid pictures of the famous dog, and also his "lead", which is a beautiful piece of workmanship, the "slip" being shaped something like a barrel and in four parts, each part being engraved with the name of one of Mr. Miller's four sons.

After the death of Rattler he was laid to rest in the Dogs Valhalla in Burley Wood, on the estate, and on his memorial were these lines:

> O Rattler bold, thy blood is cold
> And I with thee ne'er more will hold
> Thy blood and fame were always good
> And you shall lie in Burley Wood.

To those who love ancient things then the Old Saddlers' Shop is a treasure house. To the visitor to Crawley I would say be sure to visit the Middle Square and you will be surrounded by houses centuries old and none with a more interesting history than the Old Saddlers' Shop.

Next to Millers is the establishment of the Smith family. According to records the Smith family business started trading in 1724. So we have two families who have been in business consistently for over 200 years. Originally there was just a narrow space between the two establishments which became known as Ifield Lane, when customers traversed to the rear of the buildings to trade with the blacksmith. Trees were a continuation from Tilgate Forest right down the street to this point. In later years when these were cut down, one tree remained very close to Smiths shop. It has been handed down to us that when the Ifield Road was made by Mayor Pipon in 1880, it was decided to let this Oak tree to remain, but afterward it was thought the tree would cause trouble. All the branches were cut off, the top of the trunk levelled and dose of something given it to kill the tree. The Lord of the Manor (Ifield) refused to allow the soil to be disturbed, and he was angry at the destruction of the tree. Moreover, the tree was a source of revenue to the Lord of the Manor, as on Fair days, those who used it for a hitching place for cattle had to pay a certain sum. After the tree had been encased, a large iron ring was inserted, and on Fair days an oak bough was placed in the ring and the Lord of the Manor, or whom he might appoint, was allowed to sell beer up to a certain hour at the sign of the "Bough". This privilege was for Fair days only.

Though a matter of interest to antiquarians, the present day public would benefit considerably did the "Sign of the Bough" disappear, for at least three feet more space would be given on one of the most dangerous turnings between London and Brighton.

The last pay-gate house was in Ifield Road, and swung between what is now the entrances to Messrs N. Miller's Saddler, and J. Millers blacksmiths yards. The house was a long one story building and the keeper "Liner" Miles, a somewhat pugnacious individual. After the gate had been demolished, Miles assisted Mr. Miller with his ponies and dogs.

Millers shop was demolished in 1939 and Ifield Road corner widened.

This is the field where now stands Spensers Road. The cottage on the left is 10, Ifield Road.

Crawley Fire Brigade

With the passing of March (1932) passed away one of the oldest public service institutions in the County of Sussex; the Crawley Volunteer Fire Brigade passed, that is, from the "voluntary" basis to one "on the rates." It has been decided that for fire protection purposes Crawley, Ifield, Rusper and the Worth ward of Worth Parish shall combine and become a Fire Protection Committee, on the basis of a penny rate on the parishes concerned. From a purely volunteer body managing themselves, and making themselves responsible to the ratepayers of the parishes named for protection from fire, and the said ratepayers will not as in the past has been the case with many owners of property, escape with a trivial subscription, but will pay according to their possessions.

With this passing of the Volunteer Brigade a few particulars of history should be of interest.

The brigade was founded on 30 July 1866, when a Mr. R. Little presided over a public meeting held at the Railway Hotel. The meeting had been called by "Mark Lemon Esq." (the first Editor of "Punch") who resided at Vine Cottage, Crawley. We are not told what took place, except that the meeting was adjourned until 10th. August 1866. At this meeting Mr. Mark Lemon presided and announced that his friend, Mr. Thomas Bousfield, had consigned an engine from London to Crawley as a gift, with which to fight fires in the neighbourhood. Mr. Ernest Stanford writes:

> "In these days the engine would have provoked great amusement, for it was an old Phillips manual made in 1774. It was nearly a century old when it arrived in Crawley to spend its last days. Originally it was the Parish engine of St. Andrews under-shaft, London, and on the side of it was painted the name of the churchwarden of that Parish. No doubt years before it had been the pride of the parish beadle whose manifold duties, as Dickens tells us, included that of Chief Fireman."

The Brigade consisted in those days of 30 men, Captain (Mr. R. Little), president and Hon Surgeon Mr. T.H. Martin, Messrs J. Mitchell, S. Bowers, J. Ockenden, C. Smith and N. Bartley with 22 engineers, and no doubt as they drilled and waited maybe they almost hoped for the great day when they could show how proficient they were. The first fire occurred in July 1867 at Langley Farm, Ifield. "The alarm was given by the ringing of a handbell at the engine house. One can readily imagine the excitement that prevailed when the gallant 30 rushed to the Fire Station, to do or die. Many of them were shopkeepers and no doubt the fire paralysed the trade of the village, customers went unserved, work was left unfinished, and all roads led to the fire station. Horses had to be obtained from anyone who would lend them, and eventually a start was made, the villagers and children following on foot or on any vehicle that would carry them."

In this year the Brigade had three fires and in 1868, two in 1869, none in 1870 and one in 1871.

When the brigade were about to start drills, it was thought that it would be far more spectacular if music was supplied, so the Crawley Volunteer Fire Brigade Band was formed in the same month, and like the brigade has continued ever since under several names. It is now called the Crawley Town Military Band. The Snellings were the leaders of the band and continued to be so down to recent years. It is recorded that in the summer when the brigade had a full-dress rehearsal, the band marched in front of the brigade to West Green Pond for the purpose of the brigade undergoing wet drill. It was a gala day or rather evening. A large quantity of hose had been purchased following the disastrous fire at Mr. Chester's, Ifield, when it was found that the hose was not of sufficient length to reach the stream.

When the great evening came it was found that the new hose was of sufficient length to reach Mr. Spencer Smith's corner from West Green Pond, and the engine was able to throw water right across the Market Square. The band played suitable selections while the officials and brigade were congratulated on their efficiency.

During the Brigade's long period of service many amusing things happened. Once when the engine was being rushed along, pulled by a pair of farm steeds at the gallop, a farm waggon loaded with manure crossed the road and some of the firemen were flung into the waggon load, with dire results to their uniforms and dignity.

On another occasion, whilst galloping to a fire, it was discovered one of the firemen had a top boot on and one ordinary boot. Of course, this could not be allowed, so the firefighters turned around, galloped back to the fireman's abode and he soon became properly dressed. On yet another occasion the fire concerned certain haystacks, a terribly long job. The brigade was on its way when one of the superintendents found his "baccy" box was nearly empty. He suggested that as the fire would be a longish job, he should be allowed to replenish. Again a return was made to Crawley where the baccy box was well filled.

"Whether this century old engine went out of public favour is not recorded, but a few years later a more up to date engine was obtained from Hackney. This was 60 years old, and for many years gave good service in the district. This engine was housed in a better building, and in a turret above it was hung the bell which could be rung by pulling a rope in the station below. This, however, was not always satisfactory, for occasionally, when an excited messenger arrived to give the alarm, he sometimes pulled the bell so violently that the rope would break and it would be necessary for someone to climb on to the roof and swing the bell from that perilous perch, much to the amusement of the assembled folk.

On what must have one of the Brigade's unlucky days, the person who gave the alarm was so excited that he pulled the bell from its fastenings and it smashed on to the roof. When eventually the fire brigade reached the scene of the outbreak there was no water nearer than ½ a mile, and when at length a connection was made the hosepipe burst."

In those days fire fighting was often a difficult and arduous task, called out sometimes in bitter cold to travel over ice covered roads to answer the call for help. Sometimes the call had to go unanswered because of roads being impassable through weather conditions.

Many years ago the Brigade was called to a fire in a farmyard where all the straw had become ignited and was seriously threatening a thatched cottage. Naturally in the excitement of the moment the occupants thought only of the house and its contents and all efforts were directed towards saving the furniture. On the arrival of the Brigade it was discovered that a pen of sheep had been forgotten and the poor creatures were so badly burned that 40 of them had to be destroyed.

On another occasion a family was awakened by the frantic barking of a dog which happened to be upstairs with them. They awoke and found the lower part of the house ablaze and just managed to escape a terrible death themselves, but our firemen afterwards found the charred body of the dog which had perished in the flames.

Water shortage is always a difficulty in country fires and sometimes it is necessary to go quite long distances for a very inadequate supply. One mansion in our district years ago was completely demolished because of this. Sometimes the water that is available is in inaccessible places where it would be impossible for a fire engine to reach. Recently we had such an experience when certain railway property was afire. Realising that it would be impossible to get to the outbreak with an engine, we got together all available chemical extinguishers and carried them to the outbreak on the footplate of a railway engine - truly a novel fire engine!

The coming of the motor car brought a new problem for the village fire brigade. They were introduced to this new problem under very unusual circumstances. The brigade were on their way to attend a Church Parade at a neighbouring town when they saw a motor car, the engine of which was well alight. The owner of the car must have thought a miracle had happened for a brigade to come up, unsummoned and in a country road. Realising that water was useless someone must have had a brain wave. Noticing a heap of manure in a farm quite close the men ran and fetched armfuls of it and threw it on to the engine, eventually smothering the flames, much to the delight of the motorist, who, no doubt, had given all up as lost. After an adjournment to an inn further on the journey, to celebrate their triumph a much soiled and no doubt an evil smelling brigade proceeded to the Church Parade.

These are but a few incidents gathered from the records of our village brigade. Today, we boast of equipment second to none for a town our size. Gone is the bell and now the alarm is given by a powerful electric siren. We have a Turbin motor pump, capable of pumping 250 gallons of water per minute; also chemical apparatus for motor cars and petrol fires, every convenience for life saving, smoke respirators, and almost everything necessary to maintain a high state of efficiency."

Among interesting personalities connected with the brigade was Mr. T.H. Martin, who married a daughter of Mark Lemon. He was Hon. Surgeon for very many

The Crawley Volunteer Fire Brigade have held their annual meeting, at which two very important subjects came up for discussion, viz., that of obtaining horses for the engines and an increased supply of hose. These subjects are important ones, and it is to be hoped that both wants will soon be fully supplied. It is not very pleasant in case of a fire to know that two good engines would be practically useless for the want of horses to draw them quickly to the scene of conflagration, and it will be in the recollection of many that the want of hose was the cause of the fire gaining the upper hand at Ifield Park. It will thus be seen that without these necessaries the brigade will not be by any means so serviceable as they would be if they were fully and properly equipped, whilst it is quite possible that much property might be sacrificed, and possibly many lives, which would otherwise be saved. I may venture to hope that the mere mention of the fact that the balance sheet shows a deficiency of £53 19s. 3d. upon the working of last year will be sufficient to cause the inhabitants to rally round the brigade, and by their contributions show that they appreciate the services of a useful and self-denying body of men, who heartily deserve the support and encouragement of their fellow citizens.

* * * *

There is, however, another subject closely allied with the question of horsing the fire engines, which the inhabitants of Crawley would do well to take into their immediate consideration, and that is the supply of water. At present there is no public supply of water for the town, and if a fire was to occur a good fire engine and an efficient fire brigade would be of little or no use without an abundant supply of water, and it is therefore to be hoped that attention will be immediately given to this so as to be well provided for in case of any emergency.

* * * *

P.A.

Fire Station, Crawley. E638

P.A.

On parade

Funeral of Mr. Snelling - bandmaster

P.A.

1912

Decorated Float 1937 Coronation

courtesy of Mrs. Strevett

Fire!—& the Engine Was A-Weigh

By RICHARD JONES

CRAWLEY, the Sussex town which has only one man qualified to drive its fire engine, loves a joke. Within three months it has enjoyed three of the best.

The first, when it was discovered that no member of the fire brigade had a licence to drive the engine. Then three out of four men failed to pass the driving test.

Yesterday Crawley had the biggest laugh of all.

Fire broke out in Horsham-road. The syren sent its wailing note echoing over the town.

Cupboard Was Bare!

As one, 13 men raced to the station prepared to give their new engine its baptism of fire.

Alas! when they got there, breathless and excited, there was no engine! They took the trailer pump and put out the fire.

Their pride, the engine, had been taken to Horley to be weighed! And the only qualified driver, Fireman E. Strevett, was with it.

1930s

years and later was succeeded by his son-in-law Alderman S.P. Matthews, J.P. whose son in turn Dr. S.R. Matthews is now second officer. John Ockenden succeeded Mr. R. Little as Captain, and right down to the present day the Ockendens have been connected with the brigade, Bart Ockenden having just retired having reached the age of 65. A. Bowers has been connected with the brigade since its inception; Supt Charles Bowers also just retired is one of the smartest men in the brigade.

Today the brigade is considered to be the finest equipped village brigade in the Kingdom, as it has sufficient personnel to equip two brigades. Its first-line fighter, a powerful Dennis engine, can throw 480 gallons per minute when at full strength. The second engine is not so powerful as this but an excellent machine. There are a Ford tender and everything necessary to cope with an outbreak - a fire escape, ladders, and a very large amount of hose, the whole value at £2,000. This wonderful state of affairs is due to the untiring work of Mr. Ernest Stanford, whose valuable work cannot be too highly appraised.

The Old Squatters Cottage

In Small's-lane, Crawley, stands a little cottage with a history. It is only one storey high and consists of a long room with a smaller sleeping apartment at one end. The roof is very low pitched, and evidently no architect was ever consulted before the place was erected. Yet it has been a home - a real home - to the ever respected Leadbetter and Tullett families. The little place is situated in a pretty lane within a couple of stones' throw of Crawley High-street, but is as far from noise and smells of oil as though motors never existed. The lane leads from St. John's-road round into Crawley High-street.

A visitor walking past this little cottage would never dream that at one time it was the high road to West Sussex. The road left the main London to Brighton road near the "Tree", and came right through Small's-lane to the Ifield-road, where now is St. John's-road. The road from the High-street to West Green had not then been made, owing to the fact that a large pond lay right across what is now the highway, and extended from Victoria-road nearly to Small's lane. Springfield-road had not then been thought of (of course there was no railway for some 150 to 200 years after the Squatter's Cottage was built) and Goffs Park-road still consisted of meadows. This leaves us but the old main road up Small's-lane.

The "Squatter's" Cottage is, of course, built on what was once common land, and, to put it quite bluntly, land that was stolen from the public. The "Squatter," however, was but copying thousands of others throughout the land, though the word "enclosure" was used to cover the stealing of acres of public land by the "big" people. The ground on which the cottage stands is some 50 yards in length and about 12 yards wide at the north end, and tapers somewhat at the other end.

The house itself (as has been gathered from the foregoing) was built by the Squatter and his family, and it is plain that they never possessed any professional skill. The Squatter was named Tullett, and a descendant still occupies the Cottage. The late Mrs. Tullett, who was upwards of 80 at her death, was able to give first-hand information to the late Dr. Martin in respect of the traffic passing up the road. Mrs. Tullett informed Crawley's historian that "she could remember back'ards better'n for'ard." People passing along the lane should try to visualise the traffic passing up the road en route to Shoreham to fetch chalk, etc., with which to make roads, and the like. Practically everything had to be fetched from Shoreham (such as coal), this being the chief seaport of the south. This old lady was probably the last person to see traffic passing up the road. The place should be visited, for the old-world garden, is very quaint and well worth inspecting.

Before leaving the old place one must mention that one member of the family, James Leadbetter, was known far and wide for his skill with birds and vermin. Had there been an official rat catcher in those days he was the man for the task. To the whole

courtesy of Mrs Langridge

James Lidbetter's Cottage

Miss Tripp's Cottage

courtesy of P. Gwynne

of the district he was known as "Jimmy Swobber", and to call him Mr. Leadbetter would have caused much astonishment.

Turning to the right on reaching the top of Smalls-lane and walking some quarter of a mile one sees another "Squatter's Cottage". This has been more substantially built, the lower portion being of brick and the upper portion of wood, and the whole tarred over. This belonged to a member of the Leadbetter family, "Will", who also had the wooden houses (doubtless acquired in the same way) just where now stands 86 and 88, Ifield-road. From the records of the Manor of Ifield: "William Lidbetter of the Parish of Ifield hath enclosed a small parcel of land lying on the waste situate on the south side of the road leading from Crawley to the village of Ifield." dated 11 June 1827. The cottage now in the occupation of a descendant is a picturesque place with clipped yew hedges. On the opposite side of the road is yet another "Squatter' Cottage" where Mrs. and Miss Tripp now live, and the whole of the large slice of land lying between the road and the boundary ditch is acquired land.

One question has never yet been solved. The road which ran up Smalls Lane past the old "Squatter's Cottage" was a public highway. Who enclosed the road and adjacent land? And how did it become private property?

Friends Meeting House

In a quiet secluded spot about a mile from Crawley stands an unpretentious looking building, partly hidden by trees, but which for some eight months of the year is a perfect picture of quiet beauty. Few who pass would guess that they are looking at a building of historical interest, a building which should be held in veneration and pride - The Society of Friends Meeting House. The building just off the busy highway, being situated in Langley Lane, has defied the change of centuries both in structure and environment. But no one visiting this pretty spot can visualise the scenes of distress and misery caused in the past by the religious bigotry of those days.

The Society of Friends held their first meetings at Bonwycks Place, Ifield in 1646, and in the kitchen may still be seen the fixed oak seats, with panelling exactly as they were nearly 300 years ago. The Society grew so rapidly that in 1676 it was decided by George Fox, the founder of the Society and William Penn together on the necessity of building the present Meeting House.

The building material however is of exceptional interest. The walls are built of stones taken from the ruins of Slaugham Place formerly the stronghold of the great patrician family of Coverts, who at one time wielded such immense power in Sussex. The roof of the building is of Sussex stone "slabs". In the centre of the room is a massive oak pillar supporting stout oak beams which branch out again to other oak beams which support the roof. The inside fittings are of plain deal panelling with a raised gallery for

the minister at the end. Plain fixed seats run around the room and plain seats run down the centre.

Meetings for worship have been held regularly ever since it was built. They are held on the Sabbath in the same way as of old, there being no pre-arranged service, but Bible readings, preaching and prayers with intervals for private meditation. On Sunday evening a gospel service is held with plenty of singing to the strains of an harmonium.

In the early days there was great persecution of the Friends and the records often mention that the meetings were broken up and the adult members taken to Horsham jail, because under the "Conventical Act" it was unlawful to meet for worship except at the Parish Church. One can imagine the scenes when the little children saw their parents and friends dragged away to jail, their only offence being their worship of God according to their conscience instead of by Acts of Parliament.

It would appear (at this time) strange, could we witness the assembling of the congregation of those early days. Mr. Joseph Cheal has kindly given me the following particulars:

"In olden days menfolk went to the meetings on farm horses with their wives riding pillion behind, or whole families would come in farm waggons or bullock carts through muddy lanes, but now may be seen pedestrians, cyclists and motorists coming

in from many miles around. The old stone mounting blocks still remain in the yard an object of much interest."

While it was well known that both Fox and Penn were associated with Ifield, that other well known figure beloved in the Quaker world, Elizabeth Fry the great philanthropist, had no mention. But I was approached by a well known Crawley lady, who has an extremely valuable book "The Diary of Elizabeth Fry". I have been permitted to give the following extracts from the Diary:

> "This day, the last sixth day of the 8th month of 1837, I visited Ifield Meeting House and was surprised to find nearly a hundred labourers in smock frocks awaiting us. I addressed them, and later addressed another meeting in the Inn (which is nearby) and most attentive they were." On 16th October 1838 Elizabeth Fry paid another visit and in addition to addressing the gathering in the Meeting House "a large concourse had met on Ifield Common and here I gave another address."

Now we know that three of the leaders of the Quakers visited Ifield Meeting House. The Diary, too, mentions "Garton's smithy adjoining the Meeting House". According to all other available accounts Garton is described as a miller, so either there have been two Gartons or the aforesaid Garton carried on two businesses. In a book

P.A.

GEORGE FOX'S CHAIR, FRIENDS' MEETING HOUSE IFIELD 1676

QUAKER'S WEDDING AT IFIELD.—On Thursday, Mr S. J. Reynolds, of Croydon, and Miss Emily Isabel Heathcote, whose native place is Essex, but who has for some time resided at Croydon, were united in holy wedlock at the Friends' Meeting House, Ifield, in accordance with the custom peculiar to the Society of Friends. The party were conveyed to Ifield from Crawley in carriages provided by Mr P. Tracy, of the Railway Hotel. Mr A. J. Crossfield, of Redhill, acted as registrar. The marriage ceremony was witnessed by a large number of the friends of the bridal party. The wedding breakfast was served by Mrs Gates, at Ye Old White Hart Hotel, Crawley, and was of a most *recherche* character, the table being laid out in a most tasteful manner, and the repast gave the utmost satisfaction to those who sat down. The bride and bridegroom left Crawley by an afternoon train.

of Quaker stories written by Mary Robinson appears the following: "Taken from William Garton of Ifield, one payer of oxen worth £14 for a tythe of £7, nothing returned."

The well known Quaker family of Crawley, the Robinsons, donated monies from Quaker Friends to enable the West Green Schools to be built in 1831, and later bought a large plot of land in New Road again with the assistance of their friends for the British School in 1854.

Returning to the founders of the Meeting House, William Penn formerly lived at Worminghurst, Sussex, but later left Sussex and went to America where he founded the State of Pennsylvania.

Nearby to the Meeting House is the burial place, and it is an ideal resting place, surrounded by trees and with flowers springing up. No one would suspect that this pretty secluded place could be of such historical interest. It stands a monument of peace, that peace which has triumphed over all religious bigotry, undisturbed by the acts of those fanatics who would force their views upon others. Persecution, like the persecutors, have long passed away and forgotten, but the little Meeting House remains a monument to the sturdy God fearing sect.

Ifield Parish Church

The Parish Church of Ifield, dedicated to St. Margaret, is just the typical "country" church, standing in beautiful surroundings and with an atmosphere of calm and repose, "far from the madding crowd," and giving one the feeling of restfulness and peace. True, the old-world feeling has a slight shock to see a modern clock in the steeple, which, though of much use to the village, seems sadly out of place in this ancient building. That St. Margaret's *is* ancient there is, fortunately, no question of doubt, for both architecturally and documentarily the date can be fixed to within a little when Ifield first had a church, as there was a church at Ifield in 1180, but the St. Margaret's we know was founded by Sir John de Ifield and his wife, who died in 1317. The church figures in the grant confirmed by Bishop Seffrid in favour of Rusper Priory. The Bishop held the See of Chichester from 1180 to 1204: consequently there must have been a church at Ifield in 1200. This church was, however, handed over to the Nuns of Rusper at the request of William de Braose, whose family evidently built it, and may have been transformed or rebuilt by Sir John de Ifield.

In a most interesting and instructive lecture given on Ifield Church by Dr. H. Mosse (who kindly presented me with a copy) he advanced the theory that the first church was of timber built walls, and with a thatched roof similar to the church at Greenstead, Essex, which was erected 900 years ago. Dr. Mosse pointed out that there are architectural features which bear out the fact that the church existed in the closing years of the 12th century. (1) The font is late Norman - 1195-1200; (2) the practically rectangular slope of the chancel roof; and (3) the presence of three stone coffins, a feature of the 12th and early 13th centuries. Father Anselm in his little book dealing with the Catholic churches in the district gives the following: "The earliest document I can find treating at any length of Ifield is "The taxation of the Vicarage of Ifield" in favour of Rusper Priory, to be found in Bishop Sherburn's Register. It is as follows: To all the faithful in Christ who read or listen to this present writing, Master Laurence de Summercote, official of the Lord Bishop of Chichester, everlasting health in the Lord. Be it known to all men that this is the taxation of the Vicarage of Ifield, made by our authority between the Prioress and Convent of Rusper and Alan of Crawley, Chaplain, viz.: that the said Alan and his successors shall receive all tithes of corn and hay of John the son of Emme, and all tithes of Ewerthe (Howards Place or possibly Ewhurst). The said Alan and his successors in perpetuity, shall receive all tithes of the land which the said Peter (mentioned now for the first time apparently) John and Gilbert held at the time of this taxation, there being reserved to the said Nuns the tithes of all lands already cleared, or to be cleared, of wood. The said Alan and his successors shall receive,

Facing page: 1886. Yellow door is The Plough Inn.

Drawn by William Phillips ARCA   *P.A.*

nevertheless, all offerings made at the Altar of Ifield, all tithes of Mills already erected or to be erected, and all the small tithes of the said church which are not, in this document, reserved to the Nuns. Moreover, the said Alan his successors shall received tithes of the corn which the Nuns have in the Parish of Ifield, but not of the hay, while all other tithes of corn, hay, and pasture of the whole Parish of Ifield and the Principale Legatum (The Principale Legatum, or principal bequest, would seem to be the best beast, or other chattel, to which the Church became entitled on the death of a parishioner) shall belong to the Prioress and the Convent. The said Alan and his successors shall give annually, to the Sacristan of Rusper, five pounds of wax on the Feast of Palms (Palm Sunday) and shall pay the procurations, synodals and other fees. This taxation both parties agree to hold good for ever. In testimony of which we hand this present writing to each party signed with each other's seal and with the seal of Office. Dated at Rusper, 18th July, 1247.

The original church consisted of a nave only, the aisles being of later date, probably added a hundred years after. The church has many features. On the north side of the nave is an altar tomb ornamented with quaterfoils containing roses, the effigy of a Knight crosslegged, in armour of the time of Edward II resting on a lion couchant. On the opposite side is the effigy of the Knight's wife on another altar tomb, ornamented with quaterfoils, in one of which is a plain shield, with her feet on a lion and her head on a cushion supported by two angels. The two figures are in costumes of the late 13th century. "Dallaway" writes "as they coincide with the style of the church, they may be very safely considered to be the founders of the building, and probably were the effigies of Sir John de Ifield and his Lady. They are unquestionably the most interesting monuments of the kind in the Rape of Bramber." The crossed legs of the Knight would

Ifield Church.

P.A.

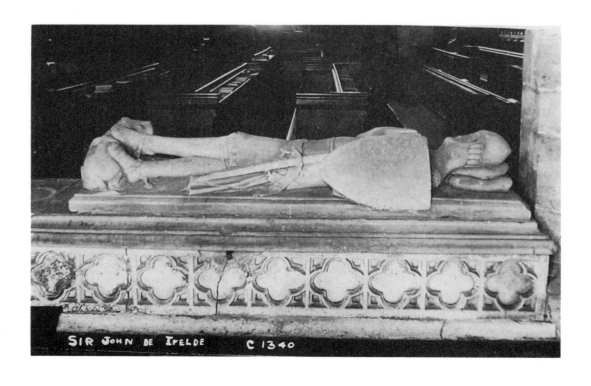

SIR JOHN DE IFELDE   C 1340

show that he was a Crusader and had fought in the Holy Land to wrest the Cross from the domination of the Crescent. Having now established our claim that "St. Margarets" is an *old* church, we will deal fully with the many interesting things connected with the sacred building.

On entering the western door, the first thing that must strike the visitor is the lofty aspect of the ceiling of the steeple, for though one would, naturally, expect it to be high, yet it gives the feeling of an enormous height. Two bells are used to call the faithful to worship, though evidently at one time only one was used, as the bells are dated 1600 and 1618 and were made by the Eldridges. It would appear that the bells have had more than one place, as at one time they hung in the gable end of the nave.

The nave roof is worthy of attention, as there is no ceiling, and the work shown is beautifully done. Dr. H. Mosse writes: "The nave being unceiled, the inner framing of the lofty and steeply pitched roof is visible and is an excellent example of the "trusser rafter" style, and is quite one of the glories of the church." There are many interesting windows, in memoriams to the Spencer and Lewin families and to Mr. Wood, of "The Court," Ifield, a one-time Lord of the Manor, and for thirty-four years a churchwarden. The memorial to the late Mr. W. Shepperson (who died in 1922) is a window in the north aisle, and also the restored side chapel. The many alterations in the church at various times have seen most interesting things done away with. For instance, it is stated that in 1755 the bow pews from St. Margaret's, Westminster, were placed in Ifield Church; but in 1884 these were demolished, and the present pews installed, this being done because the church became free and open and "box pews" not the property of certain families. The old box pews, however, were not completely destroyed, as the woodwork, or rather the panels, now line the walls of the aisles and tower.

To quote Dr. Mosse again: "Within the scararium on the south side is a defaced early English piscina but no sedilia (seat) for the ministers. There is another piscina in the north aisle chapel. The low side window is seen from the interior to be deeply recessed. Formerly it was unglazed, but closed by a shutter. Its purpose was to emit the sound of the handbell rung at the chief part of the sacred office to call the attention of the workers. The lectern is a curious piece of village carpentry of 19th century date, being made up of Caryatidean pieces of evident primo-Carolean craftsmanship representing 'The Fall' and 'The Incarnation.' It is said to have formed part of the Holy Table. The front of the Choir stalls contains portions of the former Communion railing, new 'poppyheads' being added to make up the discs in 1884. The screen set up to form the vestry in the north west corner was constructed from pieces of the old County Oak which to the great regret of all classes was felled in 1844. The poorbox, attached to a pew-end near the entrance, bears the date 1742. Within the tower hangs the Royal Arms, *temp.* George II., and an escutcheon bearing the initials of Charles II. These insignia were ordered to be set up at the Restoration (1660) - they have recently been renovated.

The north doorway has a lovely old porch entrance containing a list of the Vicars since 1288, and this entrance is typical of old country churches. Within the church lie the remains of many notable families. There is the Holles family whose founder, Denzil, was created Baron de Ifield in 1661. He was the second son of Earl Clare, whose second wife belonged to the famous Covert family, of whose huge estate Ifield formed a part. A brass tablet in the chancel is "In memoriam" to the brothers John and William Makerith, whose deaths occurred at 1595 and 1599. Other tablets record the deaths of Spencers and Lewins and another is to the memory of John and Elizabeth Seyliard. The ironmasters who formerly lived in the district are represented by memorials to the Pecks and Gales, who were notable ironmasters from the Worth district.

The churchyard has many interesting features. The lychgate is not old, but forms a fitting entrance to the beautiful God's acre. On the left, as one enters (immediately in front of the lychgate is the war memorial), is a huge Yew Tree beneath whose shadows lie honoured men and women. Between the lychgate and the Yew Tree is a simple marble curb beneath which lie Mark Lemon (of *Punch* fame) and his wife Mary; and within a few yards is the grave of the ever beloved Dr. T.H. Martin, J.P., and his wife, who was the daughter of Mark Lemon. There are many beautiful monuments in the churchyard which is not now used for burials except so far as family burial places are concerned.

On the west side of the church is the Rectory Farm and running from west to east is the great Rookery, an ideal setting for this monument of the past. The church is the object of great interest, and antiquarians frequently pay visits. Fortunately, the Church is in the hands of those who love the ancient building, which is carefully tended and watched. The surrounding district is usually known as Ifield rural, to mark it from the more busy portion of the Parish which forms the greater part of busy Crawley. At present the church is removed from scenes of stress and bustle, and enjoys an old-world repose in keeping with its old-time atmosphere.

The County Oak referred to above marked the boundary-line between Sussex and Surrey. It is on the main London to Brighton-road at a spot nearly 1½ miles north of the George Hotel, Crawley. This Oak tree is mentioned in many old-time books. Cobbett's "Rural Rides" quotes it. Why the tree was removed to Ifield Church is not known as it stood on the Crawley side of the road.

I am reminded that the effigies of Sir John de Ifield and his Lady have incorrectly been described as "A Crusader and his Lady" owing to the fact the knight is cross-legged. I did not mention this, but in all writings on the subject Sir John is given as a Crusader. Dr. H. Mosse, however, is very emphatic on this subject.

> "In the monumental effigies of the knight and his lady, Ifield possesses a most valuable and instructive memorial of past ages, one which antiquaries of the foremost rank have not failed to instance and comment upon. The knight's figure is particularly noteworthy, as it shows a transitional period of armour costume and can confidently be placed among the first score of English stone effigies. The figures lie upon table tombs, the sides of which show quatrefoil ornamentation, a 14th century feature rarely met with in Sussex. The knight is considered to be Sir John de Ifield, who passed an active life in semi-military and civilian service. We hear of him collecting 'scutage' and other taxes, of being conservator

of the peace and a commissioner of the Marshes of Kent, Sussex and Surrey, of being empowered to raise troops in those counties and so forth. He was made knight in 1324 and was representative in Parliament 1331-1333. He is mentioned 'in Nonæ Roll' (1341) as having emparked a plot of land in St. Leonard's Forest, and there is documentary evidence of his being alive in 1336, so presumably his death occurred about 1340, and not in 1317 as stated by Lower and others. Sir John was not a crusader. The fact of having his legs crossed, as in the case of nearly all effigies prior to 1350 is merely a significance of fashion. The lady wears the characteristic dress of this period. Her name was Margaret and she was the daughter of St. Henry de Apuldrefeld, of Westerham, Kent, who was the sheriff of the County in 1297 and 1298. Both figures were originally coloured, and Mr. Stothard, the artist antiquary was able a hundred years ago to delineate the arms borne upon the shield Argent, a bend or cotised gules. Traces of colour still remain in parts."

THE CRAWLEY AND IFIELD BLACKBIRDS.—This locally well-known troupe of minstrels have determined to give two entertainments in the approaching winter season: one on behalf of the fund for the restoration of Ifield Church now in progress, and the other in aid of the fund for an organ at Crawley Church. We heartily wish the Blackbirds success, and trust they will be supported in their praiseworthy efforts in a manner commensurate with the undoubted talent the troupe invariably display.

October 1883

John Jeffrey

Sussex Songwriter

n the middle of the last century there lived at Ifield a son of Sussex named John Jeffrey who had a wonderful gift of song and for hours he could entertain a company by singing songs of his own composition. His hearers could never tell what time he would sing as he would improvise as he fancied but he could always be depended upon to make the words and tune fit.

John Jeffrey of the "Old Thatched Cottage" possessed a remarkable personality, a big stout man with large features, red weather beaten face, black straight hair and dark eyes. A bass voice, loud and rasping and a habit of rolling his r's in a manner which astonished his fellow Sussexians, and to others was simply amazing. He was always clad in a smock frock set off on high days and holidays by a top hat. He lived at the "Hyde" Ifield, which although not quite so primitive as his "Old Thatched Cottage" was yet very plainly and sparsely furnished and devoid of any comfort. He went to bed by rushlight which stood near the head of his bed in one of the old Sussex iron stands. In short his "Lares et Penates" were reduced to the limits of bare necessity.

Thanks to the late Dr. T.H. Martin some of his songs have been preserved in Jeffrey's own handwriting and his spelling is also used:

"The Oald Thatch Cotage"

I have lived in the woods a great number of years

My dog drives all sorrows my gun drives all cares

I have a neat little cotage and its covered secure

I am as happy as those that has got thousands a year

My Cotage is surrounded with Briers and Thorns

And so sweet is the note of the Birds in the morn

I have a ginne in my pocket and I have plenty more in store

I am as happy as thoes that has got thousands or more

Nothing but a straw Beed for my Bones to Repoes

Thats for healing I have none but one siute of cloethes

Witch is the best of ticking, and it is stitched up secure

I am as happy as thoes that has got thousands a year.

Thats for Chares I have got none for a friend to sit down

Thats for grates I have none my fiare is on the ground

I have three leged stool which is cheaf part of my store

I am as happy as thoes that have got fine marble flours.

God bless my oald father that is now dead and gone

I hope his soul in heavien and it never will return

For he left me all his ritches and the cheaf part of his store

Beside the little oald thatch cotage that stands on the more.

A new years gift for 1873

from J.J.

MANOR OF IFIELD, SUSSEX.

NOTICE IS HEREBY GIVEN, that all persons holding any Land of or upon the MANOR OF IFIELD, SUSSEX, as FREEHOLDERS, COPYHOLDERS, TENANTS or otherwise enjoying any rights or privileges within or upon the said Manor and all other persons having knowledge or cognizance of any encroachment upon Lands of or within the said Manor by the extending of any fences, ditches or other boundaries, or by building or otherwise, or of the opening or making of any new way, footpath or crossing, or of the diversion or alteration of any way, footpath or crossing on or within the Lands of the said Manor during the period of FORTY YEARS prior to the 31st day of DECEMBER, 1921, in respect of which encroachment or extension of boundary or opening, making, diversion or alteration of any footpath or crossing, the express license of the Lord of the Manor or of his Steward in that behalf shall not have been previously obtained, ARE HEREBY REQUIRED TO GIVE NOTICE in writing to the undersigned, DUDLEY HERBERT FARNFIELD, the Steward of the said Manor, on or before the 1st day of FEBRUARY, 1922, specifying the nature and extent of such encroachment, or of the opening, making or diversion of any way, footpath or crossing, with a plan or description of the locality or place at, or places between, which an encroachment or extension of fences, ditches, boundaries was made, or the extent, direction and terminals of any way, footpath or crossing sufficient to identify the same and the name or names with their present or last known place or places of abode of the person or persons by whom such encroachment or extension of boundary, or the opening or making or diversion of any way, footpath or crossing shall have been done or made, and setting forth in all cases where the license or sanction of the Lord of the Manor is sought or required the grounds on which the Applicant or Claimant seeks such license or sanction.

AND NOTICE IS FURTHER GIVEN, that all Notices or Information given in accordance with the foregoing will, in due course, be dealt with at a Court of the said Manor, to be there decided according to Law and the Custom of the Manor, and that unless such Notice be given as aforesaid all persons holding, using or enjoying any Land encroached or taken from the Lands of the Manor without license or grant from the Lord of the Manor, or using any way, footpath or crossing opened, made or diverted within the period aforesaid, will be liable to the forfeiture of such Land and the loss of use of such way, footpath or crossing and to proceedings at the suit of the Lord of the Manor and to the rectification of boundaries according to Law.

Dated this 3rd day of December, 1921.

DUDLEY H. FARNFIELD,
STEWARD of the MANOR of IFIELD,
SUSSEX,
90, Lower Thames-street, London, E.C. 3.

Cameo

John T. Charman

I wish to place before you one that is well known to you all, Mr. J.T. Charman, "John" to everybody. "John" had fame thrust upon him at his birth, as he was the last child born in a Toll House on a main road in Sussex. This great event took place in a little house right at the top of Goffs Hill quite near and opposite to the entrance to "Springfield" and the date May 9th. 1843, so he will be 75 years of age next year.

This was "Sloe" Fair day in Sussex, that is several fairs were held that day and all were called Sloe or winterpeck Fairday. But these fairings, like the old Tollgate have been covered by mists of time and are no more. He had the misfortune to lose his mother very early in his young life. John's schooling was at the British School and when he completed his formal education, he worked on the land, as labourer and gardener, and was an auxiliary postman.

At the Christmas season John with his concertina and a friend visited all the large houses in the surrounding district, playing and singing carols, in the hope of earning a few extra pennies.

For many years John was the Verger to St Peter's Church.

Would you believe that at one time he was the most sought for man, the most eagerly awaited person in the district!

Why was he so eagerly awaited? He was the town's rodent exterminator. Yes, a rat-catcher!

But John was no ordinary rat-catcher as the following selection shows.

A VISIT TO PEAS POTTAGE CAMP

I asked for the Sergeant whose name was Bankbrook
He showed me around and I had a look.
There's a nice lot of tents 'tis a very large camp
But the weather being wet made the ground damp.
Some of the boys ride horses, while others ride mules
But all have to conform to the Officers rules.
There's a lot of Red Cross, and the Y.M.C.A.
The Lans and the Mans who all seemed quite gay.
There were some doing drill, and were called to attention
But the number of men was too numerous to mention.
There was the A.S.C. and the Medical Aid
And a large butchers shop, that seemed doing a good trade.
There were some playing football, and others at cricket
Though while I stood watching they didn't bowl a wicket.
The trip gave me pleasure, 'twas a glorious sight
But 'tis sad that such chaps should be called out to fight.
But allow me to say, although Camping is splendid
We shall be very pleased, when the War is quite ended.

J.T. Charman 1916

A bit of the Camp, Peas Pottage.

WHEN I WAS TWENTY-ONE

Things are not as they use to be when I was twenty-one
We used to play at Prisoners base and had such jolly fun.
Now it's whist and dancing that seems all the go
The lads they take their lassies and round the room they go.

We use to play at cricket they called it nip and run
If you only tipped the ball it caused a bit of fun.
And if they bowled you out why out you had to go
That was the good old days of fifty years ago.

The ladies wore the crinoline when I was twenty-one
And they use to wear a bonnet to keep them from the sun.
Now they are out of fashion, hats are all the go
Nothing like the good old days of fifty years ago.

We never played at football we never knew the game
We never rode in a Surrey Bus but mostly went by train.
And we never rode in a motor car because they didn't run
And we never had the wireless when I was twenty-one

We didn't go up in an aeroplane we never learnt to fly
We didn't go above the clouds up in the bright blue sky.
We never went among the stars and nowhere near the sun
And we never had the Insurance Stamps when I was twenty-one.

> John Charman
> 25 Albany Road
> West Crawley Sussex

LINES ON CRAWLEY FAIR

The Auction sale was held in the Croft
A few horse were sold and some not bought.
A few nice cattle fetched a fair price
The buyers were few the weather was nice.
A small lot of sheep not like other years
The cattle consisted of cows, calves and steers.
Poultry, and harness and two or three traps
And Charman as usual with his patent traps.
A little machinery and a veterinary stall
A very few pigs and that's all.

A few nice horses by the George in the town
Which trotted up to fetch another pound.
There were swings on the Green and in the Lower Square
And the usual confetti "The Fun of The Fair".
Another new game called Tango Tubum
And those that threw they knew how to snub 'em.
There was Hoop-la and darts and a Cockerel on the Green
A man selling apples near a whelk stall.

Shouting at pipes, and a gingerbread stall.
No Switchback or Roundabout in meadow or the town
Of late years the Fairs have gone gradually down.
To this account for this there is very good reason
The Fair is held in the Hopping Season.
Things went off quiet not a row in the least
Not one single case for the Crawley Police.

September 9th. 1919
J.T. Charman

John T. Charman

A TRIP TO THE NYMANS HANDCROSS
by members of the Crawley Gardeners Association
19th. May 1920

We started from Crawley about twenty to three
To view all the sights there was to see
We were taken by bus the whole journey through
Some things were old some quite new.
We were taken through the walks with the lovely flowers and trees
Mr. Comber was asked the name of these.
John the Poet thought it was interesting
He looked in the trees and startled birds nesting.
We all went to tea just before five
And sat down to the tables not far from the drive.
There was plenty of tea bread, butter and cake
Cucumber and lettuce of which you like to take.
A hearty vote of thanks was proposed by Mr. Cheal
For their kind invitation and such a nice meal.

We arose from our tea for another walk round
Where we viewed the fine weather in the lower ground.
We walked in the garden and the houses of glass
where the fruit and cucumbers looked first class.
Besides the tomatoes and lovely carnations
Which were coming on fine beyond expectation.
A good show of currants both red and black
And a fine bed of strawberries near the back.
After viewing the garden, we went on the Mound
When standing on top you see for miles around.
We then crossed the lawns as it was nigh time for home
The Lady came and shook our hands.
And seemed pleased that we had come
We got seated in the Bus and was drove to Crawley Station
Where each one got out and walked to their destination.

Nymans, Handcross. 886

A TRIP TO THE MOUNT IFIELD
by members of Crawley Gardeners Association
June 4th. 1927

We arrived at the House in very good time
A nice party went and the weather pretty fine.
The rock work was a great attraction
The Garden and lawn was well worth inspection.
We were shown in the vineary and houses of glass
When the grapes and cucumbers looked first class.
A nice lot of currants and fine rows of peas
Apples and pears on most of the trees.
A nice lot of roses some white and some red
And some very nice lupins in a side bed.
A nice lot of potatoes, savoys and Brussels Sprout
A good lot is wanted there is not the least doubt.
There were tables placed upon the lawn, we all sat down to tea
And waiters to attend our wants which was two or three.
Plenty of Bread and butter and several kind of cake
And a nice cup of tea, as much as you like to take.
A hearty vote of thanks was proposed by Mr. Cheal
For their kind invitation and such a nice meal.
Being a large party we had to go twice
We were taken up for a moderate price.
There was lovely sweet williams and nice sea-kale
Before leaving the House they gave us some ale.
Some had ginger beer and some orange wine
They didn't join us froth blowers they didn't feel incline.
It's a nice little place and worth looking round
And Mrs. Courage is a lady that's not often found
We all got back safe and each went their way
After spending at The Mount a nice half day.
Then thanks to Mrs. Courage for her kind invitation
Who was made President of the Gardeners Association.

Perhaps the best way to conclude Mr. Denman's memories of the Crawley he loved is by using part of a letter he wrote in February 1928 to Mr. James Bristow, who had resided in the U.S.A. for some 26 years and proposed to visit his hometown once more. He informs Mr. Bristow of every single change in the High Street, both by building and demolition, all too numerous to mention here, but part of his letter is as apt today as it was 65 years ago:

Mr. Bristow would not know Crawley now, as the Crawley he knew has been swept away and is no longer a peaceful haunt for the busy man to rest. The general surroundings have not altered, one cannot shift the great Downs which nearly surround us, only the north-east so to speak being open. We have the great North Downs or Surrey Hills running from west to north-east with Leith standing like a sentinel in the west. Due north we have the great chalk and sand pits shining very clearly when the sun shines. South-east to south-west we have our glorious South Downs "silent guardians against the sea." From every view point the Downs afford a glorious scene more beautiful than ever painted by human hands. Trees, trees, trees, rank upon rank, clothe the slopes to the summit, with the blue haze of the horizon finishing off nature's great picture. It is too true that thousands of trees have been cut, creating smudges on our picture.

I feel sure that one of the greatest changes that would be noticed by Mr. Bristow is the passing of the old Crawley spirit of helping each other.

With passing of the old families and the influx of the "villadom" element this neighbourly spirit has been lost. In his time it was "What can I do? What can I give?" But now it is: "What can I get?"

In conclusion, Sir, may I quote the following:

A gentleman who had been absent from Crawley 32 years made enquiries about my family and in 1926 came to see me. His visit was on a Saturday evening and we went into the High Street and he was astounded. The two bands were playing, though it was impossible to hear what it was owing to the continual noise of the traffic, the restless crowds passing up and down, the buses and the char-a-bancs, the latter with their loads of shouting and dancing passengers. My visitor said, "Dear God, Crawley, my Crawley; the thoughts and dreams of 32 years shattered within an hour, a place of peace and beauty swept away for this!"

Echoes

As I lie gazing upon pillars of concrete and glass
My eyes grow weary, but what do I see,
A great canopy of leaves are protecting me.
Trees, and more trees of every hue, and in their dappled shade
Peep primroses of delicate cream.
The haze of bluebells in the glade, the chirping of birds,
The rustle of creatures small amongst the grass
These are but echoes of my past.

Cold winter mornings which freeze to the bone
The whistle of wind amongst branches bare
The shimmer of spider's web lead to his lair.
Tinkling of water rushing merrily along,
The sharp tang of frost, the glitter of ice
Deep black holes where ghosts and danger lurks
The laughter of boys running so fast
These are but echoes of my past.

Hark, but what do I hear, the note of the posthorn
Loud and clear. Rush to "The Street" for to see
The midday coach just passing "The Tree."
Mail aboard, passengers inside and o'top.
The leaders are hitched and pawing the ground
With postboys astride a jingle of leathers
A flick of the whip, we leave at last
These are but echoes of my past.

A brass band playing in the lower Square, where villagers
Gather to shout and cheer. We look long at the moving mass.
It fades. The blast of guns, the smell of gas.
Cries from the wounded, the silence of death.
With a hiss of steam and the grinding of brakes,
I'm upon a familiar shore. Around the corner, a few steps more.
"Will, Will" the murmur runs, as my hand is clasp
These are but echoes of my past.

A leisurely stroll in the evening sun, back in the place
Where it began. A pause, to watch as bat hits leather,
There's the Doctor, Charlie and Joe again all together.
No more can I run or speed down the wing,
I lie gazing upon pillars of concrete and glass
Surrounded by friends. I hear a faint heartbeat,
For these symbols of progress will not last
Unlike my memories from the past.

N.D.H. 1992